Dream Dictionary

2nd Edition

by Penney Peirce

A Wiley Brand

Dream Dictionary For Dummies®, 2nd Edition

Table of Contents

Introduction

Welcome to a fascinating journey into your inner worlds. Whether you're already a prolific dreamer or are just peeking into the unknown, you're sure to get results from the insights, techniques, and tips provided in this new expanded edition of *Dream Dictionary For Dummies.* Not only does this book outline important dream skills, it also provides a totally unique dictionary — a fascinating read in itself — that lists the meanings of hundreds of dream symbols as they pertain to three different aspects of your awareness: the physical, emotional, and mental-spiritual.

Before you delve into the nuts and bolts of how this book is organized, it will help to understand some important points about dreams so you can use your dream life to discover more about your inner self:

» The dream world is not separate from the waking world; they are extensions of each other and are mutually supportive and cocreative.

» Everything you do in dreams is real; it's just happening in other dimensions of your awareness.

» It's normal for your awareness to constantly shift through all the dimensions; you change focus continually, day and night.

» Dreamwork is a way to discover what your whole self, the you beyond your logical mind, is doing.

About This Book

In this book, you find out how to make sense of your dreams and harness them to increase creativity, solve problems, find life purpose, and obtain accurate personal guidance. Even if you just read the dictionary definitions, you can begin to understand symbology in a much deeper way. Dreams teach us so much about what's possible in life. I want your inner dream life to help expand your idea of how big you are, how much knowledge you have to draw from, how much you can accomplish, and how interconnected you are with everything and everyone. This book is designed to help you synchronize your body, emotions, mind, and soul so that you can experience the divine sanity that underlies your life's unfolding.

In the dictionary portion of this book, you can find a unique form of symbol definition. Each word has been defined on three levels (physical, emotional, and mental-spiritual) so that you can be precise and holistic when interpreting your dreams. Sometimes symbols pertain to all the levels at once. The meanings listed in this book are accurate, useful, and modern.

Throughout this book, you encounter dream diary writing exercises that can prompt dream insights. The key to improving your intuition and success with dreams is to make your normally intangible, unconscious inner world more conscious and real. Writing about your dreams and dream process in a diary is an excellent way to do this. I strongly encourage you to record your dreams every morning. In the evening before sleep, write about your dream intentions. Your dream diary can be a record of your inner growth process. I explain tips for doing these things in Chapter 2.

Just as in any *For Dummies* book, you can jump in anywhere, move backward or forward through the material, and find enormous value. If you want a concise mini-course on dreamwork and dream interpretation, read all the chapters in order — I've designed the flow of the material as a developmental process. If you're in a hurry and want to jump right in and see what last night's dream means, go straight to the dictionary.

Here's an overview of the book content:

>> **Part 1, Decode Your Dreams:** This section gives you the basics for establishing a solid, reliable dream habit and finding the hidden meanings in your dreams.

- Chapter 1 gets you started. It gives good reasons to dream, helps you understand the basic dream process, and gives tips for enhancing your ability to dream.

- Chapter 2 helps you activate the key components of the dream process, prepare for sleep and wake up consciously, and keep a dream diary to track your personal dream process.

- Chapter 3 helps you know your dream territory and recognize and work with physical dreams, emotional dreams, and mental-spiritual dreams.

- Chapter 4 dives into decoding symbols and understanding the multiple levels of dream meaning.

- Chapter 5 takes you into deeper work with decoding your dreams, helps you make sense of all types of dream experience, and gives you a variety of methods for uncovering hidden messages.

- Chapter 6 provides some sample dreams and interpretations of them.

>> **Part 2, Dictionary of Symbols:** This section presents a unique way to understand dream symbols. You'll find each word interpreted on three levels, as it might pertain to your physical process, your emotional process, and your mental-spiritual process.

>> **Part 3, The Part of Tens:** This section provides a little "dream dessert." Here you'll find ten useful techniques for exploring dream messages and ten of the most common dreams and their meanings.

Foolish Assumptions

I made some assumptions about you as I was writing, and if true, this book will be especially useful in your quest for deeper meaning:

>> You may be disillusioned by most dream dictionaries because they seem antiquated and not pertinent to today's levels of sophistication about psychological and spiritual growth.

>> You may be interested in dreams casually but not quite understand the real power they hold.

>> You may be so busy and rushed that you don't think you have time to work with your dreams, even though they fascinate you.

>> You may remember your dreams but not have a variety of useful tools and frameworks to use in decoding them.

Icons Used in This Book

TIP

There are certain nuances of dreamwork that can increase your effectiveness. This icon alerts you to these time- and trouble-saving ideas.

TECHNICAL STUFF

The history of dreams is replete with fascinating tidbits of information. Watch for this icon to find some fun details.

REMEMBER

This icon clues you in to points you definitely should remember.

Beyond the Book

You can find the *Dream Dictionary for Dummies* Cheat Sheet by visiting *www.dummies.com* and typing the book's title in the Search field.

On the cheat sheet, you'll find a list of important things to look for in your dream, which can help you dive deeper into interpretation. I also suggest details to pay attention to and questions that can reveal major insights. Finally, there are tips for remembering dreams and keeping a vibrant, accurate dream diary.

Where to Go from Here

This little book is a powerful tool containing countless insights into the meaning of your inner and outer life. To begin the journey of discovering these secrets, start with your most immediate interest. No matter where you enter this book, you'll find something that pertains to your life and leads to the next curiosity. Doing the exercises and suggested activities will uncover more clues. Stick with it and enjoy your discoveries!

TIP

You can gather some friends for a dream support group. Dream groups jump-start and accelerate the dream process for members, and discovering so many unique, beautiful dream styles is very validating.

1

Decode Your Dreams

Understand and navigate the dream process and gain insight into the dream cycle.

Prepare for sleep and awaking consciously to increase your dream recall. Also find out how to keep a dream diary and use it effectively.

Identify the dream zones and dream territory; recognize dream symbols, actions, and emotions; and find the multiple levels (physical, emotional, and mental-spiritual) in a dream.

Decode your dreams to find hidden guidance and crack symbols open for deeper meaning.

Explore dream formats (dream fragments, recurring, and sequential dreams) and try to interpret your dreams.

Examine a variety of sample nighttime dreams and waking daytime dreams.

Chapter **1**

Opening Your Dream Door

D reams really are, in the truest sense, a doorway: to greater self-awareness, knowledge, success, and the possibility of a rich, full life. Sounds great, but how do you open and walk through that door? This chapter is a great place to begin. You'll see that there is an actual pathway, with clearly delineated steps, that can take you from wishful thinking about dreams to a reliable dream habit. You'll find your previously mysterious, invisible inner life can be revealed on a regular basis to assist you in many useful ways.

In this chapter, you'll discover some specific benefits of an active dream life, familiarize yourself with the steps in the dream process, and fine-tune your understanding of sleep and dream dynamics. This way, you can build motivation and enthusiasm, be aligned with the natural flow of dreams, and get out of your own way by becoming aware of what inhibits dreaming.

Dreaming Fully

You can engage with the dream process better after you have some ideas about what dreaming does. Scientists write dreams off as the haphazard firing of neurons in the brain, but when you work deeply with dreams over time, you begin to understand them quite differently, seeing their spiritual roots. The following sections will help stretch your context for dreaming and inspire you about their vital importance in maintaining a healthy and happy life.

The function of dreams

The best way to begin understanding more about your dream life is to first understand how dreams function:

>> **Dreams are restorative.** When you have uninterrupted sleep and go through a series of deepening dream cycles during the night, you touch into and revisit your spiritual core and life purpose. Dreaming helps you stay on track, remember who you really are, how you fit into the whole, and renew yourself with fresh life energy and motivation.

>> **Dreams are about creation; the ultimate Dreamer is your soul.** Most cultures where mystical spiritual experience is valued believe that the soul projects (think "movie projector") or "dreams" the personality and entire physical life into being. "Life is but a dream," we so often hear. When you remember that you are the soul, or the Dreamer, and not the dream itself, you have more power to change the "dream" and create a life where your destiny can unfold instead of suffering and pain. You're not stuck! Dreams show you what's possible. All you have to do is dream something different! You're only as limited as your imagination.

>> **Dreams are about learning to be superconscious — and you're learning 24 hours a day.** You're dreaming not only at night but during your daytime waking reality, too. Your nighttime dream world is as real to your soul as your daytime world. They feed into each other, inform each other, teach each other. You, the soul, are never unconscious! You're always focusing on themes and issues that further your growth, flowing through different realms of your awareness. By interpreting day and night dreams, you can discover what's going on in your innermost life.

What's in it for you?

A productive dream life begins with being fired up and motivated. You won't get started or stick with it unless you understand the benefits that dreaming provides. So I've listed some important ways you can improve your life by working with dreams:

>> **Entertain yourself and grow your imagination:** Dreams give you many interesting, fun things to talk about with your spouse, friends, and family.

   If you do nothing more than fly without an airplane or interact with dragons in your dreams, you'll be far richer than if you'd lived by logic alone. Dreams keep you childlike and open, and help promote a free, joyful spirit. Since anything goes in dreams, it's not much of a stretch to extend the same dynamic imagination to your waking reality. Imagination may be one of the most undervalued skills you have. It determines the quality of your life, since what you can imagine is truly as far as you'll let yourself go. Dreams show you it's not so hard to move beyond your comfort zone.

>> **Discover what's what in your psyche:** Dreams provide firsthand contact with the fascinating mystery "Who am I?" They teach you about your psychological process and the subconscious beliefs and fears that interfere with growth and happiness. Your dreams can show you how to be more flexible, tolerant, loving, and lovable.

>> **Tap your inner wisdom:** Dreams relay accurate, inspired advice from your higher mind, or soul — the part of you that always knows the truth. They may even warn of problems that are brewing or help you prepare for an upcoming event. Dreams reveal your unlimited creativity and notify you when you're off center and need to realign with your life purpose.

>> **Be all that you can be:** Dreams expand your sense of personal identity because you realize you're composed of energy, emotions, thoughts, and higher patterns of aware-ness. You'll start thinking of yourself as more than a physical body and have access to new realms of experience that empower you to be more, know more, and do more.

>> **Develop intuition and innovation:** Recalling dreams, interpreting them, and intending them are all acts that require intuition and imagination. The more you work with

dreams, the more you'll learn to trust yourself, and you'll realize how naturally intuitive and creative you are.

>> **Increase real-life success:** Dreams help you in real ways — with problem-solving, decision-making, improving communication, healing yourself and others, even manifesting the help and resources you need. The dream state is a fertile field awaiting the seeds you sow.

>> **Melt barriers of time and space:** Dreams expand your capacity to know things that are in the past, the future, in other locations, and other dimensions of reality. Dreams that come true or give you information you couldn't obtain by normal means can open you to know, not just theorize, that we are all much more vast than we realize.

Understanding the Steps in the Dream Process

To develop a conscious, intentional dream practice and receive the full benefit from your dreams (for more on the benefits of dreaming, see the section "What's in it for you?" earlier in this chapter), it helps to know the steps in the dream process. Each step is important, and each feeds energy to the others. Drop one step out and the whole process falls apart. The following stages are expanded in more detail in subsequent chapters. The more times you repeat the full sequence of the following steps, the stronger and more second nature your dream habit will become:

1. **Choose to remember a dream.**

The best way to launch your dream process is to have a strong resolution to know your own mysteries. Then be more specific. You can prepare your awareness to be fertile and receptive, but if you want to dream, you must have a need or curiosity that serves as an energetic magnet.

Decide what kind of dream experiences you want to have. Do you want to visit an exotic place or connect with a relative who's died? Do you want to heal psychological or physical wounds? Perhaps you'd like to go to school or to the inventor's library and learn about future technologies. Maybe you need help solving a problem. Pick something specific or ask for general guidance; then program your subconscious mind before sleep: for example, "I will remember my most important dream in the morning," or "Bring me an insight concerning which job offer to accept."

2. Sleep well; wake up well.

If you're too stressed or wake often during the night, your dream cycles will be disturbed. If you try a few pointers from the lists of dream inhibitors and dream enhancers later in this chapter, you can learn to get a better night's sleep. When you wake in the morning, take a few moments to gently rise from the depths of sleep to come back to daily reality slowly, so you can maintain a connection with your dreams. Maintain the subtle feelings and sensations in your body before your mind kicks into gear.

3. Recognize dream activity.

It's important to develop a habit of turning your attention immediately to your dreams as you awake. Let your first thought of the day be *What have I just been doing?* Dreams come in various forms: a cinematic saga, a fragment, a single symbol or word, or even a highlighted experience later in the day after you awake. Speak in present tense about dreams: "I'm swinging on a rope, jumping from tree to tree. I sense I might fall." Speaking to yourself in the past tense can distance you from the dream.

4. Record your dream.

Once you've learned to preserve your live connection with your dreams, you must do something to make the dreams real and physical to your body. This way your body, which is intimately connected with your subconscious mind, knows you meant what you said the night before when you asked to remember your experiences in other dimensions, and it will cooperate. If you do nothing, your body will think you're crying, "Wolf!" So tell someone right away, describe the dream into a recorder, or write it in your dream diary.

5. Decode the message.

Making sense of your dream is perhaps the most daunting step, but it's also the most fun. There are many techniques for discovering the hidden messages in dreams, and you will find lots of ideas in this book. This is where you will determine what dream zone you've been visiting, where you'll use the dream dictionary and penetrate into your dream symbols. This is where you'll ask yourself *How is this dream image, dream choice, dream action, dream emotion, part of a process I'm going through right now in my waking life? How are the dream elements part of a life lesson I'm learning so I can become more of my true self?* Bringing the subliminal into conscious awareness validates the process.

You're always the best interpreter of your dreams, though asking for insight from others can often be helpful.

6. **Follow through.**

If your dream contains guidance, insight, a warning, an answer to a problem, an inspiring image, or an intriguing thought, use the information. Follow through on what you receive because this is why you dreamed the dream in the first place — so you could discover more about yourself. Using dreamtime insights in daily life reinforces your intention to connect the two halves of your experience, completes the dream cycle, and frees you to move into a new phase of exploration and creativity.

7. **Do it all again.**

When establishing a reliable dream habit, your subconscious mind will engage fully and bring you dreams consistently after you repeat this process at least three times. Some people say seven times, just to be sure.

Tuning In to Your Dreamtime Dynamics

Science tells us that everyone dreams for a total of approximately two or three hours per night. Robbed of vital dream activity through sleep deprivation or stress, we become irritable and disoriented and will balance ourselves by dreaming excessively the first chance we get.

The dreams of children are shorter than those of adults and often contain animals and monsters. Nearly 40 percent of children's dreams are nightmares, which may be part of the normal developmental process of learning to cope.

The following sections explore the stages of the natural sleep/dream cycle you progress through several times each night, and I give you various ways you can improve your sleep/dream cycle.

Know your dream cycles

Every night, you rotate through four basic phases of sleep that repeat approximately every 90 minutes. During these cycles, you oscillate between awareness that's close to waking reality and awareness that penetrates deep into the collective, spiritual realms. What's important to understand here is that if your deep sleep cycles are disturbed, you may not be able to renew your vitality and sense of purposefulness easily.

>> **Phase one:** Brainwaves slow from their waking frequency, called *beta*, to the more relaxed *alpha* state, where you may feel you're floating, and pictures may drift through your mind. Your muscles relax, and your pulse, blood pressure, and temperature drop slightly.

>> **Phase two:** Your brainwaves slow more until they reach the level known as *theta*. You're now in a light sleep state characterized by many bursts of brain activity. Most dreams occur at this level, during which the eyes move back and forth rapidly beneath the eyelids. This is known as rapid eye movement, or *REM sleep*, and it lasts from several minutes to an hour.

During REM sleep, your extremities may twitch, but most of your body is paralyzed. Your heart may beat erratically, and breathing can become irregular and shallow. When awakened, you easily remember your dreams. A newborn infant experiences eight to ten hours of REM sleep per day. By age five, a child's sleep pattern has become almost the same as an adult's.

>> **Phases three and four:** In the third and fourth phases, about 20 to 45 minutes after you fall asleep, your brainwaves finally reach the ultraslow, regular *delta* frequency, which produces a deep, "dead sleep." You progress from 20 percent delta waves in phase three to over 50 percent in phase four. If awakened during either of these stages, you feel fuzzy and lost; so resist waking fully and drop back to sleep immediately.

DREAM BREAKTHROUGHS

Many people have made discoveries while dreaming. Here are some examples of extraordinary breakthroughs that can inspire you to pay close attention to the deeper meanings of your dreams:

- **Friedrich August von Kekule:** A professor of chemistry in Ghent, von Kekule had been searching for the molecular structure of benzene. In 1865, while dozing before his fire, he dreamed of a snake seizing its own tail. He awoke suddenly with the revolutionary idea that certain organic compounds are not open structures, but form closed chains or rings.

- **Melvin Calvin:** A 1961 Nobel Laureate in chemistry for his work with photosynthesis, Calvin, while daydreaming in his parked car, recognized the structure of phosphoglyceric acid in a matter of seconds.

- **William Blake:** The English artist and poet William Blake, while searching for a less expensive method of engraving his illustrated songs, dreamed his dead younger brother, Robert, appeared to him and revealed a process of copper engraving, which Blake immediately tested, verified, and began using.

- **Elias Howe:** Howe, who invented the sewing machine, couldn't figure out how the needle would work. He dreamed he was taken prisoner by natives who danced around him with spears that had holes near their tips. He changed his design to incorporate the dream's idea and it worked!

Enhance your dream ability

Like so many people today, you may be working too many hours or splitting your time between too many people and activities. You may be living on the surface of yourself, feeling frustrated, disgruntled, and fragmented. By the time bedtime comes, you're probably too keyed up to sleep well. In the morning, you may still be too tired to think seriously about the "luxury" of interpreting your dreams. Put some attention on the need to harmonize the flow of your sleep cycle and dream process by eliminating dream inhibitors and focusing on dream enhancers. By doing so, you can nurture yourself and maximize your success in all areas of your life. Familiarize yourself with the following things that either detract from or add to dreaming proficiency:

TIP

>> **Dream inhibitors:** Drugs — such as marijuana, cocaine, barbiturates, sleeping pills, tranquilizers, muscle relaxants, many mood-stabilizing drugs, as well as alcohol, tobacco, and stimulants like caffeine and amphetamines — can delay sleep, reduce your amount of REM sleep, and your ability for dream recall. Dream activity also can decrease when you are socially overactive and too stressed. Too much aerobic exercise close to bedtime tends to release adrenaline, which can prevent sleep.

>> **Dream enhancers:** Dream activity occurs more frequently when you've been engaged in quiet, private activities like meditating, reading, studying, or after a period of new learning. Eating foods like turkey, milk, bananas, or cheese that contain the amino acid tryptophan before bed can have a sedating effect. Vitamin B complex, especially B6, has been shown to produce more vivid dreams, as has the herb St. John's Wort. The hormone melatonin seems to help regulate your body clock, and even a small amount has been shown to help induce drowsiness. Ask your physician before you take any kind of supplements, however, and be sure not to exceed the recommended doses. A warm bath before bed can also lead to dreaming, since as you cool down afterward, you tend to get sleepy.

Chapter **2**

Increasing Dream Recall

B ringing dreams back from the dream world is both a science and an art. If you follow some proven principles and pay attention to your attitude and intuition, you can easily recall your dreams. The key is that the more you remember your dreams, the more you'll remember your dreams! In this chapter, I show you how to prepare to dream and how to develop a reliable dream habit.

Starting the Flow with a Positive Attitude and Open Intuition

In Chapter 1, I outline the steps in the dream process. You can maximize the results from that process by following these tips to keep your attitude positive and your intuition open:

>> **Keep your attitude positive by being enthusiastic about the power of dreams.** Start with a positive, expectant attitude. Talk to yourself about what exists: what you *do* enjoy, what you *are* doing, what you *have* now. Prime yourself with curiosity and let it percolate. A soft, receptive, nonjudgmental attitude helps the perfect dream occur. Record your dreams happily and gratefully; this tells your subconscious mind that it did a good job.

TIP

>> **Keep your intuition open by trusting yourself and the process.** Whatever you receive is just right because your soul is running the show! Stay neutral, centered in your body, and in the moment when doing dreamwork. Be true to your own sense of things, find similarities between ideas and themes, and be honest about what's real. Trust first impressions but penetrate into the core with sustained attention.

Dream recall decreases when you're stressed and anxious, yet it increases with enthusiasm. Also, dreamwork decreases with depression and increases when you're calm and centered.

Creating a Dream Motive

To facilitate your dream recall, it helps to keep your motivation strong by first clearing any blocks in your subconscious mind. These fear-based ideas can interfere with your receiving the dream insights you need to further your personal growth. First, I give you an idea of some sample blocks; then you can pinpoint your own sabotaging ideas and dissolve them. After that, I show you how to build your dream motive through heightened curiosity and the habit of noticing symbolic images.

Clear subconscious blocks

You won't let yourself remember dreams if doing so makes you scared or unhappy. True, it's uncomfortable to face your "dark side," but clearing subconscious fear brings relief, gives you permission to get more out of life, and produces an immediate increase in dream range and recall. Your subconscious might block dreams for a variety of reasons, including these:

>> You might have to admit you know more than you let on to others and yourself.

>> You might have to experience your anger concerning your father.

>> You might discover how preoccupied you are with sex and how much you're avoiding true intimacy.

>> You might dream that someone you love is going to die, and you don't want to know "bad" things.

>> You might have to admit your best friend isn't really supporting you.

Here's an exercise: To discover and clear your dream blocks, try writing about the following:

1. **Quiet your mind.** Make a list of responses to the following statements:

1. I do not want dreams to bring me information about
    _____.

2. I do not want dreams to make me have to feel _____
    _____.

3. I do not want dreams to change my life by _____
    _____.

4. I do not want dreams to overwhelm me by _____
    _____.

2. **Look at the answers and ask yourself questions like the following:** Why not? Why not have information about monsters? Why not feel what it's like to fall? Why not change my life by quitting a job that bores me? Write about how, if you allowed each thing, your life might improve.

List some trigger questions

Curiosity is a great motivator! By periodically making a list of intriguing questions — things you want to know about — you will prime your subconscious to use dreams as vehicles for answers. Later you'll work with incubating a specific dream, but for now, just work on freeing up your imagination!

Here's an exercise: I've given some examples in the following list; you can add others that address your important needs and greatest curiosities:

>> What do I need to know about my body to improve my health?

>> What beliefs are interfering with my seeing my current life situation clearly?

>> What is the next growth phase of my career?

>> How can I connect with my grandparents who died?

>> How can I improve my relationship with my spouse?

>> What is causing my child's anxiety and irritability, and what can I do about it?

>> How can I move through my writer's block and jump-start my creativity?

Notice symbolic images

Another good way to prompt the dream flow is to notice things that seem dreamlike or symbolic during the day. Perhaps you see a vibrant flower with a dragonfly on it, a person fixing a flat tire, or a child holding a large dog in their arms. Any of these could be in an actual dream scene because they contain meaning-loaded symbols.

Here's an exercise: Keep a notebook and jot down images or events that seem intriguing. By building the habit of noticing symbols, you'll increase the tendency to recall your nighttime dream symbols. When you start working more deeply with symbol interpretation in Chapters 4 and 5, you'll be speaking the language of symbols much more fluently. Here are some examples of dreamlike images from daily life:

>> Your car won't start.

>> There is thick fog in the morning.

>> A crow sits on the fence and caws at you.

>> You break a tooth.

>> You find a $20 bill.

Preparing for Sleep

To grease the wheels of the dream cycle, remember that your daytime reality connects to your nighttime reality, and the night to the day, in an ongoing continuum. By making an intentional connection between day and night, then night and day, you'll see the current themes in your life more clearly, and more cohesive information will come through your sleep dreams, daydreams, and waking dreams.

For example, you may be unconsciously involved in a debilitating codependent relationship by day, dream at night that your partner is secretly poisoning you, daydream about a past romantic partner who embodied healthy characteristics, see an animal being inordinately affectionate, and start to sob without realizing why you're so moved. All of this is your soul speaking to you in dream language about loving yourself more.

To be more aware 24 hours a day, I show you how to prepare for sleep in an intentional way and then how to wake up more consciously.

Review and complete the day

Before you drop into your dream world, take stock of what you accomplished during the day and what you wanted to do when you set out in the morning. This frees your mind to pay attention to what you do in your dreams and helps you dream more intentionally. Here are some questions to ask:

>> Did I do what I wanted to do today?

>> Am I proud of the way I behaved? Did I treat anyone badly that I'd like to make amends for tomorrow?

>> Was I wasteful? disciplined? playful?

>> What am I grateful for that happened today?

Choose to dream!

Take some quiet time to review your trigger questions, pressing needs, or childlike curiosities. What experiences do you want to have in your dreams? Do you want to visit an old friend, fly without a plane, learn more about plants, solve a career problem, talk to spiritual guides, or help others? Once you have a goal, try the following technique to align your body and mind for dreaming:

1. **Think enthusiastic, imaginative thoughts.**

   Dreams are so wonderful! It's going to be fun to dream tonight. I'm going to pay special attention to (flying)!

2. **As you prepare for sleep, sit on the side of your bed, close your eyes, and talk to yourself about your intentions.**

   Tell yourself, I am relaxed and ready. My body knows exactly how to have the perfect dream. My intuition is functioning perfectly to deliver my dream accurately to my mind. My mind knows how to recognize my most important dreams and describe them in detail. My soul knows what I really need to know. I trust all my parts.

Once you've aligned yourself, try this exercise to incubate a specific dream:

1. **Put attention at the back of your neck where your head and neck join.**

   Nod your head up and down so you can feel the spot exactly.

2. **Imagine a small ball of golden light floating in front of you.**

3. **Think about what you want to achieve in your dreams and formulate a concise sentence describing your goal.**

   Make it simple and specific. Here are some examples:

   - *In the morning when I wake up, I will remember my most important dreams.*
   - *I will fly in my dreams tonight and remember my flying dreams.*
   - *I will wake with an insight about how I can heal my back pain.*

4. **Repeat the sentence several times then visualize it.**

   Put it inside the ball of golden light. Let the light illuminate and activate the sentence.

5. **Place the ball of golden light, with its dream seed, inside the back of your neck at that magic spot.**

   Let the soft warm light gently penetrate and dissolve into your reptile brain and carry your message to the place where it can be acted upon. Relax and trust that this will occur as you sleep, and in the morning, you'll wake refreshed with the response you've requested. When you feel at ease, happy, and confident, lie down and go to sleep, smiling.

TIP

Dedicate your bedroom to dreaming. Instead of using your bed as an office, think of your bedroom as a personal sleep sanctuary. To quiet your bedroom, remove noisemakers like television, radio, and telephone. Move the bookcases to another room. Meditate in bed, sitting up, before sleep or use the time to write in your dream diary.

Waking Up Consciously

The next part of working with the continuous circuit of day and night is to complete your nighttime experience by recalling and recording your dreams and then setting clear intentions for the day, which you will review the next night before sleep. To do that, you must wake up with the least amount of disturbance. If you're jangled awake by a loud alarm or barking dogs, your connection to your dreams can easily be broken. Consider having an alarm go off in another room, waking to soft music, or having a light turn on automatically.

If you sleep like a log and wake too groggy to remember a dream, try a sequence of waking mechanisms that builds in intensity: A light goes on, music in another room sounds, and finally an alarm next to your bed rings. Before sleep, suggest to yourself that you'll notice each of the signals and wake progressively with each.

Maintain soft awareness

Leaving extra time for dreamwork in the morning pays off. Float a moment or two before your "to-do" mind kicks in. That soft, still mental state helps you stay connected to the frequency of the dream world, and your dreams often pop up magically. Here are some recall tips to practice first thing after waking:

- » Say to yourself, *What have I just been doing? Where have I been?*
- » Keep the subtle sensations in your body.
- » Scan internally for the most predominant images floating in your soft awareness.
- » Describe the images, subtle feelings or emotions, and actions you've taken in the dream in present tense.
- » Make your dreams conscious and real. Tell someone, describe the dream into a recorder, or write it in your diary. You don't have to interpret the dream right now.

Create your day consciously

After recording your dreams, turn your attention to the day. Collect yourself; be centered and calm. What's left from yesterday that you want to complete today? You're creating your day the same way you created your dreams. Tonight, before sleep, you'll review and complete your daytime goals. Make a list of your intentions:

>> What impact do I want to have on other people, and on the world, today?

>> What kind of experience and attitude do I want to have today?

>> What do I want to give and receive today?

Recalling Your Dreams by Keeping a Dream Diary

Writing about your dreams helps make them more real to your body, which reinforces the dream habit.

A diary is a great way to monitor your dreams to see what themes you've been focusing on and how your dreams have come true or been insightful. In this section, I show you how to make the most of your dream diary.

Personalize your diary

To help build the "fun" factor, which is so important to motivating yourself to have a rich dream life, make your diary a favorite object. Fill it with stimulating sensory elements, interesting things to pay attention to, and useful organization and design ideas:

>> **Are you neat and tidy?** A small, bound journal with a tasteful design on the cover, smooth paper, and narrow lines might suit you.

>> **Are you colorful, impulsive, and dramatic?** You might like a large sketchbook with pages that fall open easily with no restricting lines. Or maybe you'd prefer a cheap spiral-bound notebook from the drugstore.

>> **Type your dreams in a computer cyberdiary.** Using a cyberdiary is a speedy way for you to edit and add to your

diary, but it isn't quite as tactile and sensory as a paper journal and doesn't stimulate the dream centers as well.

>> **Divide each page in half vertically or horizontally.** Use half to record your dreams and half to divine the meaning. Or divide the page vertically to use two-thirds of the page for dreams and a third as a margin for notes.

You can capture your dream in the middle of the night by having your diary or a piece of paper handy along with a pen light.

Use your diary effectively

Think of your dream diary as a record of what's going on in the hidden dimensions of your life. You're a private eye on a stakeout, conducting surveillance. Besides recording your dreams, you can use your diary for other things as well. Try any of these ideas:

>> Write about your dream goals and your dream-sabotaging ideas.

>> Examine your sleep pattern and cycles.

>> Collect images from magazines, books, flyers, and so on that trigger dreams and make collages, diagrams, and illustrations with those images.

>> Write or copy inspirational quotes, poetry, and prayers.

>> Write about waking dreams, dream fragments, and single symbols.

>> Write the date of each dream and put a star next to important dreams.

>> Write in the present tense, recording as many details as you can.

>> Document your dream incubation statements.

>> Write about dream images that have carried over from the previous day and what happens in the days after an important dream.

Use the back of your diary

Create a section in the back of your diary where you keep ongoing lists. It stimulates your imagination to see so many ideas clustered together, and you may notice repeating themes that will factor into your interpretations. Here are some possible lists:

- **My many faces:** What myriad roles do you play in your dreams?

- **My dreamscapes:** Where do you travel and what places do you frequent in your dreams?

- **My dream teams:** Who do you dream about?

- **My dream symbols:** What images repeat in your dreams? What images surprise you and why?

- **My dream themes:** What issues concern or bother you in your dreams? What activities are you repeatedly focusing on in your dreams?

Write even if no dreams come

You'll remember dreams more consistently if you commit to writing something — a dream or pseudo-dream — in your diary every day. Here are some ideas that can make writing in your diary more rewarding:

- **Write about your emotional state.** If you can't recall a dream after you programmed one, write about the emotional state you woke up in, how your body feels, your first thoughts, or the first person who comes to mind. It's important to give your body the message that you meant what you said the night before. So, make up a dream; your body won't know the difference, and your dream habit will grow stronger.

- **Invent a dream character, a dream locale, and a dream theme.** Start your story with Once upon a time . . . . Describe the physical landscape. Ask: What does this character need? Let your character ask a question. Exaggerate whenever you can. Describe things using lots of sense-oriented adjectives and adverbs. Who's innocent, who's the bad guy, and who's the good guy? Have the characters learn something. Create a title a five year old would like.

TIP

Take your dream diary with you when you travel. Most people report that dreams are more active when they are away from their routine and sleep in new places.

IN THIS CHAPTER

» Find out how to move among the
dream zones

» Practice focusing on a physical,
emotional, and mental-spiritual dream

» Connect symbols with different
kinds of dreams

Chapter **3**

Identifying Dream Activity

As you prepare to find the meaning of your dreams, you'll want to know what kinds of dreams are possible. Identifying the categories and focus of your dreams is one of the first steps in dream interpretation. Dreams appear both at night and during the day, and they occur within several distinct realms or zones of awareness, fulfilling various functions. In this chapter, I show you the differences among, and how to work constructively with, the physical, emotional, and mental-spiritual dream zones.

Knowing Your Dream Territory

Dreams cover a lot of territory, bringing useful insights about mundane things like solving problems at work and preventing illness to loftier issues like clearing emotional problems and staying on purpose spiritually. Dreams also reveal ways your energy and awareness can be stuck through repressed, blocked emotions, or locked-in beliefs you've never examined. During the night and day, your dreams speak to you on one or all of the following levels:

>> Your subconscious mind (suppressed fears and ideas that block soul expression) and your superconscious mind (wisdom and love that free soul expression)

>> Your body and physical life, your emotional life, your fixed beliefs and important new ideas, and your spiritual destiny and life purpose

>> Your individual growth process, other people and their growth processes, the evolution of your relationships, and society's collective process of evolution

Notice waking dreams and daydreams

Your soul dreams your entire waking world into existence, and no Hollywood director can rival its mastery over plot, dialogue, timing, and special effects. When you need a wake-up call or a clue to a new direction, your soul can create an experience — a waking dream — that gets your attention through shock, drama, humor, or amazing coincidence and synchronicity.

A *waking dream* is a real-time standout symbol or experience that seems like a "sign," or a short series of images tied together in an attention-getting way. These experiences have an emphasis that makes you want to pay closer attention. In Chapter 2, I ask you to notice dreamlike images during the day to prime your mind to focus on symbols so you can bring more symbols back from your nighttime dreams but also so you can begin to interpret waking dreams and daydreams.

There are hidden messages in waking dreams, and they can be interpreted just like nighttime dreams. Here are some examples of what waking dreams might mean:

>> **Waking dream:** You're not sure you should go out with your old lover, and the day before your date, your car's clutch breaks and you can't drive.

Possible meaning: You're telling yourself that being with this person again could handicap your full self-expression.

>> **Waking dream:** On a driving trip, you see three dead owls on the roadside in an hour.

Possible meaning: You're drawing your attention to the need to focus on the wisdom of your body, mind, and spirit.

>> **Waking dream:** You've been criticized for being insensitive. In the early morning as you're jogging, two spotted fawns cross your path and aren't afraid of you.

Possible meaning: You need to feel more innocent and share your heart energy with others more.

>> **Waking dream:** Your sink, dishwasher, and toilet back up and overflow.

Possible meaning: You need to clear an emotional block that is clogging your creative flow and life force.

Daydreams may be a little harder to recognize at first because you tend to be absent-minded or "spaced out" while they're occurring. See if you can catch some of your flights of fancy, subliminal conversations with imaginary characters, or unconscious visions and wishes and then write about your underlying concerns, desires, and growth themes in your dream diary.

TECHNICAL STUFF

If it takes less than five minutes to fall asleep, you're probably sleep-deprived. The ideal drop-off time is 10 to 15 minutes, meaning you're tired enough to sleep deeply but haven't been exhausted all day. Sleep apnea or deprivation can sometimes cause overactive *hypnagogic* visions as you're falling asleep, or *hypnopompic* hallucinations as you're waking up. For example, you may hear a dream's soundtrack, feel things that aren't there, or glimpse vivid dream fragments while you're half awake.

Notice the dream zones

All dream experiences are real at some level. Dreams are always about a process of growth, and they occur in one of the *dream zones* or dimensions of awareness:

>> Physical

>> Emotional

>> Mental-spiritual

When interpreting your dreams, you'll start by identifying what part of your growth process you're working on. Is your dream about a problem in your physical world, like needing to sell your house? Are you focusing on your emotional world and a fear of displeasing someone, or how angry you are about a betrayal? Are you focusing on your mental-spiritual realm, wanting to receive new information and inspired guidance? By knowing the dream zone, you can more easily pinpoint the source of the issues you're trying to understand, dissolve, or create.

Notice movement between zones: Flying, falling, diving, climbing

During both day and night, you move constantly through the dream zones, shifting your awareness up or down in frequency. When you "space out" during the day, for example, you're actually ascending into higher zones, and when you shudder suddenly, you're descending to the physical world in a rush of consciousness. At night, the movement between dream zones might be symbolized by flying, falling, climbing, or diving. Ascending with or without a vehicle is a representation of the mind expanding to a higher zone or dimension. Descending via an elevator or staircase or by free falling is a symbol of your mind returning to the "lower, slower" physical reality.

REMEMBER

The most important part of dream interpretation is being able to track what your inner awareness is doing. The basic movement of your consciousness between zones accounts for many of the symbols you will encounter.

Recognizing and Working with a Physical Dream

Many dreams deal with the functioning of the physical world. Some of the topics of physical zone dreams are

>> **Daily residue:** You watch a scary movie before bed, argue with your mate, or bring a problem home from work; then you process the situation further in a dream.

>> **Health and healing:** You receive information about a disturbance in your energy flow, or body, so you can avoid a budding health problem. Martha dreamed she entered a rehab center, and the counselor gently took a glass of wine out of her hand. She hadn't realized she was drinking too much.

- **Problem-solving and decision-making:** You receive guidance so you can proceed in your life. An interior designer needed an innovative focal point for a large wall and dreamed of using ladders in an odd, interesting arrangement.

- **Skill development:** You accelerate your learning by practicing in your dreams a new ability you're trying to learn in waking life. Jenn, a new professor, worried about being good enough in front of her large classes and dreamed repeatedly of public speaking until she was totally comfortable.

Recognize physical symbols

As you learn to work with symbols in the next chapters, it will help to recognize images that pertain to physical processes. Here are some examples of physical zone symbols:

- **State of your body:** Jar, earthenware pot, bowl, cup, glass, cave, basement, house, room, closet, train, bus, car, trailer, motorcycle, bicycle, tree, bodily organs, tumors, body parts, aura

- **Body processes:** Eating, drinking, chewing, urinating, defecating, vomiting, washing, shaving, swelling, growing, flowing, breathing, stoppages

- **Health issues:** Hospital, clinic, doctors, nurses, surgery, massage or bodywork, energy healing, acupuncture, bandages, casts, X-rays, injections, construction, digging, sculpting, jogging, exercising

Make a physical dream work for you

Try the following writing exercise to track your "daily residue" dreams:

1. **Look through your dream diary for dreams that might have been triggered by something that happened in daily life.**

   Did the dream provide further insights that you applied? What happened right after you had the dream? Write about these things in your diary.

2. **When you find a connection between a perception in waking reality and a similar dream, write about the underlying theme.**

What was it about the original trigger experience that made you focus on it so much that you needed to dream about it? What is your soul telling you?

Recognizing and Working with an Emotional Dream

Every time you express or deny intensity of feeling, you can be sure there is fodder for a powerful emotional dream. Though dreams from the emotional zone can be disturbing, they provide guidance about clearing blocks to superconscious experience. Some topics of emotional zone dreams are

>> **Psychological processing:** You root out fears, pain, vulnerabilities, blind spots, and subconscious blockages so you can become conscious of what holds you back, clear it, and be courageous and free. You may dream about fears of being powerless, in pain, unworthy, unsuccessful, out of control, overwhelmed, victimized, rejected, losing loved ones, changing, dying, or facing the void.

>> **Taboos:** You explore forbidden territory, inhibitions, and suppressed desires, often about sex, crime, or antisocial behavior, as a way to free self-expression. Cheryl, a sensible accountant by day, dreamed of wild sexual trysts with rock stars by night. Joe acted out his secret vengeance thoughts about his self-centered brother.

>> **Relationship dynamics:** You receive insights about how you relate to others and how you give and receive so you can improve your ability to love. This includes learning to balance your internal yin and yang energy. One woman dreamed she was a helpless passenger in a car driven by another, aggressive woman. Another dreamed she took her obnoxious neighbor a cake instead of reporting him to the police.

>> **Past life memory:** You travel in time to revisit memories of other lives or to clear blocked energy where emotion is stuck. You re-experience, in a dream, a previous death,

trauma, remorse, deep grief, terror, or a situation where you had too much ego.

>> **Precognitive warnings:** You receive forewarning of sudden change or upheaval: A loved one is about to die, you are soon to lose your job or partner, or the world is about to experience a shocking event like Pearl Harbor, Kennedy's assassination, or September 11. Or you are shown an omen to watch for that is a clue to success in a new endeavor.

>> **Out of body travel:** You collapse time and space and visit a distant sick friend you're worried about, have a visitation from a dead relative with a message for you, or travel with a friend who's actually in India.

Recognize emotional symbols

With a little practice, you can figure out how to immediately sense the "charge" that's often present with emotional zone symbols. Here are some examples of images that pertain to emotional processes:

>> **State of your emotions:** Water, lake, ocean, river, pool, swamp, flood, tidal wave, swimming, diving, fishing, drowning, boats, rafts, water vehicles, fire, house burning, forest or brush fire, campfire, fire in a fireplace, smoke, explosion, storm, tornado, hurricane, earthquake, volcano, mudslide

>> **Emotional processes and issues:** Babies, children, fish, snakes, lions, tigers, bears, sharks, dolphins, puppies, hummingbirds, otters, horses, elephants, sex, relationships, celebrities, battle, betrayal, hiding, hoarding, being drained, being chased, exposure, nudity, poison, suffocation, paralysis, prison, weapon, trap, losing or finding important items or money

Make an emotional dream work for you

Use your diary to press into emotional issues and explore deeper feelings with the following exercise:

1. **Write about a relationship dream, a nightmare, and a sex dream, asking yourself these questions about each:**

● If I accept what's happening in the dream and extend the action further, what happens?

- If I let the dream take an odd turn, what might happen that I never expected?

2. **Write out three of your wildest fantasies about sex, taboos, the dark side, or death.**

   It's okay to be politically incorrect! Write about what you learn.

TECHNICAL STUFF

Teenagers and small children need about ten hours of sleep, while those over 65 need about six. For the average adult, eight hours is optimal. Some studies suggest women need up to an hour's extra sleep a night compared to men, and not getting it may be one reason women are more susceptible to depression.

Recognizing and Working with a Mental-Spiritual Dream

Many dreams deal with patterns and processes in your mental and spiritual realms. Some of the topics of mental–spiritual zone dreams are

>> **Mental clutter:** You become aware of fixed mental beliefs, worries, and rigid ideas, as well as information that doesn't belong to you, so you can dissolve it and expand into greater self-expression. Donna dreamed she was to inherit the possessions of the women in her mother's lineage. Instead of great treasures, she received tiny restrictive shoes, primitive sewing implements, and raggedy clothes. She realized she needed to clear a belief system based on limitation that she inherited from her mother.

>> **Guidance:** You receive instructions or guidance, often from historical figures, spiritual guides, dead relatives, or animals, to know how to proceed or that you are supported. Susan dreamed she was putting on mascara but had the mascara with the wand she didn't like. There is another kind she just bought that has a perfect wand. Where is it? From this fragment, she realized she wanted her new business to be the way *she* wanted it to be, not the way others were telling her it *should* be.

>> **Teaching others:** You teach others so you can see how wise you really are. Steven, a car mechanic, dreamed he was

teaching a large class, gesturing with a piece of chalk. On the blackboard were scrawled complex mathematical formulas. He realized he must know about math and have teaching ability that he'd never tried to develop.

>> **Creativity:** You experience creative genius to remind you of your potential and how much you love innovation and artistic expression. Dennis dreamed he was painting the air, and a scene from reality revealed itself with each brushstroke. He realized the paintbrush was his own perception and that he could create his reality as effortlessly as he painted the air.

>> **Interdimensional communication:** You connect with loved ones who've died, historical figures, extraterrestrials, or your *soul group* (people who feel like spiritual family) as a way to remember your multidimensional nature. Mary dreamed her dead father brought her a birthday present. Inside the box were numbers she somehow knew were the vibrations of her true self.

>> **Parallel realities:** You explore other worlds and parallel realities that reveal new aspects of yourself. A housewife had regular dreams about being part of a Mission Impossible–style team in which she was a courageous, undercover operative. She realized she was smarter and had more power than she thought.

>> **Extrasensory perception:** You develop expanded perception, like clairvoyance, telepathy, time travel, materialization, teleportation, spiritual healing, and enlightenment to find a higher viewpoint. Paula dreamed she was watching the television news and it was reporting that Michael Jackson had just died. When she woke, it hadn't happened, but a year later she saw the same report on the morning news and it was true. It helped her understand that clairvoyance was real.

>> **Spiritual awakening:** You learn to regulate your awareness to open to more enlightenment. Jack dreamed he had to fly through a shallow band of energy with lots of little explosions in it. Jack stretched out flat and held steady so he wouldn't hit the sparks. He passed through easily. He realized he was learning to tune out negative thoughts so he could reach spiritual truth.

>> **Global-collective visions:** You see trends and events that pertain to the earth and people as a whole over long periods of history and into the future. Rob dreamed he saw an ancient time when the Egyptian pyramids were surrounded by water and was surprised later to find reports that it may have been true.

Recognize mental-spiritual symbols

Let's look at the symbols that represent mental processes and spiritual growth. Here are some examples:

>> **State of your mind:** Air, wind, storms; things that fall from the sky like hailstones or satellites; caged birds, low-flying birds like owls, crows, jays, or sparrows; ruler, tape measure, closed box, hourglass, numbers, calendar, spider web, spider; library, university, books, dictionary, elementary school, exams; attic, hat, headband, scarf on head

>> **Mental processes:** Flying close to earth, airplane, hang glider, sailplane, balloon, jet, elevator, tall buildings, skyscraper, high-tension line, ladder, tower, futuristic technologies, geometric patterns, spoken words, written language; crystal, diamond, jewels

>> **Spiritual growth processes:** Rocket, spaceship, UFO, flying high above earth, white birds, feathers, hummingbird, eagle, hawk, dragonfly; climbing tall ladders, staircases, or mountains; lotus flower, standing snake, spiritual teachers and guides, religious figures, angels, spiral, city, colony, conference; grids of light, sun, planets, galaxies, northern lights, stars, outer space, the void

Make a mental-spiritual dream work for you

Use this dream diary exercise to find insight about your mind's dynamics and discover messages from spirit:

1. **Pick five recent dreams and write about them. Ask these questions:**

   ● If this dream were talking to me about my mental clutter, what beliefs or worries might I eliminate?

- If this dream were talking to me about the fixed ideas that are holding me back, what might they be?

2. **List your three most pressing questions.**

Imagine that a wise guide, teacher, animal, or historical figure comes and gives you advice. Write out your dialogue as though it is a dream sequence.

FUN DREAM FACTS

You may be intrigued by a few of these interesting facts about dreaming:

- To fall asleep we must cool off; body temperature and the brain's sleep-wake cycle are closely linked. The blood flow mechanism that transfers core body heat to the skin works best between 64 and 86 degrees. Later in life, the comfort zone shrinks to between 73 and 77 degrees — one reason older people have more sleep problems.

- The luminous rays from a digital alarm clock can be enough to interfere with the sleep cycle. The light turns off a neural switch in the brain, causing levels of a key sleep chemical to decline within minutes. Scientists have not been able to explain a study showing that a bright light shone on the backs of our knees can reset the brain's sleep-wake clock.

- Men tend to dream more about other men, while women dream equally about men and women. Over two thirds of dreamers report experiencing déjà vu in their dreams, though it's more common in women. All mammals dream, and other animals may also dream. Elephants sleep standing up during non-REM sleep but lie down for REM sleep.

- You cannot snore and dream simultaneously! Sleep apnea, or strangulated breathing, occurs often as muscles relax deeply in REM sleep and the body then tends to wake suddenly from an adrenaline-fueled need to reopen the airways. This interferes with dreaming.

- Flying dreams are found worldwide and have existed since ancient times, long before the invention of the airplane. Dreams are penetrable; it has been found experimentally that you can communicate with a person who is dreaming.

Chapter **4**

Unlocking the Secrets in Symbols

ymbols are the language of dreams — an intuitive shortcut your soul uses to talk to you. They convey a vast amount of encoded information that always pertains to your own process of living and evolving. Every symbol is somehow about you. In a typical dream scene composed of a group of symbols, you can find clues to how you're developing, what you want to create, how you need to heal, or how to make correct choices. In this chapter, I show you different types of symbols and how to interpret them.

Discovering How Symbols Can Come Alive

Everything is a symbol, really, and conveys underlying meaning. What do your clothes, car, furnishings, cologne, business card, phone message, hairstyle, and body say about who you are? The symbols that appear in your dreams are just as indicative of you as those in daily life. Do you dream of outer space or eating French pastries? Are your dreams populated with cats, babies, mobsters, angels, or large insects with shiny eyes? Dreaming about a hummingbird instead of a bald eagle reveals as much about your inner self as your real-life choice of a pickup truck over a sports car. There's a good reason those symbols appear in your daytime and nighttime reality when they do; they represent characteristics or aspects of spirit you want to activate in yourself.

To truly understand what a symbol represents, you must *feel into* or merge into the symbol, pretend to be the thing, and speak from its point of view about what it knows. This way, you enter the direct experience of what it is to *be* a daisy, a polar bear, a set of lost keys, or a school bus. And the symbol comes alive. Once you become the symbol, it's easier to see how the image is a part of you and your life process.

Try the following writing exercise to practice merging with, becoming, and speaking as a symbol:

1. **Pick an object from your house.**

   Choose anything, such as a vase, an easy chair, the sheets on your bed, a broom, the welcome mat, a candle, a statue.

2. **In your imagination, step into the object.**

   Align your energy with it, feel its life, what it knows, and where it comes from; tell its story, and why it's in your life right now; write directly from your intuition in first person and present tense, allowing anything to come.

Familiarizing Yourself with Kinds of Meanings

Every symbol has an archetypal definition, a meaning that describes universal themes common to all people in all cultures. Additionally, it can have a personal definition and mean something unique to you alone. Kayaking in a fast river might mean a fluid emotional process archetypally, but because you flipped over in a boat and almost drowned, to you it means, "Danger!"

Notice archetypal meanings

Archetypal meanings of symbols often have sweeping themes that describe spiritual truths and processes, like the hero's journey into the underworld to face and conquer fear; the nurturing relationship between divine mother and divine child; or death, rebirth, and transformation into a brilliant new spiritual form. You can find great archetypal insights about symbols by exploring the classic myths and legends of the world.

The following exercise will help you identify archetypal meanings:

1. **Make a list of ten dream images, either single items or a snapshot of a scene.**

   For example: Going to the doctor, a bruised apple, swimming across a lake, a black-and-white dog.

2. **For each one, imagine a spiritual teacher or guide is giving you insight about what it means as a soul lesson or spiritual process.**

   For example: Going to the doctor — you're working with spiritual guides to change the way you run energy through your system; bruised apple — you're healing an emotional wound that caused you to not develop or offer your talents to the world; swimming across a lake — you're beginning a sustained spiritual quest; black-and-white dog — you're examining ideas about good and evil, right and wrong, especially as connected to friendship.

Notice personal meanings

The following exercises give you a variety of ways to become more familiar with personal symbols.

TIP

Here are several methods for imagining personal symbols:

>> Make a list of your positive character traits, the things you like about yourself. Next to the words, list images that represent those characteristics.

>> For example, for *free* you might list horse, eagle, wind; for *industrious* you might list ant, bee, beaver, hammer.

>> Pick the traits about yourself you'd like to represent to the world. What do you want others to notice about you? Imagine, describe, or draw a logo for yourself.

>> Imagine, describe, or draw a meditation symbol that represents your essence.

TIP

Symbolizing someone else can help you discover personal meanings as well. Try these methods:

>> **Make a list of ten people you've seen in the media.** Write their first and last names in your diary. Then ask yourself, *If these people had different names that conveyed their essences or important qualities of their personalities, what would they be?* Don't be logical. Take the first impressions you get. List the pseudonyms next to their present names.

>> **Pick three people you know.** For each one, ask, *If this person were a tree or an animal, what would they be? What kind of music would they be? What kind of car would they be? What is this person's secret fantasy? What does their bedroom look like? If this person were a geometric symbol, what would they be?*

Experiment with titling your dreams as a way to develop personal meanings from symbols:

1. **Make a list of ten past dreams, or recent situations in your waking life that seem like dreams.**

2. **Use your imagination by letting the most colorful images and whimsical actions in each dream connect and form a poetic title that captures the spirit of the dream and makes it instantly meaningful to you.**

   For example, sauna jailbreak, colorful lost dogs, vegetable windfall, gummy and toothless, healer mom.

Cracking Symbols Open

There are several ways to unlock the meanings in symbols. In the sections that follow, I describe a few methods and give you a chance to practice them.

Find archetypal meanings vertically

Symbols exist between the reality of the body and the reality of spirit. They represent messages from the soul to your mind and personality, and messages from your body and emotions to the mind and soul.

The meaning behind every symbol eventually helps you determine the actions that are most purposeful for you.

You can find the archetypal meanings of a symbol by moving your awareness *vertically* — "up" into the symbol's highest essence or "down" into the symbol's deepest core. You can distill a universal meaning by asking questions like *What's underneath this meaning? What came before that idea?* or *What is the highest spiritual experience this symbol provides?* Try the following exercise to interpret a symbol vertically:

1. **Pick a dream fragment or a piece of a longer dream.**

   Focus on the symbol that seems most important and describe it in a short phrase. For example, *(Blue Pegasus) is a symbol for the image I see of (a flying blue horse).*

2. **Ask yourself, *If I could feel what it's like to be blue, without fear or reservation, what sensations and emotions would I experience? If I could feel what it's like to be a flying horse, what sensations and emotions would I experience?***

   Write about the experiences, in first person and present tense, using as many sensory and emotional words as possible. Try to include vision, hearing, touch, taste, and smell.

3. **Ask yourself, *If I were a flying blue horse, aware of all its sensations and emotions, what would I naturally know about myself, the world, and life? What insights would I have?* Write about your answers.**

4. **Ask, *If I had all the sensations, emotions, and knowing of a flying blue horse, what lesson would I be teaching myself? What purpose would I be fulfilling?* Write about your answers.**

Find personal meanings horizontally

You can find the personal meanings of a symbol by expanding your awareness *horizontally* or sideways across the world. You can uncover associated ideas that are similar to the symbol, that have a meaning specific to you, by asking questions like, *What does this symbol remind me of? What memories do I connect with this image?* Traveling the horizontal path to a symbol's meaning is a totally subjective journey; symbols hold different meanings depending on how much love and fear are connected with the viewpoint. To discover the personal meanings you have with a symbol, you must trust your subconscious mind.

The method of free association can help flush up a symbol's related meanings from your subconscious. With this horizontal method, you describe the thoughts, impressions, and feelings you receive when you think of the symbol, no matter how silly.

TIP

When looking for associations, look also to your opinions and judgments. Your most forthright, candid, and judgmental ideas are often most revealing. Logical assumptions about what symbols stand for are often boring and only skim the surface. Look for emotional reality, or that special intuitive "hit" that makes you pause a moment. Omit the enticing details that wander tangentially away from the point, or you'll get bogged down. The association you find may be an episode from your life. Summarize the story in your diary, then look for a key word that stands out. This word is often tied to the meaning of the original symbol.

The flower petal technique helps you find connections and personal meanings without going off on a tangent of increasingly irrelevant associations:

1. **Close your eyes and imagine a large open flower with many petals.**

2. **In the center of the flower, place a symbol you'd like to decode.**

   Let's use a snake. Focus on the image and be willing to receive any ideas.

3. **Move your awareness out to the first petal. Imagine another image, idea, personal memory, or word on that petal, something that's related to snake and note the idea in your dream diary.**

   The first thing might be "poisonous."

4. **Return to the center and connect with the snake symbol again. Then go to the second petal and see what idea or image is there and note it in your dream diary.**

   Maybe this time it's "sexuality."

5. **Return to the center and feel the symbol before going to the third petal.**

   This time you get "ancient wisdom."

TIP

6. **Continue going back to the center, then out to a petal, until you've exhausted the meaningful associations.**

Don't jump from petal to petal or you might start associating the associations with each other. Soon you should have an intriguing list: poisonous, sexuality, ancient wisdom, dangerous, slippery, sensual, "snake in the grass," dragon, cold-blooded, sacred, teeth, sheds skin, constrictor, transformation, kundalini.

7. **Review your collection of words, feelings, memories, and concepts.**

As you write, ask yourself, *How are these ideas like me or my life right now? How do these ideas relate to each other and fit together to describe a situation in my life?*

TIP

Often a symbol's personal meaning pertains to a traumatic or confusing event in your past. You can find associations to memories and thematically interrelated experiences by following these steps:

1. **Pick an image from a recent dream and let it appear in your imagination.**

2. **Ask, *What does this image remind me of that is present in my life now?***

Let yourself receive one or more associations. Write them in your diary.

3. **Ask, *What earlier similar experience is tied to these present ones through an association in my subconscious mind?***

Let yourself receive one or more associations. Write them in your diary.

4. **Ask, *What earlier similar experience is tied to this one through an association in my subconscious mind?***

Keep asking until no more come.

5. **Examine the string of connected experiences to find common themes leading into the present.**

What core emotions are at the heart of the experiences?

DREAM DICTIONARIES OF THE PAST

Dream interpretation dictionaries figure prominently in the literature of history. Ancient Egyptians, Mesopotamians, and Greeks used them, as well as Muhammadan scholars. The *Beatty papyrus,* written around 1350 BC and discovered at Thebes, is the oldest dream dictionary existing today. It lists the interpretations of many dream images, as well as incantations and rituals to prevent nightmares. Special dream-interpreting priests were called "Masters of the Secret Things" or "Learned Ones of the Magic Library."

After the printing press made books more widely available to the public in the mid-1600s, a dream dictionary called *Oneirocritica (The Interpretation of Dreams)* by Artemidorus became one of the first bestsellers, comparable only to the Bible in popularity. On the other hand, Sigmund Freud's best work, *The Interpretation of Dreams,* now read by many as a foundation for dreamwork, sold only 451 copies in two years after being published in 1900.

Older dream dictionaries are notorious for listing obscure meanings of symbols that may have made great sense in the more distant past but don't quite compute today.

Unlock a group of symbols and find the message

Sometimes it helps to pretend you're describing the symbols to a friendly ET-type extraterrestrial who's trying to understand what they're observing on earth. For example, a woman dreamed *I'm in Europe and have made a huge amount of money, in cash, that I want to bring back into the United States, but I don't want to declare it at customs. I don't want it to show up on the X-ray machine. I'm paranoid and frustrated that I have so much money but may not be able to use it.*

This woman identified three key symbols: a large amount of cash, a foreign country that is the origin of the money, and customs and its X-ray machine. The following list shows you how to unload these symbols to their basest meanings.

>> **What is a large amount of money?** Money is a reward. Money brings opportunity, security, and power. Money is strength and energy. A large amount of money means I can have and do a lot. A large amount of money means I have done something well or been very good.

>> **What is a foreign country?** A foreign country is a place I don't normally live. It's a place where I'm not limited by what everyone thinks of me. A foreign country is exciting and offers unusual opportunities and adventure.

>> **What is customs? What is an X-ray machine?** Customs is a guard dog. Customs is the suspicious consciousness at the outside edge of the place I live. Customs will take things away from me if I have too much. An X-ray machine sees through the outside covering of things to reveal what's underneath.

After this woman could sense the underlying meanings of the individual symbols, she tried merging into them to find out how they might be a part of her current life process. Chapters 5 and 6 delve into interpreting dreams in more depth, but for now, see if you can feel how this woman put the individual symbols together to reveal an issue in her innermost self that she hadn't been aware of previously.

This woman sensed that the foreign country was a new kind of self-expression that was unfamiliar but exciting, a way of having permission to be more of herself and be more successful. The large amount of money felt like a validation of her natural talent and the rewards that could soon be coming to her. Her paranoia about customs felt like an old fear she'd had that everything good would be taken away from her or she'd be criticized if she showed herself fully to the world. So when this woman put all the symbols together, she realized her soul was sending her a message: Move past old limitations, show up for who you really are, be creative in a totally new way, and let your wealth of talent be known.

Chapter **5**

Finding Dream Meanings

This chapter gives you basic principles and techniques for drilling down to find your dreams' core insights. Be sure to check Chapters 4 and 6 for more techniques for exploring dream messages.

Examining Dream Formats

TIP

Dreams come in many shapes and sizes — some vague, some detailed, some frightening, some inspiring. They all contain encoded messages aimed at improving your life. Here are some tips for working with dream formats you might encounter:

» **Vague impression:** Try meditating and receiving any subtle feelings about the impression. Note related thoughts, moods, and sensations in your body. Follow a sensation to a feeling, to a memory or association, to an insight.

» **Single symbol or dream fragment:** Try merging into the single image and speak as the symbol or dialogue with it.

» **Story:** Try breaking the story into scenes; look for the main lesson or message in each piece by asking trigger questions about the elements and analyzing the symbols. Then put it all back together and see how the whole thing is about your current growth process. Look for insights about where the process wants to go.

» **Recurring, incomplete:** With recurring dreams, especially scary ones, there's a subconscious block that needs to be faced. When a dream is interrupted or feels incomplete, try redreaming it in a meditation and take it to a new conclusion.

» **Sequential:** When a dream is part of a series where information is revealed over time, treat the separate dreams as scenes in a longer story dream.

» **Stream of consciousness:** When the dream contains a long string of images, look for the relationships between the symbols to find a process that relates to your personal growth.

Getting Started: Things to Look For

In interpreting a dream, remember that you're first looking for insight about an issue or theme the innermost you is concerned about, working on improving, learning, or creating. You're looking for this wisdom so you can grow and become more of your truest, highest self. In finding that key message, you're likely to receive modifying details that will help you make the necessary changes and fine-tune your understanding of the lessons at hand. In addition, you may find insights about other people or society at large, and these will always pertain to your own life, too.

Remember that in dreams, time is malleable, so you may receive information about the past and future as though it is in the present.

In the following sections, I give you a loose framework for looking at key components of dreams that can help you see through the surface to what's happening underneath. Use any or all of them — they're tools for exploration.

Looking for fear and love

Dreams deliver messages from your subconscious and superconscious mind. Looking for fear or love in the dream can give you a clue about your process: Are you trying to clear a blockage or move forward from your soul's clarity?

>> **Subconscious dream content, related to the past and fear, arises so you can clear the way for more soul expression.** Personal symbology is often connected to these dreams. By looking at contracted fear responses, both in the dream and after, you can discover your subconscious blocks. One woman's dream, which forewarns of the emergence of breast cancer, shows subconscious content: *A snake has gotten inside my body, and now it's in my chest and laying eggs all over. I can't get it out!*

>> **Superconscious dream content brings guidance from your soul, access to love and wisdom, or understanding of a process shared by all people.** Typically, negative emotion is not present. These dreams feel expansive, loving, open, neutral, and informational. Archetypal symbology is usually related to these dreams. In one man's dream, his soul self is reassuring him that he's entitled to abundance and nourishment: *I'm riding in a car. As I round a curve, a passing truck swerves and vegetables fall onto the road. I stop and pick them up. I'm excitedly stuffing them into my pack — lettuce, carrots, celery, and tomatoes.*

Dreams deliver messages from your subconscious and your superconscious mind. Looking for fear or love in the dream can give you a clue about your process: Are you trying to clear a blockage or move forward from your soul's clarity?

One woman dreamed: *I'm looking over a pilot's shoulder as he guides a commercial jet in for a landing. I'm frightened yet exhilarated when he flies between skyscrapers in a big city, then finally lands safely in a lake.* She determined that she was descending from the mental-spiritual zone into the emotional zone. And when she looked at how the dream fit all the categories, she realized some things:

>> **As a physical zone dream:** She needs to develop new skills for navigating more masterfully in her life.

>> **As an emotional zone dream:** She needs to take risks to move forward in life, and she's anxious about crashing emotionally if she doesn't stay centered.

>> **As a mental-spiritual zone dream:** She's bringing higher knowledge carefully down past various fixed mental constructs, so it can be applied in her emotional life. She feels she has help from guides and teachers.

In the end, the woman decided her dream was primarily based in the mental-spiritual zone. She had been depressed and needed to refine the quality of her emotions by opening to greater spiritual understanding.

TIP

Dreams can deliver messages or instructions verbally or in written form, via a disembodied voice or a few printed words. Mental-spiritual zone dreams originate in realms that are abstract, pattern-oriented, and often devoid of symbols or scenes from daily life.

Looking into the symbols

List the main symbols in your dream; then look for the archetypal and personal meanings, as I explain in Chapter 4.

REMEMBER

Archetypal meanings of symbols take you straight to the core and give insight about universal themes, while personal meanings add insight that has particular relevance to you. Once you understand how each symbol is about a part of you, you can put them together to discover something about your personal growth process.

Looking for new information

Dreams routinely bring information that can help you in daily life. One woman dreamed that a friend insisted she drink hibiscus tea, so she actually bought and brewed some and found she liked it. Another woman dreamed of a ray of light shining through the window onto the left side of her abdomen; within weeks, she discovered she had a cyst on her left ovary.

Looking at the change points

You can find interesting insights when you examine how your dreams start, shift, and stop. The change points carry clues about your inner dynamics. Ask yourself these questions:

>> *At what point do I enter the dream action?* This can tell you something about your main concerns.

>> *What choices do I make in the dream?* This can show where you're passive or aggressive, what you're afraid might happen, or how you unconsciously react to situations.

>> *What causes one scene to shift to another?* You may discover the power you've given to others to control your life or the unconscious links between beliefs you hold.

>> *What's happening when the dream ends?* This can point out where you typically withdraw from situations or become unconscious or how you want a situation to turn out.

Asking Questions That Trigger Insights

Sometimes, you just need to be conscious of details you'd normally gloss over for meanings to become evident. Start by asking questions about the following main elements:

>> **What are the key elements?**

- How would you describe the dream structure? Did the dream have a beginning, middle, and end? Was it just a fragment? Was it a stream of consciousness, a string of images or episodes that are related to each other in some odd way? This gives you hints about what decoding techniques to use.

- What were the main scenes and settings in the dream? Were you inside or outside? Was it urban, rural, or unearthly? How many scenes were there? To notice details, ask yourself how this setting is different from others like it you've seen before. This helps you understand your process — internal, external, worldly, spiritual, stages of growth.

- Was there a sense of time or direction? Was it day or night? Were you in the past or the future? Were you facing one of the four directions? This gives insight about information being unconscious, conscious, frozen, or projected, and shows attitudes you're coming from and needing to develop.

- How was the dream lit? Were the scenes full of sunlight, in color, or lit by a spotlight? Was it foggy or dark, in sepia, or black and white? Were you aware of specific colors? This indicates what you're paying attention to, what's real to you, and the overtones you associate with things.

- What was your viewpoint? Were you a participant or playing the role of another person? Were you an observer or commentator? Were you above the action, at eye level, or below? This gives insight about how engaged you are in life and how you use authority.

- What characters were present? Were you alone or with other people, animals, or spiritual beings? Were there peripheral characters who never showed up but had an impact on the dream? This tells what aspects of yourself you're developing; shows how you cooperate, give, and receive; and what sort of help you need.

- What were the primary images, objects, symbols, or patterns? Was the dream filled with the objects and imagery of normal life? Or was it more otherworldly, abstract, or geometric? Here you can dive directly into symbol decoding.

- Did numbers occur in the dream? Did you see three wasps, seven puppies, numerals on a house, or lottery ticket numbers? Did someone tell you their phone number or the date or time? More symbol decoding.

>> What are the motivations?

- What actions were taken, and by whom? As each action was taken, what goal was pursued? This shows what you're doing in your life and the mistakes you're making or avoiding.

- What choices or decisions were made, and by whom? Action proceeds from choices and intentions. What motivated each action in the dream? This shows your soul desires, subconscious fears, and interfering mental structures.

- What outcomes were reached? Did actions lead to results? Were you satisfied with the outcomes? Did you resist them or not notice them? This shows what you want to accomplish or think you should accomplish.

- At what speed was the action occurring? High speed is a different kind of awareness than slow motion. This shows how you're processing your experience. Slow motion indicates deep understanding physically and emotionally, while lightspeed pertains to direct higher mental-spiritual knowing.

- What statements were made? Orders given? Questions asked? By whom? Pay attention to standout declarative statements and questions. Watch for words or phrases you see in print. This indicates key ideas or messages to explore, accept, or dissolve.

- What was left incomplete? Were certain actions ineffectual or interrupted? What interrupted the flow? At what point did the action stop? This reveals places you avoid experiencing something.

- What impressions did you have about the dream while dreaming? It's common to comment about a dream to yourself while you're dreaming. For instance, "This is a continuation of that other dream I had six months ago." You may have forgotten the previous dream in waking life, but your dream self keeps track. These impressions reveal ongoing deep processes your soul is facilitating.

›› What are the feelings?

- What feelings did you or other characters have? Was there an underlying mood running through the dream? Did you experience mild or intense emotion? When exactly? You may want to amplify and exaggerate a mild feeling so you can see what it's really about. This helps you see where your fear and pain lie and how you react or protect yourself.

- What senses were you using to perceive? Were you primarily aware through vision? Or did you feel someone touching you, taste food, hear music, or smell flowers? This shows preferred modes of knowing and how deep in your body you're processing something.

›› How is each part about you?

- What do you have in common with each symbol and character? Assume there is an aspect of your own emotional makeup, belief system, and behavior that the symbol or character embodies.

- How do the emotions, decisions, and actions parallel something in your own life? There are always parallels between the dream and your waking life, perhaps in a different area, about a different subject, or involving different people.

Putting It Together: A Sample Interpretation

While writing one of my books, I dreamed: *I'm walking at night on a city street, slick with rain, in a bad area. I'm following sheets of paper being spit out one by one from a copy machine that act like stepping stones or a breadcrumb trail. They keep appearing, and I have to pick them up. They're leading me into a dangerous area with many derelicts. Because I'm concentrating on the "paper trail," the derelicts aren't bothering me, but I must not lose focus or look directly at them. Ahead is a hole in a wall at the end of an alley lined with bums; through it is a muddy swampy hellhole area where the bad men come from. I decide I'm not going farther, and I wake up.*

Here's what I made of it, picking the previously listed interpretation tips that stood out to me the most:

>> **Subconscious or superconscious:** I'm looking at a *subconscious* process because there is darkness and anxiety throughout the dream.

>> **Dream zones:** The dream fits all the zones. As a *physical zone* dream, it relates to my writing, and how I must keep on, one page at a time, and not get ahead of myself. As an *emotional zone* dream, I see my writing is taking me into deep emotions, fears, and primal experiences that I hadn't expected. As a *mental-spiritual* dream, it's showing me that the book's content (and my life itself) will flow, and I'll receive the next piece (experience) just as I need it, and that by staying focused in the moment and on the creative process, I remain stable and safe from distortions or biases caused by fear.

>> **Dream categories:** Skill development, psychological processing, creativity.

>> **Dream symbols:** Several images stand out strongly:

  * *A city at night, bad part of town:* What is a city at night? It's the dark side of a collective consciousness — a part of the mind filled with desperation. Archetypally, the symbol focuses on collective subconscious fears of being attacked or perhaps fear of the unknown. As a personal symbol, I may be dredging up memories and associations

I have from living in New York City as a young woman in a period of my life fraught with difficulty and rejection.

- *Rain and a muddy-swampy hole:* What is rain, mud, a hole into a swamp? It's a flood of emotion that I can get stuck in and confused by. Archetypally, the symbols focus on emotional paralysis and overwhelm, going into the deepest part of our fear. As personal symbols, they remind me of a vague fear I have of losing direction and freedom through emotional negativity or victimization.

- *Derelicts:* What is a derelict? It's a person who's out of touch with the soul, who feels victimized by life. Archetypally, the hopeless, downtrodden, needy, possibly violent men relate to a negative, suppressed side of our masculine, manifesting energy. Personally, the symbol reminds me of an anxiety I have about poverty swallowing me up. How are the derelicts *me*? They are the starved parts of my own creative-productive self that are overworked, cut off, unappreciated, and unrecognized. They might turn on me, suck me dry, and destroy me and my book if I don't replenish them with play, respect, and warmth.

- *Copy machine:* What is a copy machine? It's a part of my awareness that translates material from other dimensions to my mind and onto the page. Archetypally, it represents the production process. Personally, the symbol reassures me that I have help in my creative endeavor.

- *Manuscript pages:* What are pages? They are formed ideas and manifested communication. Archetypally, the symbol focuses on the finished product of a writing process. Personally, the pages feel like precious jewels and a core part of me.

>> **The actions, choices, and lessons:** I follow the pages, pay attention, listen to my intuition to stay focused and steady. I learn that if I even *look* at the derelicts, I'll draw their attention and be in danger: a basic principle of how to use the mind? Don't lower my personal vibration? I see I don't need to force the creative process; I am receiving material at a speed I can handle, and I only need to pick up the pages one by one. I learn I'm being guided into deep territory, and the process will keep me safe no matter where I go. Why do

I decide *not* to go through the hole into the swamp? Honest response: I don't need to. It might shift me so much it would stop the flow of my creative process; it's not what I'm doing in my life right now.

>> **Conclusions:** To write the best book, I need to trust the natural flow of creativity and stay in the moment. As my growth process leads me deeper into my core, I will face fears, but I don't need to resist them or they'll get stronger. I must work more with feminine energy and nurture my worker bee self. I can explore beyond my known rational world into the swampy origin place when the possible repercussions won't interfere with a worldly commitment.

Trying Your Hand

This section includes a collection of exercises and techniques you can use to work with various types of dreams.

Delving into body, emotion, mind, and soul

Use the following three exercises to listen to your body, emotions, mind, and soul.

Find body messages by following these steps:

1. **Pick a few dreams and write about them as though they are messages to you from your body.**

2. **Ask how the dream might relate to your body's energy level circulation, assimilation, or elimination systems.**

   Is there a message about your health? Is there an action you should take?

You can sleuth for subconscious emotional blocks by doing the following:

1. **Pick a few dreams and see if there are any images that might have been triggered by fears or blocks in your subconscious mind.**

2. **Make a list of the images, emotions, and actions you took in the dreams.**

   Write about what the underlying themes are and how these emotions are connected to events in your daily life. Also write about how the themes you discover might be connected with each other.

Find hidden spiritual guidance with these two simple methods:

1. **Pick a few dreams and look for teachings about improving the way you use your mind and heart.**

   Could a spiritual guide or angel have been working with you to help you become aware of a new principle of consciousness?

2. **Write about what your dreams might mean.**

   Did they originate from the collective consciousness and were they pertinent socially?

Work with dream fragments

The following two exercises can help you interpret dream fragments.

Find insights by conversing with a dream fragment using the following procedure:

>> Pick a dream fragment and focus on the image or experience. Be your conscious mind asking questions, then be the image/fragment and respond. Record the questions and answers in your diary.

>> Ask the fragment these things: Who/what are you? What's your special gift? What do you do? What's your function or role in my life?

>> Ask the fragment, why are you appearing in my dream? What emotions do you want to trigger in me? What message do you have for me? What do you need, or want, me to do?

>> Ask the fragment, are you the representation of something else, like a kind of energy or belief system? If I integrate the quality you represent, how might I change?

By tracking your feelings about a dream fragment to a best or worst possible scenario, you can find interesting and helpful insights:

1. **Ask yourself these questions:**

   What feelings or sensations do I have concerning this image?

   What else comes to mind as I experience the image?

2. **If you reach a fear-based idea, ask these follow-up questions:**

   What would happen if the situation I'm trying to avoid occurred? If you reach a positive insight, ask the next question.

   What would happen if the good situation occurred? When you get the answer, ask the next question.

   And then what would happen? Continue to ask: *And then what?* until you arrive at a final outcome; then ask the last question.

   If this worst or best possible scenario happened, what might I learn?

Make sense of recurring and sequential dreams

Recurring dreams and nightmares typically end midstream without a satisfactory resolution. Sequential dreams seem to be connected in a progression over time. Stream-of-consciousness dreams contain strings of images that form a process. The following exercises will help you work more effectively with these dream categories.

Complete an incomplete or recurring dream by following these simple steps:

1. **Pick a recurring or incomplete dream.**

   Review it in your imagination from the beginning to the point where it abruptly ends. Write about what emotion, feeling, or quandary you're stuck with.

2. **In a meditation, continue the dream as though it's a movie you haven't finished watching.**

   Don't will it in a certain direction, but let it evolve naturally in your mind, and keep going until you feel the aha! Then write about what lesson you're learning.

Try this exercise to find wisdom in a dream sequence or stream-of-consciousness flow:

1. **Look for a series of dreams where one picks up where another leaves off (sequential) or dreams that contain a long string of oddly connected images.**

   Make a list of these dreams or symbol-strings.

2. **For a series of sequential dreams, write about the gist of each dream.**

   Can you sense a progression from one to the next? Is your soul revealing different aspects of an issue to you? Are you showing yourself the next appropriate action in your process? For a stream-of-consciousness dream, look for and write about how the symbols' meanings connect logically to one another in a progression. What process is being described?

3. **Write about how the dreams parallel your waking reality and the themes or life lessons you've been working on.**

TECHNICAL
STUFF

Just months before the start of World War I, Carl Jung dreamed Europe was engulfed in a great flood in which thousands drowned, and the water turned to blood.

Chapter **6**

Sample Dreams Interpreted

To find the meaning — and *meanings* — of a dream, dream fragment, waking dream, or daydream, it helps to drop below your ordinary, relatively superficial conscious mind. That first layer often says, "This dream doesn't make sense; it's crazy. It's too vague or disjointed. It's gross or frightening; I don't want to think about it. It doesn't matter anyway." When you focus more inwardly, you move into insights about how you think and believe, feel and sense, and how you can evolve more effortlessly to know your most authentic self.

Some dreams have a literal meaning, yet most reveal something you can do to heal, find new direction, make better choices, materialize a vision, help others, or develop a higher personal vibration and unlimited consciousness. These are messages from your higher self/soul to you-the-personality.

This chapter examines the hidden messages in ten sample sleep dreams and ten "waking dream" experiences. You can use these to sense how to find the golden symbolic nuggets of insight you're giving to yourself.

Making Sense of Sleep Dreams

To assist you in finding a helpful perspective for viewing and understanding the hidden meanings in your nighttime dreams, I asked friends and clients to contribute one of their dreams. For each, I provide insights that relate to the symbology and a deeper summary of what the dreamer may really be focusing on.

Beautiful Dresses

Dream: E just took early retirement from an isolating and demanding job. She dreams: *I'm in a cabin in the woods, looking through a Nine West catalog and there are beautiful dresses and jewelry on each page. I can pull the actual dresses and jewelry off the page! I hand them to 12 friends. They put on the outfits; I take photos and make a collage. I take the last dress, number 13, for myself.*

Insights: E is experiencing her new freedom in a simple cozy cabin (reality) that feels like her core self. The Nine West catalog involves 9, which represents completion and revisioning. West is the direction of letting go and deep rest. This is what E needs to focus on now. She is connecting with feminine energy (dresses and women friends) and how much she values generosity and not having to control life. Number 12 relates to the completion of a cycle, which is where she is in life. In addition, E validates her friends by recording their uniqueness (photos), then helps bring them together as a harmonious group (collage). Thirteen, the number of the last dress, is associated with feminine wisdom as well as the start of a new cycle.

Summary Message: E is giving herself guidance about how to proceed into this new phase of her life (relax, enjoy her space and freedom, trust intuition). She validates her innate generosity and ability to have good friends. She reminds herself of her love for beauty and art, and of making an idea real (2D images becoming 3D) — a longtime buried interest she might revisit.

The Magic Watch

Dream: C is actively pursuing a spiritual path. She dreams: *I'm in a large home with many rooms that lead to even more rooms. It's enormous and I'm enjoying the things left by prior owners — books on shelves, children's wooden toys, candies, sculptures. I come to a futuristic* *watch that's unlike anything I've seen before. It's silvery blue and some-how alive; it has actively swirling colors and no clear dials. I can look into it and know things beyond time. It morphs comfortably around my wrist and feels exciting.*

Insights: C is showing herself how big her potential reality is and how many interests and talents she could pursue (home with many rooms). She enjoys a variety of things from the past, yet her attention turns to what's possible to know — beyond linear time. What can she know about different dimensions? She realizes she has the ability to do this.

Summary Message: C is validating her innate love and appreciation for ordinary life and the people who have come before her. This enables her to move on and become aware of what's possible with higher levels of consciousness: time travel, clairvoyance, multidimensional knowledge. She shows herself she has the ability (the living, conscious watch that fits her perfectly).

A Rare Special Seed

Dream: R is looking for a new home and which of many project ideas to begin. She dreams: *I am visiting a monklike man, a specialist in plants, in an outdoor sanctuary. I ask for advice, and he gives encouragement quietly with few words, but not an "answer." He gives me a rare seed that is oval and as large as my hand with a sort of pocket in the top. In the pocket are many small glowing seeds. I'm happy but don't know where to plant it. He doesn't tell me where.*

Insights: R is tapping into her soul wisdom (the master gardener), receiving guidance about how to grow things (the next creative phase of her life). Without verbal direction, she must decode a multilayered symbol. The large, rare seed (her own self) reminds her that she is also rare and special and has many special tiny "light-seeds" (new positive creations) within that can grow to fruition and beauty. Not knowing where to plant the seed reflects her confusion about where to live and how to begin her new process of growth and unfolding.

Summary Message: R is telling herself to look past advice from her left brain to the intuitive right brain, feeling the new "higher" senses she is developing. She first needs to find the right home in which to plant herself, and then the glowing seeds of her renewed creativity will sprout.

Gun Battle with Six Men

Dream: M is dealing with egotistical work colleagues who try to sabotage him. He dreams: *Six men with guns break into my house and threaten me. One says he is with the KGB and asks who I am. I don't answer. A few start shooting at me, but I can see the bullets in slow motion — they're golden — so I can easily avoid them. I take my gun from the closet and kill all of them.*

Insights: M is surfacing suppressed frustration at being invaded, dominated, and belittled. He doesn't fit with his colleagues vibrationally, so both he and they feel threatened. Six represents harmony and safe intimate groups that feel like family, which is what he wants. The dream invaders act out the opposite of that yet send him high-frequency insights (golden bullets) about the polarization trapping them all. He doesn't catch (receive) the insights and instead retaliates and eliminates the "others," mirroring their behavior.

Summary Message: M is showing himself he has missed the mark — there are valuable, "golden," spiritual insights he has been avoiding and not allowing himself to physically feel and integrate that can help heal the split. Instead of looking more deeply into how his own thinking contributes to the opposition, he shows himself how he escalates and perpetuates the situation.

Healing a Young Boy

Dream: P is developing her empathic ability. She dreams: *I'm in a doctor's office and an Asian man and his young teenage son come in. I intuitively know they are real people who live in Asia. I'm some sort of doctor and the father wants me to help his son. I take the boy to a mirror, then somehow enter his body and look in the mirror as him. I don't know how this has occurred, but I know what to do for the boy - for "me." I walk us to a sink and cause him/me to throw up. Out comes a long column of gelatinous black seeds. I realize he is an opium addict. Now he is clear of it, and I separate from him and tell the father he will be fine.*

Insights: P is surprised she can share personal space like this with another person without hurting or dominating them. She didn't know she could heal, especially in this odd way, but learns she can understand others by respectfully and neutrally merging with them then separating again. She reports no sense that this is symbolic of her own health or mental/emotional issues; it felt literal to her.

Summary Message: P is showing herself how it is to be another person and see through their eyes without judgment. There is a oneness that guides her to do what she and the boy did — together. This is what allowed the healing. P realizes some part of her knew how to do this and that they were working in a higher dimension.

The Mudslide

Dream: A is dealing with her father's mental decline and is caught in family dramas. She dreams: *My father is taking our family on a drive when we realize a mudslide is coming down the mountain toward us. My father gets out of the car and goes back to the house. I move to the driver's seat and take the rest of us to safety. At home, I walk outside to investigate how dangerous and close the mudslides are. I want to know how they function. I realize I'm about to be caught in a new mudslide, just as snow starts falling. It freezes the mudslide and stops it, blanketing it in whiteness.*

Insights: A shows herself how her father is avoiding reality and how truly responsible — perhaps overly responsible — she is. The mudslide is a huge wave of heavy, thick, released emotion (water and earth), possibly burying her family in an oppressive situation. She begins to examine the dynamics of the subliminal emotional density, to get at the root causes, but she stops because snow (frozen emotion) freezes the issue and "snows it under."

Summary Message: A is showing herself that she is ready to be clear of her family's fearful, suffocating emotional beliefs and habits. She takes a few steps forward but her own anxiety stops her, and she glosses over the problem. The purity of the snow, however, hints at a sort of neutrality she could adopt to help her start excavating without having to avoid her father's upsetting behavior.

Past Life Memory

Dream: H, a woman, dreamed this in vivid detail as a preadolescent. *I am a Native American male and am with others of my tribe trapped inside a fort. We're locked in a room with a narrow high window that faces outside. After starving ourselves and waiting until nightfall, we escape by squeezing through the window. Once outside, we stay low and quickly reach the water's edge. We swim under water until we reach land, which has many trees and bushes that allow us to slip away undetected.*

Insights: Years later, H visited St. Augustine, Florida. She says, *When we walked around the Castillo de San Marcos National Monument, I could intuitively sense, deep in my body, how the fort and grounds would lay out before me. The dream flooded back just as I turned the corner near where we'd been trapped in the fort in my dream. I could feel and actually see the path we took to escape, where we entered the water, and where we ran through the trees in the distance. Inside, the tour guide pointed to a room and shared how some Native Americans were imprisoned there and escaped. The relief of escape that I felt in the dream felt fresh again.*

I later found online that in 1837, the Seminole leader Coacoochee ("Wild Cat"), was imprisoned at Castillo de San Marcos by U.S. forces. He and 19 other Seminoles escaped by fasting to lose weight, then squeezing through a narrow barred ventilation slit. Wild Cat reportedly said that they "slipped through the bars like eels" and "escaped in the night from a narrow hole."

Summary Message: H was validating to herself the reality of reincarnation and her love of Native American culture. She was reinforcing the idea that she could be, and was, truly free.

I Don't Fit Here Anymore

Dream: G was an attorney earlier in his life. He dreams: *I am working at the law firm on an important project and have determined to stay all night to finish. I brought clothes to wear the next day. In the early morning, I emerge from my office wearing only a blanket draped over my head and around my body. Surprise! The office is teeming; everyone is there and already working. I gasp. I'm in deep trouble! I shouldn't have slept here. I should be presentable and I'm wearing nothing but this blanket! I am mortified and feel overwhelming shame.*

Insights: G is facing judgment by his peers and realizes much of their approval is tied to how he presents himself. His efforts at being clean-cut, hard-working, professional, and Ivy League have helped him be successful there. Yet if he shows his authentic "imperfect" self (almost naked looking like a rumpled homeless person), he may be black-balled and lose his job — in spite of all he has achieved.

Summary Message: G is showing himself that he doesn't fit with that lifestyle and group of people. They're incapable of valuing his true self. He wants to be with people who see him for all of who he is. He wants to feel more joyful and natural. Being naked, wrapped in a blanket, signifies his true, pure self and his desire for nurturing and comfort. The dream is instrumental in his decision to leave law and pursue a totally different career.

Holographic Rapid-Fire Video Game

Dream: L dreams: *I am in a conference room with a group of young Japanese women and men, working to perfect a special kind of video game. We're sitting at the conference table, some on each side, leaning forward and staring into a 12-inch high, 3D hologram happening between us like a minimovie. It's a living reality, the result of all our minds and choices combined. We pay intense, close attention to the hologram's action and contribute our input mentally to further the development then others do the same, modifying what we've added. We have to respond instantly and register the changes and respond again, playing off each other. It's complex and mesmerizing!*

Insights: This is a symbolic representation of the way life really works. We live in a cocreated world that is constantly being revised by the split-second choices we all make. Overall, there is a companionable tone, not a destructive one, to the playfulness of the player-creators because negativity slows the game and distorts the flow. All contribute equally to the split-second realities of the hologram, enjoying the surprising ideas others contribute. The Japanese players represent a unified, mutually supportive way of thinking.

Summary Message: L is showing herself how to live joyfully by being authentic and expressive without blocking the flow of life with ego, fear, or hesitation. She must trust and be improvisational without being aggressive; she doesn't need to worry about being hurt by others' actions or offending others with her own when she remains in joy.

Pressure to Hold It All

Dream: D is an artist and coach, looking for inspiration for her growing business. She dreams: *I'm at a training in a huge auditorium. We're given lots of information about codes, constellations, images, and patterns, what they mean, and how to use them. I have lots of notes and sketches and feel very overwhelmed with much homework to do. I am told I need more testing or "revealing."*

I'm now in a clinic and am given a flat glass disc 3-inches in diameter. I lick it to reveal that it's covered in symbols. They represent my past lives, and I can see myself in those lives by putting the disc on a machine. Then, everywhere I look there are symbols and codes, embedded in things. I can't communicate with my logical mind, but if I relax I can see the energy flow of the construction of beings, thoughts, and forms. I'm trying to hold so much, but I'm dropping things, forgetting, overflowing uncontrollably. I experience panic.

Insights: The training represents a collective consciousness or soul group focused on working with symbols, patterns, and mathematical or vibrational codes to understand how life works from higher, more abstract levels down to the physical.

Summary Message: D is showing herself that she's part of this group that works with right-brain imagery and patterns to educate people about higher consciousness through creativity. She's experimenting with trying to hold all the knowledge represented by these symbolic carriers or translators of higher wisdom in her logical mind. She realizes it doesn't work. She can let it all pass through her because she already contains it all and can't forget or lose it. Information will come when necessary.

PRECOGNITIVE DREAMS THAT MATTERED

We all have dreams that give us important information about the future or that solve problems we've been chewing on. Here are a few:

- The tune for "Yesterday" came to Paul McCartney in a dream. Early one morning in 1965, McCartney heard a classical string ensemble playing in his dream. He has said, "I woke up with a lovely tune in my head. I liked the melody a lot, but because I'd dreamed it, I couldn't believe I'd written it. I thought, 'No, I've never written anything like this before.' But I had the tune, which was the most magic thing!"

- Abraham Lincoln, a few days before his assassination, dreamed he heard mourning and sobbing in the White House, got up to look for the source, and found a body wrapped in funeral vestments in the East Room. Soldiers were standing guard. "Who is dead in the

White House?" Lincoln demanded of one of the soldiers. "The President," was the answer. "He was killed by an assassin!" Lincoln recounts, "Then came a loud burst of grief form the crowd, which awoke me from my dream."

- Novelist Robert Louis Stevenson said of his classic story *The Strange Case of Dr. Jekyll and Mr. Hyde* that it was "conceived, written, re-written, re-re-written, and printed inside ten weeks," and was conceived in a dream. He said, "For two days I went about racking my brains for a plot of any sort; and on the second night I dreamed the scene at the window, and a scene afterward split in two, in which Hyde, pursued for some crime, took the powder and underwent the change in the presence of his pursuers."

- Golfer Jack Nicklaus found a new way to hold his golf club in a dream, which he credits with improving his golf game. "I dreamed about my golf swing. I was hitting them pretty good in the dream and realized I wasn't holding the club the way I've been holding it lately. I've had trouble collapsing my right arm taking the club head away from the ball, but I was doing it perfectly in my sleep. So when I went to the course, I tried it the way I did in my dream and it worked!"

Decoding "Waking Dream" Experiences

So often, we have odd snippets of experience or see something special that stands out against the background of ordinary daily life. These are as loaded with insight as your nighttime dreams. This section includes some real experiences I've interpreted for you so you can be more alert to these additional ways your inner self is talking to you.

The Perfect Eagle Feather

Experience: S was having a tough few days, grieving for her father who died unexpectedly two years prior. It was his death-day anniversary. She says, "I was caught up in the loss and quietly asked for help to soothe my contracted heart and mind. I live in the Pacific Northwest, and later that afternoon as I pulled into my driveway, I noticed something in the grass. It looked like a large leaf. When I stooped to pick it up, time stopped. Reality expanded. I burst into tears. Here was a pristine, perfect eagle feather on its edge, like a knife cutting through the green blades. Here was my father, reassuring me that he — and I — are well and good. I got the message in my mind, 'I never forget you.'"

Insights: The feather from such a powerful, high-flying, clear-seeing bird is often a sign denoting a message from a loved one who has died, a spiritual guide, or angel. These omens on death-day anniversaries are not uncommon.

Summary Message: S is showing herself that what she needs is always provided, the beings in the invisible realms are indeed real, and she is still intimately connected with her father; he is not gone.

The Enlightening Echo

Experience: K was practicing being deliberate about sharing positive energy with others. She went to an acupuncture appointment and noticed how beautiful the practitioner's face was, so she shared, "The skin on your face is so gorgeous! It's so smooth. What do you do for it?" Pleased, the woman told K about her regimen. Next, she went to get her nails done. The manicurist said, "Your skin is so beautiful; what do you do for it?" K was surprised in an amazed, entertained way to have the two experiences mirror each other so perfectly and in such close proximity.

And *then*, as she left the building, she started to smile at a man coming in, thinking it might make him happy, but didn't quite get a full smile to happen. She felt self-conscious about what she must have looked like, just as the man turned and said, "Thanks for the smile!" and winked at her. Now she couldn't help laughing.

Insights: K could see how her generosity of spirit and warm-heartedness allowed others to experience the same thing in themselves. It felt good! She was actually sharing positive energy for her own pleasure.

Summary Message: K is showing herself that gratitude and reciprocation occur, not always immediately and not always from the same person, and some people reciprocate by validating the core motive, if not the act itself.

Greetings from an Otter!

Experience: P was gardening in her back yard, digging and planting vegetables. Suddenly out of the bushes at the edge of the property, a smallish, dark animal came running toward her. She thought it was a feral cat. Just as it came parallel with her, it stopped, sat up, looked straight at her, and seemed to be smiling. Then it ran on. Its long sleek body was a deep, rich, shiny brown and it moved in a wavelike flow. "I think that's an otter!" she exclaimed aloud to herself. "But how can it be? I'm nowhere near the ocean." It made a strong impression, turning her mind from work and accomplishment to pure joy. Later, she discovered it was a river otter that lives in ponds, wetlands, and estuaries.

Insights: Otters symbolize curiosity, emotional freedom, playfulness, good luck, friendship, grace, empathy, and ease. They also represent adaptability, resilience, and being happy with the present moment.

Summary Message: P is showing herself that she has these qualities, too, and needs to remember this, use the traits, and benefit from the otter's gift, which was so pointedly communicated to her.

New Car Starts Itself

Experience: L was experimenting with manifesting. She successfully "created" a great deal on a fancy new car with many high-tech bells and whistles. She and her husband were getting ready to drive several hours to visit a friend and were discussing whether to take his truck or her new car. She really wanted to drive her new vehicle. As she came downstairs, she heard a strange low revving noise outside. She checked and her new car was idling in the driveway. Her husband didn't start it remotely and neither did she.

To add to the eerie sense they both had, when L got in the car, she was unconsciously humming John Lennon's song "Nobody Told Me" and said, rather flippantly, "Strange days indeed!" She turned on the radio and that very song was playing.

Insights: L saw that when she focuses clearly and simply on wanting something, feels it physically, then relaxes, the right moment arrives to act and meet up with the experience she wanted. The process can flow easily, without snags or logic. And her mind is tuned in to something deeper, talking to her in code (song lyrics) — and with a sense of humor.

Summary Message: L is showing herself that the process of materializing her desires can occur faster now than ever before, and that more things are possible to do than she had imagined. She is reinforcing a sense she has had that she's connected with nonphysical beings — like angels and helping souls.

A Pine Cone Opens

Experience: In a meditation, K asks to be shown symbols that are important for her. What appears in her mind's eye is a small tightly closed pine cone. She asks her deeper self what it means and receives the idea that her pineal gland is lighting up and opening to improve her intuitive knowing. A few days later, K and a friend visit a quaint thrift shop where she happens upon a basket of large, fully opened pine cones.

Insights: K immediately sees the contrast between her first internal, tightly wound image and this new physical, open, expanded version. A developmental, personal growth process is implied.

Summary Message: K is showing herself, by the correlation of a nonphysical and physical image of the pine cone, that she wants to expand her ability to experience higher levels of consciousness by opening her pineal gland. She needs to pay attention to working with visualization and spiral paths of growth.

Power Animals "Speak"

Experience: N opens her front door, and on the welcome mat is a large, perfect, dead dragonfly — one of her favorite creatures. A few days later, the welcome mat contains a perfect dead Monarch butterfly — so beautiful! And soon after, a gorgeous 10-inch hawk wing feather is waiting for her. She arranges them on her hall console table.

A week later while on a walk, she sees two hummingbirds (which only briefly migrate through her area), a thin 3-foot garter snake slowly crosses her path, a great white egret flies low, right over her head, and she stops her car to carry a large painted turtle off the road.

Insights: N is overwhelmed by the number of creatures appearing near her — almost as though they're giving themselves to her or relaying messages. *Dragonflies* symbolize new perspectives, transformation, and going with the flow. *Monarch butterflies* also represent rebirth, hope, and release of the old. *Hawks* symbolize vision, intuition, clarity, and strength. *Hummingbirds* represent joy, beauty, overcoming limitations, and agility. *Garter snakes* are associated with transformation, letting go of limitations, and protection. *Great egrets* mean grace, purity, harmony, and good fortune. And *painted turtles* represent wisdom, longevity, determination, and patience.

Summary Message: N is ready to receive guidance from a higher realm — in no uncertain terms — telling her it's time to make a leap in consciousness that will change her reality. And yet, it won't be difficult because she has much help.

Repeating Numbers

Experience: J frequently sees his birthdate numbers, 3/25, on digital clocks, as well as double-digit and triple-digit numbers, like 11, 22, 333, 444, and so on, in a wide variety of places, including dreams.

Insights: Each single number carries a meaning—a particular kind of consciousness and energy. Among other things, 1 might mean a focus on individuality and motivation; 2 on connection, balance, and patience; 3 on self-expression and creativity, 4 on physical form and discipline, 5 on freedom and change. When the numbers repeat, as in 333 or 444, the meaning is intensified and raised to a more collective or spiritual level.

Summary Message: When J sees his birthdate number, he can interpret the meaning of each number and remember how he needs to use those kinds of consciousness. He can also remind himself, "I am new (born) in this moment!" When he sees multiples of the same number, he's showing himself that he's ready to do more of that particular kind of consciousness.

Credit Card Compromised

Experience: B's credit card company notified her that six suspicious charges were made to her account; were they legitimate? No! A long process ensued to straighten things out, and for B to notify all the vendors of her new replacement card number. In the next few months, the same thing occurred two more times! Now B is incredibly frustrated and somewhat scared.

Insights: B may not have been paying enough attention to what she was spending, and this was a wakeup call. Similarly, she may have been lax in creating complex, nonrepetitive passwords. Time to fix things?

Summary Message: B is showing herself that she isn't occupying herself fully, and her unconsciousness allows others to invade her "space" and take advantage of her. Also, spiritually, she may be ready to release attachment to her personal story and identity, especially as it feeds ego or slows self-expression. She may be pointing herself to a more expansive identity as her soul, with enhanced powers of intuition, observation, and presence, which will help keep her safe and abundant.

Appliances Are Breaking

Experience: Within a month, S experienced the breakdown of her sink disposal, refrigerator's icemaker, and stovetop heating element. Then she lost her phone and several garden tools — they were somewhere in her home but she couldn't find them. After that she noticed she was dropping and spilling things, like an egg, cutlery, a cup of tea, and an open bag of rice.

Insights: Each appliance represents part of B's inner life. The disposal reminds her to make sure she's fully releasing old habits and beliefs that were cluttering her self-expression. The refrigerator's icemaker draws her attention to any "frozen" behaviors and thoughts that might need to "melt" and be released. The failing stovetop heating element points to her recent feelings of low energy and lack of enthusiasm.

Summary Message: B is showing herself how she needs to let go of old patterns and habits that have been holding her back. She's practicing letting go by actually dropping things and temporarily losing things — to feel what it's like to do without, to have some open space. She is reminding herself these things need to be fixed to free her authentic energy flow.

Lost Dog Returned

Experience: Z's beloved Cairn terrier, Amy, got out of the yard and ran away. Z searched everywhere, put up signs around the area with the dog's picture, called animal control and the animal shelters, and posted notices on online bulletin boards. A week passed with no responses. He was worried yet knew he had done what he could, physically, to find her. He decided to drop the worry and imagine her happy, healthy, and with him again; he needed to let go and relax. The next day the doorbell rang and standing there, with a wiggling Amy in his arms, was a man from a lawn care service, his coworkers eagerly watching from their truck. "I think we may have something of yours," he said with a grin. "We found her a mile away, exploring a housing development. Saw one of your posters. . ."

Insights: Z experienced just how much he loved Amy — unconditionally — and what that kind of love truly felt like. He saw how because he took actions to reconnect with her so she would be safe and decided to release control and have faith in her and her desire to return, life somehow engineered that outcome.

Summary Message: Z is showing himself that loving kindness is a powerful force And worry and negative thinking are a waste of time that may contribute to negative outcomes. He saw that his physical actions, taken with attention on Amy being back in his arms, acted as catalysts for the string of events and the lawn service crew's kindness that brought Amy home and fed the hearts of all involved.

Lost Dog Seminar

2

Dictionary of Symbols

Find a wealth of common and not-so-common dream symbols with thoughtfully derived meanings and interesting nuances.

Find three levels (frequencies) of interpretation for each word.

Dictionary

A

abortion: Physical: You're focusing on your own partially completed project, dream, or vision and realizing the timing may not be correct or something isn't quite aligned. You need to let go of a cherished aspect of a new reality for now. Emotional: If you're pregnant or your partner is, you're focusing on your response to the shock of loss: grief, anger, guilt, even relief. Mental-Spiritual: You need to pay attention deeply to the experience the souls are having, to the higher-good reasons the action needed to be suspended. Look for the deeper spiritual purposefulness in all participants.

above/ascend: Physical: If an object or person is above you, you're giving your power or energy away. If you're above, you feel you have greater influence and power. Emotional: You admire or resent someone above you or feel in control or superior when you're above them. Mental-Spiritual: If something is above you, you need more perspective and understanding concerning that idea. It might be an important missing piece of your life purpose. If you're above, you have keen insights about the issue below. Ascending signifies a desire for the big picture, that your attention is on future goals, or your awareness is moving into higher states of consciousness.

abyss: Physical: You're facing the void, the unknown, or the idea of infinity. You're in liminal space between phases of your life and need to stay there until things shift naturally. You're about to experience a significant opening into a new level of consciousness.

You need time to meditate, stop the internal dialogue, and just be. Emotional: You feel anxiety or panic about where your life is going and what's coming next. You're dealing with a primal fear of possible nonexistence or annihilation. It's important to stay centered and breathe! You need to totally release something you've defined as all-important for your survival. Mental-Spiritual: You're extremely close to realizing you're the soul and understanding how "life" in the nonphysical realms functions and feels. By allowing yourself to be with the spaciousness of the void, you discover great truths.

accident: Accident dreams aren't necessarily something you can sense before they happen. Physical: If the dream has intuitive "weight" (totally subjective to you), it could indicate a potential problem. You're probably sensing a mistake in the works: — an energy flow or process needing revision before you go too far and get in trouble. Slow down and evaluate things. Emotional: You're too emotional, or attached, or a situation is about to go out of control, and you're feeling anxious about what could happen. Mental-Spiritual: You need to pay closer attention to something. You lack key knowledge or are out of alignment with your purpose. Consider your deepest motives and wisdom.

acorn: Physical: You're looking at your potential, what you can accomplish, how much talent and endurance you have, and how ready you are to act. You're looking at the idea of how much value can be concentrated in a small act, or how the first step of a process influences the outcome. Emotional: You're feeling motives and inner strength, reassuring yourself that you can do what you intend. If there's a stash of acorns, you're hoarding what you consider valuable or need to conserve resources. Mental-Spiritual: You're touching into your core self, into your life's destiny or blueprint, sensing your purpose and what you're built to do.

acrobat: Physical: You're showing yourself how joyful it is to be fluid, flexible, and in control of dramatic movements. You're focusing on making exercise fun or enjoying ordinary daily activity as though it uses the same kind of concentration and release as gymnastics. Emotional: You need more variety to spice up your life or more intensity, discipline, and practice. You want to express more joy. Mental-Spiritual: You need more focus, choice, trust in the flow, and precision in the way you think. You're beginning to feel the lightness of spiritual reality and the freedom to move as you please.

actor/actress/acting: Physical: You're looking at your personality and how you live your life and present yourself to the public. If you're acting, you're examining the roles and qualities you portray to your "audience" in daily life. Look for tips about improving your performance. Emotional: If you're uncomfortable acting, you may feel superficial or forced to please others. If you've forgotten your lines, you may feel anxiety about a real-life situation. A phenomenal performance means you're showing yourself how to be uninhibited and unselfconscious. Mental-Spiritual: You're ready to expand your self-expression, experience more joy, and allow the energy of others, your audience, to help you be your most dynamic self. You're exploring the idea that you can understand anyone by walking in their shoes.

addict/addiction: Physical: You need to face your addictions, even if they're relatively innocent. This calls for you to look deeper: What feelings or experiences are you avoiding by using a particular substance or behavior? You're focusing on the sensation that comes just before you indulge in an addiction, so you can change the response. Emotional: You're looking at being out of control and how it feels. You're feeling how an addict can drain your energy. You're facing your weakness or cowardice about experiencing the deeper fear that fuels addiction. Mental-Spiritual: You're focusing on how any addiction, or addict, can block your true soul expression and how habits are not the source of security.

adversary/enemy: Physical: You're facing an aspect of your life or body that you physically fear, a situation you can't control, an illness, or an addiction. Emotional: You're dealing with a repressed part of yourself or may feel threatened by someone or a situation. Whether you fight or flee, and how you feel about the action you take, tells you what you need to do. Mental-Spiritual: You're integrating an important part of yourself that needs to be loved and understood. What seems negative holds a hidden gift or talent.

advisor: Physical: You're seeking guidance from someone you trust who has the wisdom, character, and experience you're ready to embody, whether it pertains to sports, job, rehabilitation, or a new life skill. Emotional: You're upset about something, needing help from someone who has the emotional perspective to help you recenter into stability without simply commiserating with you, which would perpetuate the wound or pain. Mental-Spiritual: You seek assistance from a counselor or therapist who can put your situation into a new perspective that alleviates the confusion about ego, beliefs, thoughtlessness, or defensiveness. Spiritually, you receive guidance from a nonphysical being, teacher, angel, or relative who has died, helping you rise to a higher level to see pain or problems as gifts to help you evolve.

affair: Physical: You need excitement in your relationship life. Something is out of balance in your reality, and you seek answers outside yourself. You're trying to reveal or discover a new part of yourself. Emotional: You want to feel "young" again, more adventurous, or classy. You're avoiding emotional pain by distracting yourself. You're seeking a source of happiness and fulfillment through another person or trying to activate a character trait in yourself represented by the partner. You may be punishing someone else by making them jealous or hurt. Mental-Spiritual: You're avoiding your spiritual life by looking outside rather than inside yourself. You're involved in a lack of transparency, keeping secrets, telling lies, or inadvertently hurting others through disrespect and selfishness.

air: Physical: You need to improve your vitality with more oxygen, by breathing deeply, or by improving your circulation. You're focusing on the breath of life, the health of your lungs, or oxygenation of your blood. You may be telling yourself to get outside, increase movement and energy, and breathe deeply of fresh air. Emotional: Floating on air indicates a need for contentment, whereas not having enough air means you feel lack of support for your self-expression. You're focusing on restricted freedom or the need to lighten up your emotions. You need to feel more open and flexible. Mental-Spiritual: Traveling through the air denotes movement through streams of thought and bodies of knowledge, from the lower realm of individual thought to the higher, shared collective consciousness where there's freedom from limiting beliefs. Encountering anything in the air represents fixed beliefs based on fear, interferences to clear thought, or specific ideas you should pay attention to. You're focusing on restricted freedom or the need to lighten up your emotions. You need to feel more open and flexible.

airplane/airport: Airplanes represent your focus within the mental and spiritual realms. An airport represents a departure point for a transition in your life. Physical: A small plane means you're focusing on a localized reality. Taking off shows a new venture is ready to occur. If a plane can't get off the ground, the venture may be stuck or held back. Landing signifies bringing inspiration, ideas, or energies back to incorporate into your life or body. Missing a plane means you're missing an opportunity. Emotional: A hang glider represents an experience of personal joy and inspiration. The way you feel while riding in or piloting an aircraft shows how you deal with the unknown. Having to fly a plane when you don't know how indicates you're reaching for heights you haven't attained before and are anxious. Mental–Spiritual: You're focusing on your freedom and power to rise above challenges and obtain higher perspective. A plane crash signals the end of your involvement with a series of beliefs. A jet represents concepts you hold in common with many other people. A rocket indicates you're moving rapidly toward spiritual knowledge. A UFO symbolizes a collective consciousness catalyzed by many souls of similar developmental awareness.

alarm: Physical: If you hear an alarm, you're warning yourself to pay attention to your health, habits, and inner tensions and pain or how you act in the world. Emotional: You're bringing an alarming situation to light. Someone is not who they seem to be or something that seems safe might not be. Mental–Spiritual: You are telling yourself to wake up, be aware of inner truth, and be more alert to a new period of heightened creativity, and you're giving yourself a message of guidance.

alchemist: Physical: You're focusing on your ability to change or transform yourself and your life. You want to "turn lead into gold" to drastically change your financial picture from scarcity to wealth. You don't want to put in the effort to materialize a goal; you want instant results. Emotional: You're are focusing on clearing yourself of fear, limiting beliefs, and negative emotions. You're seeking true authenticity. Mental–Spiritual: You're learning that by purifying your consciousness, you have many revelations, visions, and new abilities. You're beginning to experience the "elixir of life": your own soul's love and wisdom.

alcohol/drunkenness: Physical: With drinking, especially if it becomes a habit you can't control, you're directing attention to dealing with an actual addiction of some kind. You need to cleanse your body or shift gears, let go, and relax. You want an excuse to do something wild, different, or out of context. Emotional: You feel upset at a deep level and are trying to distract or numb yourself. You want to escape an overwhelming, painful situation or feelings of guilt or sadness. You don't want to be responsible for your behavior. You feel isolated and want to feel more connected socially. Watching others get drunk and act out means you have judgments about that behavior. Being the sober one in a group of drunken people means you feel like an outsider or superior, you need to examine your friendships, or you are wrestling with ending an addiction of your own. Mental-Spiritual: You're bored and want more excitement, fun, mental stimulation, self-expression, and exchange. You need to jump-start your imagination and creativity. You're avoiding your spiritual growth and need to get serious.

aliens: Physical: You're focusing on how your body could function more elegantly or on part of your anatomy as represented in the exaggerated features of the alien. Big eyes might mean you're trying to see something more thoroughly and deeply. Emotional: You're focusing on your experience of being an alien, feeling like a stranger in your social setting; there are aspects of yourself you've defined as foreign that need to be familiarized. You need to experience a situation freshly, as if you're from another planet. Mental-Spiritual: You're focused on your own higher awareness, possibly with a technological orientation or multidimensional wisdom. Listen for the message or teachings.

alley: Physical: You're transitioning to a new phase of life, taking a nontraditional route, changing plans as you go, and possibly hiding from public view. An alley is a shortcut or escape route on your path through life. Emotional: Alleys — behind houses, narrow, and often containing refuse — represent the subconscious mind and experiences that are slightly negative or dangerous. You feel anxiety about being attacked or heading into a dead-end. Mental-Spiritual: Something is "right up your alley" or perfect for you. You're looking behind the scenes of the normal view, seeing what's revealed in the inner lives of others.

alligator: *(see crocodile)*

ambulance/paramedics: Physical: You're on the verge of a physical problem or in a situation that needs expert helpers. Emotional: You're having an emotional crisis and urgently need help or want to help someone else. If an ambulance is taking you to the hospital because of a heart attack, for example, you may be experiencing a broken heart. Mental-Spiritual: There is an urgent need to tune into your intuition and inner wisdom. You're reassuring yourself that there's always help when you need it and you can relax, trust others, and let yourself receive.

ambush: Physical: You're experiencing an unpleasant surprise, unanticipated challenge, or showing yourself how a situation is blocked or that people are working against you. Emotional: You feel overwhelmed by unforeseen circumstances or betrayed by friends or colleagues. If you're doing the ambushing, you might want to prevent a situation by taking things into your own hands. Ambushes are also unconscious fears surfacing suddenly or upcoming loss and emotional upheaval. Mental-Spiritual: You're showing yourself that you may need healthier personal boundaries. You're experiencing a sudden breakthrough to higher awareness that you hadn't expected.

amputation: Physical: You're experiencing the radical removal of something from your life that's no longer necessary. Losing a body part points to the need to take care of that area of your body. You're neglecting an ability symbolized by the amputated part. Losing your right arm might mean you need to pay more attention to how you manifest results. You're cut off from a source of vitality. Emotional: You have feelings of separation, loss, helplessness, disempowerment, or even punishment concerning the function or misuse of a part of your body. You're separating yourself from an old wound. Mental-Spiritual: You want to experience wholeness in spite of a loss in your life. You're overcoming fragmentation.

anchor: Physical: Dropping an anchor means you're focusing on one thing and being grounded. Pulling up an anchor means you're ready to begin a new phase of growth and creativity. Emotional: An anchor securing a boat signifies that you feel stable concerning emotional self-expression. Difficulty dropping anchor means that you feel unable to center yourself and calm down or that you're drifting slightly out of control. Mental-Spiritual: You're showing yourself that there's a way to drop straight through emotional distractions into your core purpose and heart.

angel: Physical: You're refining your physical functioning and energy or drawing in healing help. You're aligning your efforts in the world with a more divine pattern. Emotional: Angels are the messengers of God to humanity and thus symbolize a bridge between the superconscious and subconscious minds. There's an important message or blessing trying to get through to you that will ease your suffering. Mental-Spiritual: You're focusing on qualities of purity, goodness, faith, protection, and guidance; you're asking for help or developing these qualities in yourself. You're attuning to your soul vibration, remembering who you really are.

animals: Physical: You're focusing on your instinctual nature. You're strengthening the part of yourself represented by the animal; look to the natural traits of the animal for clues. Emotional: If the animal is injured or trapped, you need to heal or free a part of yourself. If an animal threatens you, you need to develop that animal's strength or express your own wildness. Mental-Spiritual: Animals are spiritual guides. If you're bitten by an animal in the dream, the animal may be important as a teacher, guide, or protector. You're about to develop talents associated with the animal's expertise: the eagle's vision, the wolf's loyalty, the butterfly's transformational ability.

ants: Physical: You're focusing on diligence, hard work, and foresight. You need to work more closely with others, or perhaps you're losing your individuality by conforming to social pressures. Ants inside your body can be toxins that need to be cleansed. Emotional: Something may be bugging you, especially if ants are invading your house. You're irritated or in turmoil. Biting ants symbolize unkind acts and words. Mental-Spiritual: You are experiencing a collective consciousness that operates in harmony for the good of all.

antlers/horns: Physical: You're focusing on aggressive, belligerent, masculine energy. You're sexually aroused or stimulated. Emotional: You're looking at how you defend yourself or "horn in" on others. Mental-Spiritual: Antlers refer to intellectual powers and access, as through sensitive antennae, to ancient wisdom in higher realms. You're working with mature masculine wisdom.

apple: Physical: You're focusing on good fortune and the realization of the fruit of your work. An apple's connection to health may mean you need to pay attention to your nutrition. Emotional: Rotten apples or apple cores mean that your goals have little value or may even be harmful. Beautiful ripe apples mean you are experiencing pleasure and beauty. Mental-Spiritual: Apples represent fullness, wholeness, and knowledge and are a sign of spiritual health — that you have much vitality, wisdom, and richness to offer the world.

architecture/buildings: Physical: You're focusing on your life vision, environment, or the context in which an experience can occur. Houses represent the self, particularly the body. A building's style shows how you think of your foundation, inner structure, postures, or how you appear to others. Parts of a building symbolize parts of your body. Emotional: The condition of a building's architecture — in disrepair, ostentatious, or welcoming — shows how you feel about your personality and lifestyle. Mental-Spiritual: You're focusing on collective beliefs, worldviews, or the habits of a group. Movement between floors symbolizes rising or falling in status or awareness. Skyscrapers denote mental structures that can lift you into spiritual awareness. A cityscape indicates a complex belief system involving a collective consciousness.

arm: Physical: You're looking at your ability to reach out for what you want and to embrace others and life. Arms show how you send and receive energy, make things happen, and hold what's important to you. If the arm is damaged, you're limited in your ability to create. Emotional: Arms block attacks, defend, and strike others. You're tired from fending off hostility or from holding a heavy load. Perhaps you've been afraid to hug someone and show affection. Mental-Spiritual: You're lifting an ordinary idea up into the light. Reaching to heaven invites revelation and joy.

arrow/bull's-eye: Physical: If you're hit by an arrow, look to that area of your body; tension, pain, or congestion could be building toward a problem. An arrow punctures a blocked area and releases pressure. If you miss the bull's-eye, you need to focus and be in the flow before you act. Emotional: An arrow symbolizes a thought that seeks connection and understanding. A bull's-eye is a goal or "Aha!" If you're shooting, you feel confident about achieving a goal. If you hit a bull's-eye, you feel successful. If you've been shot, you could be wounded by sharp words or the selfish actions of others. Being shot by Cupid's arrow opens you to love and romance. Mental-Spiritual: An important message is trying to make itself known to you. Your soul is trying to make something known through you to the world. Hitting the bull's-eye means you know where to place the insight and how to deliver it.

artery/vein: Physical: An artery shows how your creativity moves into the world, while a vein shows how you receive from the world. You're looking at how much nourishment is reaching your organs and tissues. Blocked arteries can be literal problems or blocked self-expression. The circulatory system represents your network of contacts and avenues for expression. Emotional: You're seeing how nurtured and expressive you feel. A severed artery or vein means you feel panic about a loss of sustenance or support. Mental-Spiritual: You're looking at how you receive light and energy from your soul and the divine and how much you give back through gratitude and praise.

artist/artisan: Physical: You're focusing on your creative abilities and life. You need to get in touch with your body, let more energy and ideas flow out of you, or take a break from work and engage your creative, sensual side. A new project wants to be born. Emotional: You're remembering how inspired and creative you are, how joyful and enlivening your creative flow can be. You need to rekindle playfulness, spontaneity, and concentration on craft. Mental-Spiritual: You're in touch with the collective consciousness, from which all creative urges and forms emerge effortlessly. Feel the magic, the smooth flow, the innate beauty in yourself and life.

ashes: Physical: You're focusing on the remains of an old form or structure that has outlived its usefulness. You feel drained and need a fresh supply of fuel. You're dehydrated and slightly toxic. Emotional: You're looking at old values, beliefs, worldviews, and habits from which you no longer derive benefit. You feel bereft at the loss of something — a relationship, job, motivation, or loved one who has died. A loved one's cremated remains means you are processing feelings about that person or trying to communicate with him or her. Mental-Spiritual: You're letting go of the old, purifying yourself, and moving into a new phase of greater wisdom.

astrology: Physical: You're working with the fundamental energies in your body, aligning with optimal functioning and growth cycles. Important changes are ahead. Emotional: You're seeing your whole personality, accepting all of yourself. Seeking an astrology reading means you're looking for reassurance and understanding. Mental-Spiritual: Astrology signs, planets, and charts represent specific energy patterns and the desire to understand your future. You're seeing the big picture of your life, potentials, life lessons, and action plan.

attic: Physical: You're looking at old behaviors and habits you might want to integrate fully or discard. Emotional: If you're emotional while browsing through mementos, you're ready to face emotional wounds. Mental-Spiritual: An attic stores memories and beliefs from the past and is associated with the subconscious mind. Playing in the attic means you're imagining realities. Clearing or renovating the attic into a living space means you're opening your mind to inspiration, ready to live more spiritually.

audience: Physical: You're focusing on the people who receive your self-expression. You are looking at how much physical affection or assistance you receive from, or give to, others. You're showing yourself there is a market for your creations. Emotional: Your attitude toward the audience shows how ready you are to show up in your life in a bigger way, or how judged or self-conscious you feel. Mental-Spiritual: You're learning how intimately connected we all are, how others fuel you, and you them. There is no separation and nothing to fear from the outside world.

auditorium: Physical: If you're onstage, you're worried, nervous, or excited about giving a performance to a large audience. You're looking at the level of your talent and energy. Are you prepared to be exposed? If you're in the audience, you're opening yourself to new knowledge, experience, entertainment, or aspects of yourself. Emotional: You're focusing on your self-worth, doubts, and true motivations. You need to be open and nonjudgmental about what you receive, whether it's as a performer or an audience member. Mental-Spiritual: You're experiencing a space designed for the focus of attention, to be part of a gathering of aligned yet diverse beings or to learn or experience something evolutionary.

aunt/uncle: *(see grandparents)*

aura: *(see halo)*

authority/boss/teacher/parent: Physical: You're working out specific issues with real authority figures in your life. You're contemplating your own authority. Emotional: You're looking at hidden, unresolved issues with your father or mother. The symbol shows how you give your power away or deal with internal and external authority. Mental-Spiritual: You're facing issues of confidence and leadership in yourself, showing yourself how to grow spiritually.

autopsy: Physical: You're examining your health in general and the health of your organs and bodily systems in particular. Emotional: You feel disconnected from your emotions or invaded by others in your most vulnerable, private areas. Mental-Spiritual: You're focusing on letting go of your habitual identity story. You need to review a project or experience to understand what you learned and what mistakes you made. You're receiving insight into how you've been living.

avalanche: Physical: You're experiencing a sudden release. Your life is about to progress rapidly, or your body is about to precipitate a sudden change, like a healing crisis. Emotional: You feel overwhelmed by emotions that have been piling up and denied. You're doing too much and need to stop and let go. Perhaps you're facing a period of emotional upheaval, of feeling buried or swept along by circumstances out of your control. Mental-Spiritual: You're experiencing a breakthrough and release of old patterns that have kept you frozen and immobile too long.

award: Physical: You need to receive or are receiving a tangible validation of your talent, work ethic, character, accomplishments, or excellence. If you're giving an award to another, you're focusing on your gratitude, appreciation, and ability to determine the value of someone or an accomplishment. Emotional: Witnessing an award given to another means you're focusing on what you can improve in yourself or on what you envy or triggers a sense of failure or unworthiness. Mental/Spiritual: Receiving an award means you're triggering a positive, lucky attitude and state of being in yourself. You're validating yourself for wise, noble action, reaching a spiritual goal, or living at a higher frequency of consciousness.

B

baby: Physical: You're looking at a new idea, potential, or phase of life that's just beginning. You're concerned about an actual pregnancy or a desire for a child. Emotional: You're clearing your dependent behavior or infantile desires to be babied or pampered. Mental-Spiritual: You're in touch with innocence, unconditional love, vulnerability, and fresh perspective. You're focusing on new information about life purpose.

back/behind: Physical: The back of the body symbolizes your strength to handle life's difficulties. There may be literal back problems or issues concerning physical support or finances.

Emotional: Being behind someone else shows your comfort about following and not receiving recognition. The back also indicates stubbornness. Mental-Spiritual: Anything in back of something else, like a backyard, indicates a private, personal area, something not revealed to the public. You're focusing on something that is just about to become conscious.

ball: Physical: You're focusing on cells or atoms, your energy field, a specific reality, or a possibly reality. Throwing a ball indicates good communication or missed communication. Ball sports represent luck, skill, fluidity, playfulness, or cooperation within a group. If the "ball is in your court," you need to take responsibility for an action. Emotional: Balls often connect to childhood memories (pleasant or unpleasant). You're experiencing oneness, peace, and wholeness. A good game of catch denotes a harmonious rhythm that can bring joy. Mental-Spiritual: A ball represents a specific mental focus or state. You may be exchanging ideas with someone. A high-flying ball can represent movement into higher-frequency consciousness.

balloon: Physical: You're releasing old ideas or toxins from the body. Emotional: You need to celebrate, feel free, or release pent-up feelings. If you're holding the strings, you're afraid to let go. A deflated balloon indicates energy drain or disappointment. Mental-Spiritual: You're contemplating and forming creative ideas, hopes, wishes, fantasies, and prayers.

bank/bankrupt: Physical: You're concerned with physical stability and security. Something you have needs safekeeping. You have great resources at hand. Emotional: You're afraid or rigid. A bank robbery means that what's valuable about you is not respected or safe with others. Bankruptcy indicates emotional exhaustion. Mental-Spiritual: You have a wealth of ideas and talent. There is abundance in the universe to draw from.

banquet: Physical: You're focusing on having more abundance and social connections. You want to show others your power, wealth, and sophistication. You want to experience more hospitality and community. Emotional: You're focusing on your sense of hunger, greed, or need for more sustenance of all kinds. You feel vulnerable in large groups, guilty about being unable to provide, or uncomfortable about being an outsider. Mental/Spiritual: You're grateful for provision, community, and good energy. You're focusing on experiencing unity, communion, gratitude, generosity, inclusion, and reverence. You want spiritual revelation and fulfillment.

basement: Physical: Because a basement contains equipment, like the furnace and water heater, its condition hints at your physical condition. You're exploring issues concerning sexuality. Emotional: You're focusing on your subconscious where repressed ideas, memories, fears, and dangers lurk. Mental-Spiritual: You're examining the foundations of your life, where you keep what needs to be worked on. Here you access the inner resources you need to maintain your world or handle emergencies.

basket/bowl: Physical: You're focusing on how much you have and need, particularly concerning nutrition and energy. A full basket or bowl represents the harvest of your labors. Emotional: An empty bowl means you feel depleted and need love and nurturance, as these symbols represent the womb. Mental-Spiritual: Bowls and baskets hold abundance and the essence of soul. You may be offering your gifts to others. A begging bowl shows your faith in being provided for.

bathroom/bathing: Physical: You need to purify, renew, or cleanse yourself, care for your body, or eliminate toxins or tension. Emotional: You're allowed to focus privately and totally on nurturing and tending to yourself. You're cleansing harmful emotions. An overflowing tub shows emotional flooding and feeling overwhelmed. Mental-Spiritual: Toilets indicate the elimination of old ideas. You are entering a period of spiritual rebirth.

battle/fight: Physical: You're remembering actual past conflicts, or forces and energies in your body are not working harmoniously. It could indicate an attacking illness like cancer. Emotional: You feel threatened and defensive about your ideas and rights. Another person triggers a denied part of yourself. Mental-Spiritual: You're in conflict with yourself, trying to balance personality traits, or your mind is divided.

beach: Physical: You are telling yourself to relax and play, to take a vacation from what's difficult. A life change is imminent. Emotional: You're nurturing yourself, connecting with the rhythms of life and deeper, more universal feelings. You need more space and freedom. Mental-Spiritual: The shore is the boundary between the ego and unconsciousness. You're looking for inspiration; your goals are far-reaching and visionary.

bear: <u>Physical</u>: You're focusing on strength, instinct, a strong mother figure, or the feminine aspect of nature. <u>Emotional</u>: You're dealing with someone who is overbearing, ill-tempered, unpredictable, or playful. You want to withdraw from life. <u>Mental-Spiritual</u>: You need more introspection and patience to center inside yourself. You're working with a spiritual teacher of great wisdom.

beard/mustache: <u>Physical</u>: You're hiding part of your self-expression. Beards represent male courage, energy, and the power to manifest goals, especially if the beard is pointy or long. You're focusing on the father archetype. <u>Emotional</u>: Specially shaped facial hair shows how you portray yourself to others; a goatee is intellectual or artistic expression, whereas a beard with no mustache accentuates verbal communication or sensuality. Shaving indicates a willingness to be seen and vulnerable or fear of losing power. <u>Mental-Spiritual</u>: You're releasing habitual behavior, prejudices, or an old identity.

beaver: <u>Physical</u>: You're focusing on productivity, efficiency, hard work, and staying busy. <u>Emotional</u>: You're damming up the flow of your emotions to feel secure or avoiding feelings by overworking. <u>Mental-Spiritual</u>: You have a busy social life, easily overcome challenges, have a good design sense, and care for family.

bed/bedroom: <u>Physical</u>: You're focusing on regeneration, love, death, or birth. You need more sleep. <u>Emotional</u>: You need a womblike retreat, more space, or nurturing in your inner life. You want romance, marriage, sex, and a healthy intimate relationship. The bed represents your emotional condition and innermost secrets. <u>Mental-Spiritual</u>: You're trying to connect with your inner realms. Anything under the bed shows what subconsciously threatens your peace.

bees/beehive: <u>Physical</u>: You're focusing on fertility, industriousness, creativity, and how you organize your life. You're looking at the power of hard work and cooperating with others to get a job done. A healthy, humming hive means you're headed for an increase in success and material comfort. <u>Emotional</u>: You've been hurt or have hurt others with gossip or stinging words. You need to let others support you and you support them. Swarming bees reflect feelings of annoyance and bother or a need for significant change. Fear of being stung shows you feel you might be injured emotionally. A diseased or empty beehive means you feel sad, alone, or without purpose, or you may be depressed and worried about close relationships or finances. Mental-Spiritual: You're focusing on the opportunities you need for success or fulfilling the role you were built for. You're focusing on the harmonious functioning of an organization in which each individual is happy performing its job for the collective good.

beggar: Physical: You're focusing on your confidence and initiative level, looking at how much you want to achieve. You've lost control of a situation or of yourself. You're being too lazy and need to pick yourself up and get going. Emotional: You feel insecure, undeserving, like a failure or outcast, or that you will lose favor with people and be rejected. You feel no one will help you. You need a way out of depression. Mental-Spiritual: You're examining your scarcity thoughts and how you think you've been victimized. You need to develop either more humility or self-confidence to understand something about yourself. You need to focus on trusting that the spiritual realm and other people will provide just what you need when you need it to live well and evolve.

bell: Physical: Hearing a bell can mean you're being called to begin or complete something. You're focusing on a point in time. You're put on notice to pay attention to something coming into your reality or about engaging in an upcoming choice or action. Emotional: Hearing bells, as on a bicycle or with windchimes, means you're clearing negativity from your path or home. Mental/Spiritual: You're invited to a meeting or gathering of people you may already know or may not know yet or of nonphysical beings in higher spiritual realms. The sound of bells ringing carries you to higher dimensions and creates spiritual harmony and awareness of divine presence.

below/descend: Physical: You're experiencing a decline in energy or status or a return to what's fundamental. You're dropping into your body fully. Emotional: If you're below someone, it indicates humility, service, yearning, and growth potential as well as feelings of inadequacy or depression. You feel compassion or disdain for what is below you. Mental-Spiritual: You're moving through your subconscious mind on a journey of self-discovery.

bill: Physical: You need to put forth effort to create balance for what you've received, or you need to collect what is owed you. Emotional: You need to be more responsible, generous, and keep your promises. You feel stressed about your image or resources. Mental-Spiritual: Life is handing you the bill for past mistakes, karma, and bad decisions so you can face up to the lessons you need to learn.

binoculars: Physical: You need to take a closer look at a situation or bring an aspect of your life into focus. Emotional: You're looking ahead, feeling anxious about the future and the potentially dangerous or negative outcome of a situation. Mental-Spiritual: You want to see things that are far off or understand the specifics of a coming process or event. You need to evaluate your choices and decisions. You're developing intuition and precognitive ability, seeking a vision or spiritual insight. Your focus is too narrow; you're missing the big spiritual picture.

birds: Look to the species of bird for meaning nuances. Physical: You want greater lightness and freedom in your body. Singing birds bring good news. Emotional: Birds represent the way you love. Caged birds mean you aren't expressing yourself joyfully or freely enough. Migrating birds are about homesickness. Mental-Spiritual: Birds represent the ability to reach higher realms of awareness. Like angels, birds serve as messengers of the divine and are symbols of the soul. Look for the messages birds bring.

birth/birthday: Physical: Giving birth symbolizes the beginning of a new project, ability, or stage of life. It relates to the desire for a child or anxiety over pregnancy. Your birthday focuses attention on how you're living your life. Emotional: You feel reborn. You're focusing on feminine, nurturing energy. Birthdays remembered or forgotten by others show how significant you feel as an individual. Mental-Spiritual: You're receiving new ideas, attitudes, plans, wishes, or parts of your destiny, and emerging into new levels of wisdom. Your birthday centers you in your sense of soul and life purpose.

bisexuality: Physical: You're focusing on finding clarity about your own sexuality. You're are trying to understand the physical experience of being intimately open to male and female partners. Emotional: You're focusing on possible repercussions of revealing your sexuality to others. You need to find others you can relate to happily and safely. You want to overcome obstacles and integrate bisexuality into a healthy lifestyle. Mental/Spiritual: You're focusing on balancing and integrating aspects of the masculine and feminine in yourself, unconditional love, or being nonjudgmental and open to all people.

black: Physical: Your body may be unhealthy, blocked, or feeling somewhat comatose. Black portends death or the end of something, as well as gestation. Emotional: You're focusing on your unconscious, the underworld, evil, fear, grief, or negative feelings. You might also feel elegant, formal, strong, and authoritative. Mental-Spiritual: You're aware of the death of old ideas, the mystery, deep space, the void, receptivity, or protection by or absorption into the divine feminine.

black hole: Physical: You're focusing on a person or situation that drains you and sensing how to be involved or not be involved. You need to stay centered and fully present, without allowing your energy to be hijacked. Emotional: You're are facing a fear of annihilation, a sense of losing yourself. Mental/Spiritual: You're contemplating death. You're fascinated by the unknown that exists in other dimensions. You're focusing on the experience of simply being, without thought, feeling, or personality.

blanket: Physical: You need more heat or "fire element" in your body. Emotional: You need to feel protected and safe, hidden, or loved. Mental-Spiritual: You want a period of introspection and self-discovery, where greater self-love can develop.

blind/blindfold: Physical: Open your eyes and use them, connect with reality. Emotional: You aren't aware of something important or don't want to see something. Someone is deceiving you or you are deceiving yourself. Mental-Spiritual: You need to direct attention deeply within to experience a more spiritual or sacred connection with life. Don't be distracted by the superficial.

blood: Physical: You're looking at your vitality and life force as well as danger. Bleeding to death means something is draining your creativity and energy. Menstrual blood symbolizes fertility or cleansing. Emotional: You're focusing on a denied emotional wound, anger, hatred, or fear a loss of part of your life. Bloody violence indicates emotional upheaval. Mental-Spiritual: You're aware of the source of all life, what makes you strong.

blue: Physical: You're too cold or have a sluggish appetite, metabolism, and circulation. Or you're too keyed up and need calmness. Emotional: You feel sad or depressed. Or you feel clean, precise, serious, masculine, or corporate. Mental-Spiritual: You have, or need, clarity, insight, truth, loyalty, justice, or neutrality. You're detached from emotion, perhaps living in an overview. You need to receive or give a soothing action or a communication based on faith and hope.

boat: Physical: You're focusing on your life's journey, wanting to make a change, or to reach the other side. Emotional: Boats show how you traverse an emotional experience or `help` protect you from being overwhelmed by one. The kind of boat shows how you deal with emotional situations: A powerboat rushes or pushes through, a canoe gives time to think in your own space, a tugboat moves slow and steady to get the job done. Sinking boats indicate fear of water or an overwhelming emotional encounter you're afraid to, or need to, experience. Mental-Spiritual: You're embarking on a new spiritual journey. Being becalmed or drifting aimlessly with no paddle shows apathy or lack of purpose.

bomb: *(see explosion)*

bones/skeleton/spine: Physical: You are focusing on your stability, courage to take a stand, inner strength, and the structures you live by. Broken bones represent disrupted energy flow in a particular area of the body. Emotional: You're too hard or emotionally fossilized. You need to release rigidity and resistance. You feel unsupported and weak. Mental-Spiritual: You're getting to the essence of something. Skeletons pertain to death, either literal or metaphorical. You're examining how you receive from your unconscious and transmit energy from your lower self to higher self and vice versa.

book: Physical: You are ready to receive news or are integrating your life experiences. Emotional: Opening or closing a book symbolizes opening or closing a stage in your life. Mental-Spiritual: You're learning or reviewing your knowledge and wisdom; you're looking for guidance about life issues. Old books represent neglected or forgotten knowledge, an earlier chapter of your life, or even ancient wisdom. You're examining the book of your life — your destiny throughout time.

boss: *(see authority)*

bouquet: Physical: You're focusing on receiving or giving an expression of affection, love, caring, or fond remembrance. The choice of flowers or plants in the arrangement can convey extra meaning. Emotional: You want to express feelings that are difficult to put into words and want to rely on a "go-between" to help. Mental-Spiritual: You're focusing on an offering to higher consciousness and evolved nonphysical beings to convey how much you honor and trust the help and truth that comes from beyond your current sense of reality.

box: Physical: You're focusing on your body, a particular commitment, task, or goal. You need order, definition, and less or more structure. Emotional: You're offering a gift to others or receiving one. An empty box means you have lost something, had something stolen by others, or can't see your own resources. Mental-Spiritual: You're unlocking secrets and mysteries or forming ideas into strategies and goals.

brain: Physical: Pay attention to your head. Emotional: Don't make all your decisions with your head alone, or don't be too hot-headed and impulsive. Mental-Spiritual: You're looking at how you process information and perceive concepts. Make better use of your intellect, pay more attention to facts and details.

brakes: Physical: Using brakes to stop a vehicle implies you should immediately stop or withdraw from a situation before there are disastrous consequences. You're going too fast, not taking care of your body's needs. Emotional: When the brakes don't work, you feel out of control about a situation, too much ahead of yourself, and helpless. Mental-Spiritual: You're focusing on how to regulate the flow of your self-expression.

bread: Physical: You're focusing on nutrition and a need for greater simplicity. Emotional: Bread is basic nurturing and sustenance. Bread crumbs show lack of abundance or a process leading to greater abundance. Burned toast shows nurturing that was unappreciated and wasted. Moldy bread indicates you may be wasting important nourishing resources. Mental-Spiritual: Bread is sacred, the "food of life," representing patience, humility, and other godly qualities. Fresh-baked bread shows luck coming. Offering bread to others demonstrates compassion and an open heart.

break: Physical: Breaking things means you need to change an area of your life, like breaking away from a relationship or job. Emotional: You need to break through a barrier into an area of yourself that's been repressed or release an emotional attachment. Mental-Spiritual: Broken objects signify shattered ideas, hopes, or goals. It can also mean you have broken through limiting thought structures to a higher dimension.

breasts: Physical: You're focusing on fertility, motherhood, and nurturing or female beauty, sexuality, seductiveness, and power. Breasts that are too large and heavy represent a burden of feminine responsibility and a challenge to physical health. Emotional: You're looking at the experience of comfort, safety from being close to another's heart, or you're focusing on sexual exploitation. Small breasts may represent feelings of unattractiveness. Losing a breast or breasts due to surgery means you're focusing on wholeness and identity, as well as experiencing loss and gratitude for life. Mental/Spiritual: You're becoming aware of your essential self and abilities that lie beyond child-bearing and sexual attractiveness, based on your spiritual nature and heart. You're rediscovering a higher level of caring, nurturing, and attractiveness.

bridge: Physical: Bridges indicate literal travel and life transitions. The condition of the bridge shows the type of journey it will be and your way of entering new territory. Bridges also represent relationships. Emotional: You're making an emotional transition and looking at ways to avoid feeling overwhelmed by emotion or the unknown. You're finding helpful connections between yourself and things you fear. Mental-Spiritual: You're linking life experiences or realms, like conscious and unconscious, and dealing with unresolved contradictions and paradoxes.

brown: Physical: You're focusing on toxins, waste, or excrement, indicating you need better elimination. Emotional: You feel depressed, negative, or sluggish, or you want more comfort. Mental-Spiritual: Brown suggests thought processes involving greater stability and the animalistic nature, or your mind is muddied with distorted thinking and other people's ideas.

bubble: Physical: You're releasing something from your physical system or are experiencing indigestion with gas or bloating. Emotional: You want to feel lighter, more childlike, effervescent, celebratory, fun, and spontaneous. You're releasing worries, difficulties, or negative emotions. Mental-Spiritual: Bubbles symbolize wishes or unrealistic expectations, as in "bursting one's bubble." They also show true hopes and ascendant thoughts.

buffalo: Physical: You're focusing on abundance and plenty or survival. New opportunities are coming your way. Emotional: You're being too obstinate. A buffalo herd symbolizes peace and increase, as well as family loyalty and safety in groups.

<u>Mental-Spiritual</u>: You're focusing on how much you honor what you've been given, and whether you show gratitude for your life.

buildings: *(see architecture)*

bull's-eye: *(see arrow)*

burning: <u>Physical</u>: You're purifying, or something is disintegrating so you can move on unencumbered. <u>Emotional</u>: You're releasing anger, criticalness, or intense emotions. You feel passionate. You're living through a trial by fire or a loss beyond your control. <u>Mental-Spiritual</u>: You're focusing on bright new ideas and spiritual purity.

bus: <u>Physical</u>: You're looking at the many aspects that make up your personality. You're focusing on achieving a goal where other people are involved. You're antsy because your progress is too slow, you're being stopped by setbacks, or the quality of your experience is substandard. <u>Emotional</u>: You're uncomfortable in a crowd. You feel you aren't receiving enough recognition. You're frustrated. You need to show more patience and less selfishness. <u>Mental-Spiritual</u>: Driving a bus means you're responsible for other people's safety or leading a group. You're focusing on collective consciousness, collective ideas, and energy. You and a group are working in the spiritual realms to learn, remember, and make progress toward a new reality.

butterfly/caterpillar: <u>Physical</u>: You're transforming yourself in a fundamental way, growing in stages. You need more freedom. <u>Emotional</u>: You're reminding yourself to lighten up and be more tender and gentle. A flitting butterfly suggests social or romantic activity, possible infidelity or superficial involvement with others, yet with a happy attitude. <u>Mental-Spiritual</u>: You're focusing on becoming your most beautiful self. Butterflies represent the soul's essence.

buy/bargain: <u>Physical</u>: You're expanding and fortifying yourself with the tools and opportunities you need in life. <u>Emotional</u>: You feel you don't have enough love or support and are easing anxiety with new possessions. Finding a bargain means you feel lucky, or you're not valuing yourself enough. <u>Mental-Spiritual</u>: Buying indicates the acceptance of an idea or situation. You're focusing on a fair exchange of value, or that you need to receive as much as you give.

C

cactus: <u>Physical</u>: You feel crowded; someone is invading your space. You need better boundaries and more privacy. <u>Emotional</u>: You're defensive, too prickly, and isolated emotionally. You need to be flexible and express more emotion instead of feeling so dry. <u>Mental-Spiritual</u>: You've adapted yourself to a difficult situation or need to apply a tougher attitude. The resources you need are stored within.

cage: <u>Physical</u>: You're focusing on restriction and limitation in an area of your life. You're alerting yourself to a blocked energy or circulatory flow in your body. You need to break some habits and add more variety to your life. <u>Emotional</u>: You feel confined by someone or a condition that holds the keys to a fuller life, and you're sad or frustrated that you've lost your freedom. You feel inhibited, helpless, victimized, or handicapped. A caged animal or bird means you fear or hold back your wildness, joy, and instinctive urges. You're facing repressed emotions or caught in an escapist attitude. <u>Mental-Spiritual</u>: You need to free an aspect of your self-expression and creativity. You need to focus on your deeper self to realign with your truth. You think freedom lies outside, or spiritual growth happens in a particular way, but you're showing yourself it can happen anywhere.

calendar/datebook: <u>Physical</u>: You're planning on creating or doing something that has an end date. <u>Emotional</u>: You're worried about a deadline or having enough time to do everything you need to. <u>Mental-Spiritual</u>: You're learning to be more grounded in time. You're looking at how you use your time and plan your life — how organized and prepared you are. Crossing off days on a calendar means you're marking time until an event happens.

camel: <u>Physical</u>: You're preparing for a journey. You need to conserve resources and energy. You can handle big problems and responsibilities with patience and perseverance. <u>Emotional</u>: You're carrying too many burdens. You need to express and release emotions you've been holding too tightly or practice forgiveness. <u>Mental-Spiritual</u>: You're capable of going the distance and finding resources within when things in the outside world look bleak or hopeless. Something good is coming to you from a long distance.

camera: Physical: You need to pay attention to what you're doing and notice how others see you. Emotional: You're fixated on a particular reality, resisting change, or lost in nostalgia for the past. Mental-Spiritual: You want to stop the action, gain more information, or capture hidden meanings in a situation. You're involved with your worldview, attitudes, or credo. Taking snapshots represents daily perceptions, observations, or decisions. Old photos point to something you need to remember from another time.

cancer: Physical: You don't necessarily have this disease, though it could be a warning. A condition in your life may be out of control, consuming your energy and vital resources. Emotional: An emotional issue has been denied too long or an emotional habit is out of control. You feel your life is wasting away. You feel too negative, critical, or hopeless. Mental-Spiritual: You're obsessing about an idea. You need to examine how fully you're living your life and how to uncork your creativity.

candle: Physical: You want a cozy, comfortable, warm ambiance to relax in, lit by candlelight. You want to celebrate a birthday or marker point in someone's life. Looking into a candle flame brings peace, self-realization, and insight. Emotional: A candle burning at both ends means you're under pressure, doing too much, and time is running out. A candle's light can signify a beacon of hope, that someone is home, that a destination is within reach. Mental-Spiritual: Lighting a candle for someone who is sick or has died means you're consciously remembering and caring for them. You light a candle to offer a prayer or to represent the truth of the Light of spirit.

captivity: Physical: You need to stop running around and focus. Something important needs attention. You may be too sedentary and need to get out and move your body. Emotional: You may feel trapped by circumstances, as though you're a victim with no choices. You may feel you're being punished. Don't give your power away to others. Mental-Spiritual: You've forgotten about free will and that it's okay to say "no." You're remembering that your soul will restrict you when you need to face important issues.

car: Physical: You're focusing on your daily life and life direction or on your body and personality. Mechanical problems indicate blocks in your body or forward movement. Being stuck or backing up means you feel this way about your progress. The condition of the vehicle gives an idea of your health condition. <u>Emotional</u>: Driving indicates you're in control. Riding in the passenger seat or back seat means you're deferring to another's influence or feeling out of control. <u>Mental–Spiritual</u>: How you drive shows your ability to navigate through life, your ambition, confidence, and ability to make decisions. Your car gives clues to your identity. A stolen car is a loss of identity. Being hit by a car means you're in conflict with another person or way of doing things.

cards: <u>Physical</u>: Playing cards indicates you are using, or need to use, luck and the skills of strategy and timing in a current project or phase of your life. The number and suit of the cards provide clues to the meaning. <u>Emotional</u>: You feel you're gambling in some way or that success is a matter of luck. <u>Mental–Spiritual</u>: Clubs mean taking action and getting down to business. Spades mean sadness, disappointment, or the presence of an obstacle. Hearts symbolize love, positive emotion, and relationships. Diamonds relate to your concepts of material and inner abundance and resources.

castle: <u>Physical</u>: You're hoping for great success or preparing to fortify yourself for an endeavor you see as difficult but rewarding. <u>Emotional</u>: You need to protect yourself from attacks, even from your own internal critic. Castles represent a warring, defensive nature. If the drawbridge is down, you're receptive, ready to face the forces of the outside world. There is also a connotation of fairy tale rescues where you're either the hero or damsel in distress. <u>Mental–Spiritual</u>: You need to examine the idea that the world is hostile, you need power over others, or isolation by being above it all.

cat: <u>Physical</u>: You're focusing on qualities of independence, power, self–sufficiency, mystery, magic, feminine energy or the anima, sexuality, grace, and cunning. When beautiful, a cat means you will meet a charming new person. <u>Emotional</u>: You feel others are fickle and uncaring, seductive, ominous, "catty," or aggressive. A black cat means you're hesitant; you use your intuition. Kittens symbolize unchanged, bothersome, astral plane beings. <u>Mental–Spiritual</u>: A cat's nine lives symbolize good luck and longevity.

cataclysm/catastrophe: <u>Physical</u>: Natural disasters and upheavals symbolize sudden shifts or releases of energy in your body or in the world. <u>Emotional</u>: There's emotional instability, and you're facing an upsetting experience that could change your reality. You're worried about basic survival issues. Mental-Spiritual: You're about to have a breakthrough into a more enlightened state as you let go and have faith.

caterpillar: (*see butterfly*)

cattle: Physical: You're focusing on good luck, the goddess, maternal nurturing, and fertility. Cattle feeding in a pasture signify an easy flow of income. Herding cattle means you're working harder to maintain your income. Emotional: You're focusing on your individuality and going along with others too much or too little. You feel you're too passive, docile, or contented with your life. Mental-Spiritual: You're focusing on your intrinsic value and what you're capable of producing.

cave: Physical: A cave symbolizes the womb, childbearing, new life, creativity, or an empty place in you that needs more energy and attentiveness. Emotional: Crawling into a cave may mean being overwhelmed by a present situation or that you need to protect yourself. Living in a cave means you feel deprived or isolated, or you need sustained privacy to regroup and renew. Mental-Spiritual: You're focusing on your deep inner self, the place of ancient wisdom, contemplation, rites of passage, initiation, the earth, and your feminine side. Coming out of a cave is the emergence of a new self and desire to be involved.

ceiling: Physical: You're looking at the limits you or others place on your progress. A ceiling means protection, if it's also a roof. Emotional: You're focusing on safety and self-expression. A leaky ceiling means an intrusion of unwanted emotions or other people's values that affect you negatively. High ceilings give you room to expand, whereas low ones make you feel stooped and stunted. Mental-Spiritual: You're looking at how you use your thoughts, how open you are to change, how imaginative and resourceful you can be, or how far you have to go to the next floor. A glass ceiling means you can see farther than you can actually go physically right now. Something unknown holds you back. Being on the ceiling looking down gives you the soul's perspective on a situation.

celebrity: (*see fame*)

cellular phone/telephone: Physical: You're focusing on establishing and maintaining connections and on developing telepathy and clairaudience. Emotional: Losing your phone means you've lost touch with your true feelings or inner self and, to the degree you are dependent on it, how capable you are of being alone. If it's ringing constantly, you need more quiet, gestation-meditation time. You're looking at the balance between extraversion and introversion in yourself. Mental-Spiritual: You're working with a soul group or collective consciousness. You're receiving new information, setting up events in the near future.

cemetery: Physical: You're focusing on the end of a phase, project, relationship, or habit. You're looking at your family lineage and how it affects you. Emotional: You're tapping into memories that carry emotions like sadness, nostalgia, grief, anger, anxiety, fatalism, hope, and deep love — pertaining to a past or anticipated loss. Mental-Spiritual: You're seeking to understand death and dying. You're reviewing your history or the history of a culture or the planet. You're communing with higher dimensions of consciousness, connecting with people who have died, or completing old death-related fears. You're focusing on inner peace. On rare occasions, a funeral or open grave may be a precognition of the passing of a loved one.

chase: Physical: If you're being chased, you're avoiding a situation that's potentially dangerous or unwanted. You have an answer someone needs. If you're the pursuer, you're chasing after a goal, trying to right a wrong that's been committed against you, or trying to gain attention from someone who's rejected you. Emotional: Being chased means you feel indebted to someone or that you're being driven away from involvement with others. It means a rejected part of you needs to be acknowledged and reintegrated into your personality. Mental-Spiritual: You feel pursued by disturbing, fearful ideas that you don't want to experience. The pursuer may have a message for you. The pursuer may be you!

cheat/steal: Physical: You're picking up hints that someone is not being truthful or committed, or you're trying to take the easy way to greater comfort. You have compromised your beliefs or integrity and are wasting time on fruitless endeavors. Emotional: You feel you aren't meeting the expectations of others, and you're experiencing insecurity and lack of trust and self-esteem. You feel envious of someone else's talent or fortunate circumstances. Mental-Spiritual: If you're cheating at a game, you probably aren't being honest with yourself. Cheating on tests, or stealing, indicates you think you lack knowledge, creativity, or a natural talent and that no one will help you, so you have to take what you want.

chess: Physical: You've found a worthy opponent or a perfect match in love or in your professional life. You're looking at how you use your resources to accomplish goals. Emotional: You're showing yourself how to be more deliberate and less impulsive concerning your interactions with others. Mental-Spiritual: You need to think through a situation or problem more carefully before deciding or taking action. You're looking at the greater plan for your life. *(see games)*

chest: *(see heart)*

chicken: Physical: You're focusing on idle chatter and gossip, what people are saying about you, or what you're saying about others. Emotional: You're looking at qualities of cowardliness, erratic helter-skelter emotion, or lack of willpower. You're acting like a "mother hen," being too concerned about others. Roosters represent cocky, show-off behavior with little regard for others. Mental-Spiritual: Since chickens aren't known for intelligence, you're telling yourself to be more serious and focused. Hens with eggs represent new life and possibilities. Hearing a rooster crow is a wake-up call.

child: Physical: You're activating a new beginning, fresh perspective, latent talent, spontaneity, or trust in yourself. You're eager to learn, need simplicity, or purity. Young people symbolize lost vitality, so you may need rejuvenation. Emotional: You want to return to a life where you had little responsibility and fewer worries. You're pointing to your own immaturity or the need to receive unconditionally. A childhood anxiety or long-buried issue needs to be resolved. You're nurturing your vulnerable self. Mental-Spiritual: Innocent, loving children represent the true self or child within. You're recalling old memories or getting in touch with your playful creativity. Saving a child signifies saving a part of yourself that's in danger of being lost.

chin: Physical: You're "leading with your chin" and not listening to others enough. Emotional: You may need to be more or less assertive or stubborn. Mental-Spiritual: A strong or weak chin signifies how you cut through to the heart of situations and represents your determination and resolve.

church: Physical: You're looking at your mistakes and how to rectify things in your life. You need to treat your body as a temple. Emotional: You're looking for guidance, to be uplifted and nurtured, to forgive or be forgiven. You need to be appreciated by those you love. Mental-Spiritual: You're focusing on a spiritual context or space, your value system and the things you hold sacred, religious beliefs, or attitudes toward organized religion. You need to pray for yourself or others, or receive grace, spiritual nourishment, or atonement.

circle: Physical: You are going in circles or have come full circle. You're looking at the idea of being complete as an individual in each moment. You're are looking for satisfaction. Emotional: You're anxious or enthusiastic about beginning a new cycle or completing an existing one. You want the right circle of friends. You feel vulnerable and are imagining a circle of protection around you, like a shield. Mental-Spiritual: You're experiencing centeredness, wholeness, fullness. You seek the experience of oneness and peace.

city: Physical: You need more privacy or more social involvement. You're dealing with community issues involving cooperation and interdependence. Emotional: To be alone in a city means you feel rejected or overwhelmed by others. A city in ruins means you're neglecting social relationships. Mental-Spiritual: A city with tall skyscrapers indicates you're dealing with collective thought and belief structures and worldviews.

cliff: Physical: You've reached a jumping-off point where you're faced with a major life change. Emotional: You're facing your fears and overcoming the need to retreat. Mental-Spiritual: You're at the edge of consciousness and the unknown, a point of heightened understanding and awareness, where you need to surrender and have faith to proceed farther. You have an expanded view.

climb: Physical: You're making steady progress toward a goal, requiring persistence and strength to overcome obstacles. You experience an increase in social, economic, or artistic pursuits. Emotional: How and what you climb shows your courage, fear, and enthusiasm for growth and the expansion of your worldview. Mental-Spiritual: You're focusing on the specifics of your intellectual and spiritual growth, your strategy on your path forward in life.

clock/watch: Physical: You're aware that your biological clock is ticking or that time is passing, and you need to overcome procrastination about achieving life goals. You need to speed up or slow down. Emotional: You're anxious about being on time, meeting a deadline, or falling behind. Mental-Spiritual: As with any circle, a clock represents wholeness, but also the present moment, all time, and immortality. Note the hour and minute and look for meaning in the numbers.

clothes/costumes: Physical: You're focusing on the façade, or layers you put between yourself and others, how you portray yourself, your role in life, and how you like to feel personally. Changing clothes or costumes suggests a need for change, or adaptation to a new way of being in the world. New clothes mean social or economic improvement. Emotional: Being undressed to various degrees indicates feelings of vulnerability or not fitting in socially. Underwear connotes hidden sexual issues. Too many clothes show layers of protective identities. Mental-Spiritual: You're examining beliefs about how to express yourself, what you need to do to receive approval, and how vulnerable you can be.

clutter: Physical: You need to let go of or discard something. Emotional: You need more clear space so you can calm down and not be worried about so many things. You're afraid of being alone. Mental-Spiritual: You need to sort through your beliefs and see how many thoughts actually belong to other people and get rid of them. There may be parts of the self you've rejected that need to be reclaimed.

cobwebs: Physical: Old spider webs and dusty conditions indicate that an area of your life has been neglected or that you've been ignoring an issue for too long. You need more exercise, better circulation, and detoxification. Emotional: You're apathetic, depressed, or afraid to experience emotions from the past. You need to clear emotional blockages. Mental-Spiritual: You're telling yourself to dust off some aspect of yourself, reexamine old beliefs, and clean house so you can see yourself clearly again. You're making connections between ideas and experiences — how your ideas mesh with other people's thoughts and how individual experience connects with spiritual insight.

coffee: Physical: You're talking to yourself about waking up and becoming more conscious in your life. You need more energy and ability to focus. You're alerting yourself to the advent of fresh, new ideas that are just "brewing." Spilled coffee means a wasted resource or opportunity. Emotional: You need to take comfort in a routine. Or you may feel stuck in a rut and need new stimulation. Sharing coffee with friends means you want more warm-hearted, interactive social activity. Too much coffee points to addiction and the need to calm down. Mental-Spiritual: Drinking coffee means you're open to ideas and visions, activating your motivation, and experiencing a wake-up call to pay more attention to your spiritual path and intuition.

cologne: (*see perfume*)

colors: Physical: A pale tint of a color indicates an early stage of development or weak energy, while a dark shade conveys strength, density, toxicity, or blocked energy flow. Emotional: Muddy, clear, intense, light, or dark color tells you about the qualities of your current emotions. Mental-Spiritual: Bright, clear color indicates a heightened sense of reality, even a precognitive or visionary dream. If an object in your dream has an unusual color, you're seeing an extra overlay of meaning. Complex colors, like olive green (green and brown) or turquoise (green, yellow, and blue) contain qualities of each color.

column: (*see pillar*)

competition: Physical: You are anticipating a competitive event or are involved in improving your performance under pressure. You need to grow and expand or rest from an intense competition that's ended. Emotional: You're focusing on being more assertive, persevering, and ambitious. Watching a competition from the sidelines means you feel others are passing you by. Mental-Spiritual: If you win a competition, you have the necessary skills to accomplish a goal or solve problems. You're examining the need to win and what winning and losing means.

computer/laptop: Physical: You need to get out more, vary your routine, and be more sensual. If the peripheral components malfunction, you're frustrated that you aren't supported or producing effectively. Emotional: If you lose your laptop, examine how dependent you are on external systems to give life meaning, and how you can develop more emotional richness within as well as real-time relationships with others. If you have a virus or someone is hacking into your computer, your privacy is being invaded or you feel you're at the mercy of another. Mental-Spiritual: You're looking at how you structure your awareness, how your mind works. You're connecting to global knowledge and examining your life record and identity. If the computer crashes, you're overloaded and need to take a break from being so mental. If you expand the memory or speed, or get a bigger monitor, you're jumping into new capacities and self-expression.

cooking: Physical: You're focusing on improving your diet and nutrition, developing your cooking into an art, or using cooking to lose or gain weight. You're tired of cooking and want someone else to do it for you. You're "cooking up" plans for a new endeavor. Emotional: You're cooking or baking to show your appreciation and gratitude to someone. You're upset about the price and quality of meals at restaurants and want to focus on craftsmanship and economical food. Mental-Spiritual: You're fascinated with how cooking can change basic ingredients or focusing on transforming yourself or helping someone else transform via greater attention to health. You're focusing on healing and personal growth by blessing your food, cooking with consciousness, and sharing it with others.

counselor: Physical: You need to listen to your body. If the person being counseled is not you, you may identify with that person's issues or be concerned about their psychological health in waking life. Emotional: You're seeking support and direction. Pay attention to what the counselor is saying and doing. You need to look within to explore feelings, gain insight about a particular issue, or understand your motives. Mental-Spiritual: You're receiving guidance from your soul or a higher collective consciousness.

countryside: Physical: If your dream has a country setting, you need to focus on physical activity and more wholesome, natural values and goals. You need more space to find clarity or a slower pace. Emotional: You're telling yourself to return to the basics and simplify your life. You need to feel more generous and patient. Mental-Spiritual: You're experiencing an expansion of thought beyond separate structures into communion and oneness.

courtroom: Physical: You or someone else needs to be held accountable for an action. You're waiting for a decision from an authority about your next step. Emotional: You're upset that you must face something you were trying to avoid or that you must make restitution for. Mental-Spiritual: Are you a lawyer taking the defensive side or prosecuting side? This alerts you to a dominant habit of thought. If you're the judge, you're attuning to law and the spirit of the law. You're focusing on morality and what's fair and just. You're focusing on universal principles and whether you're in harmony with them.

crab: Physical: You're looking at your inability to effectively move forward, how you sidestep or avoid difficulties and unpleasantness. Emotional: You're pretending to be tough or looking at your "crabby" personality. Claws indicate a desire to cause pain to others, or fear of being hurt, as well as a tendency to grasp and cling. Mental-Spiritual: As with all water-dwelling animals, the crab represents issues in the unconscious.

crash: Physical: Being in a vehicle that crashes or is about to crash indicates that a situation in your life is out of control. It also means you simply arrive suddenly and dramatically at a new level of achievement. Crashing into the ground from the air means you're descending rapidly from the mental and emotional realms and coming back to your body, or you need to be more grounded. Emotional: Crashing into a similar vehicle means a confrontation with someone else's physical presence (car, motorcycle), emotional values (boats), or belief structures and opinions (planes). Mental-Spiritual: You're going too fast, being impulsive and inflexible, listening to incorrect advice, and need to pay attention and regulate your mind. You're experiencing a spiritual chiropractic adjustment or opening that will catalyze a new phase of your life.

criminal/outlaw: Physical: You're exploring your animalistic side. Emotional: You feel the rules don't apply to you, that you're above others. You take what you want because you feel no one will help you, that others have more than you. You are experiencing guilt over something you've done and feel anxious over being found out. Mental-Spiritual: If you or someone else is breaking the law, you feel too boxed in by customs, expectations, and authority and want to break through limitations.

crocodile/alligator: Physical: You're focusing on hidden danger, deceit, or evil-minded people. The crocodile represents your own aggressive behavior or negative, snapping attitudes. Emotional: You feel you could be swallowed up by chaos, greed, gluttony, hidden violence, or dark, stifling emotions. Perhaps you've displayed false emotion and shed disingenuous "crocodile tears." Mental-Spiritual: You're focusing on your deepest subconscious, primal mind, your beliefs in evil and lack of safety in the world, and your survival instincts. You need to look for ways to be more sincere.

crossroads/fork in the road: Physical: You're breaking physical habits and seeking new direction in life. Emotional: You're dealing with anxiety about making the right decision, facing the unknown, or separating from loved ones. Mental-Spiritual: You have a choice to make, and it often involves an intuitive component. You're at a powerful point of integration of diverse ideas.

crow: Physical: You're reminding yourself that what seems negative (dark) is also positive (light) and often important. You're remembering that crows mate for life and are loyal to their well-organized flock (a clear expression of wise collective consciousness), are extremely smart, and are protective of loved ones, even certain people. If you're kind to a crow, it will remember you and the flock can become friendly toward you. Are you similar or dissimilar? Crows engage in "mobbing," loudly warning, as a collective, about danger to others. How much like a crow are you? Emotional: You're ready for an important shift or period of growth. You're focusing on bravery, allowing yourself to be open to guidance that at first might seem threatening. Mental-Spiritual: Crows are seen as messengers between the physical and nonphysical realms, bringing guidance or warnings, often the announcement of someone's impending death or major change. Are you open to receiving what a "sentinel" crow is saying? Why has it come to you? You're activating important information, and even ancient wisdom, in yourself. You're recentering into the experience of your own spiritual transformation.

crowd: Physical: You're looking at your own authority, leadership ability, or questioning your role in society. Emotional: You feel you're being swallowed up by other people's ideas and emotions, or you need greater anonymity and privacy. Mental-Spiritual: A crowd indicates that you're participating in a group mind or collective consciousness.

crown: Physical: You've received recognition, or want to, for a job well done or for your innate abilities. You are acknowledging your own competence and power. You're about to receive greater responsibility. Emotional: You're dealing with your relationship to authority figures. There can be issues of vanity, envy, resentment, and need for attention. Mental-Spiritual: A crown symbolizes spiritual authority, often indicating an initiation. It's a transmitter of knowledge from the collective consciousness to your conscious mind.

crystals/crystal ball: Physical: You need to cleanse your body or listen to the messages your body is bringing you. Seeing a crystal in the body means that area may be blocked and needs to receive and transmit energy more fully. Emotional: You're telling yourself you need greater inner peace and transparency (honesty and vulnerability). Mental-Spiritual: You're accessing higher wisdom and opening your intuition, developing clarity of perception and removing illusions. Look for the visions, take note of the messages.

cut: Physical: If your body is cut, or you cut someone else, you're showing yourself an area that needs to release pent-up energy, pain, and contractedness. Cutting yourself indicates a need to release feelings of turmoil by experiencing physical pain. Emotional: You're focusing on severed relationships, cutting off from feelings or other people, sarcastic remarks, or anger and rage. Mental-Spiritual: You need to cut through to the heart of an issue, be honest, and see clearly with spiritually based insight. Having your hair cut means a loss of vital power or a focusing of your consciousness to be aligned with your personal expression.

D

dam: Physical: The energy or circulation in your body is blocked. You're hoarding something. Emotional: You're focused on repressed emotions, holding back a flood of tears, panic, or anger. A dam breaking means you're releasing past fears and emotions. Mental-Spiritual: The dam itself represents the reason you hold back your self-expression, whether that be family or cultural beliefs, an unexamined habit, or stubborn resistance to change caused by fear.

dance: Physical: You need more exuberant, spontaneous movement and exercise. You're focusing on romance, sexual exchange, freedom from constraints, participation in life, pleasure, frivolity, and gracefulness. Emotional: If dancing with others, you're looking at partnership dynamics, fluid cooperation with others, and how well you fit in and interact in your social setting. A dance performance shows how confident, talented, joyful, and comfortable you feel expressing yourself in the world. Mental-Spiritual: You're focusing on psychological and spiritual release and sacred communion with the rhythms of life, especially if you're dancing alone. You're integrating the masculine and feminine sides of your nature.

danger: Physical: You're warning yourself about something you've been overlooking. To escape danger portends success. Emotional: You're anxious about a situation in your waking life and need to use intuition to feel what's really happening below the surface. Mental-Spiritual: Confronting danger means you're overcoming fear and learning from the situation. What is dangerous in the dream is something you haven't integrated into your totality.

datebook: (*see calendar*)

daytime: Physical: When a dream setting is during the day, you're experiencing things clearly. What you need to do is obvious. You know where you're going in life. Emotional: The sunnier the scene, the more the activity represents something beneficial, or something you need to see as a good part of yourself. Mental-Spiritual: You're dealing with material that has already become conscious, or you're shedding light on an important fact.

deafness: Physical: You're closing yourself off from new experiences. You don't want to hear something you need to acknowledge. Emotional: You feel secluded or excluded from the world. You're too stubborn and resisting change or other people's realities. You aren't sharing your emotional reality with others. Mental-Spiritual: You need to withdraw from the chaos of the world into a quiet inner sanctum to find your own still, small voice of guidance and truth. You need to develop greater flexibility and openness concerning ideas.

death/dead people: Physical: Dreaming of death is not necessarily a literal omen, and it's untrue that if you die in your dream, your body will also die. You're focusing on the end of a phase in your life or a part of your identity, getting ready for rebirth, renewal, and growth. Dying slowly or seeing a corpse represents a devitalized condition or lifeless routine. Emotional: You're experiencing anxiety about endings. Dreaming of another person's death means you're letting go of the quality or emotion that person represents, or you feel the possible loss of that aspect and want to activate it more in yourself. Mental-Spiritual: Talking to a person who has died is resolving incomplete communications, and it helps activate the qualities the person represents to you. You're active in the higher, more telepathic realms of your awareness, receiving guidance from your soul. Seeing yourself after death reassures you that you are eternal.

deer: Physical: You're focusing on your ability to be agile, graceful, and alert. You need to be more responsive to a situation, notice subtle cues, and be quieter. Deer often represent friends and what kind of friend you are to others. Emotional: You need to experience gentleness, kindness, compassion, innocence, purity, and willingness to surrender. "A deer in the headlights" means you need to break free of a brain freeze and take immediate action on something important. To see a dead or dying deer, or to kill a deer, warns of a betrayal by a friend, or that you have acted without heart. Mental-Spiritual: Deer are considered divine messengers that help open the heart. Pay attention to where they lead you, and what they say or convey with their eyes.

descend: (*see below*)

desert: Physical: You're dehydrated or lacking in important nutrients. You need alone time away from the overstimulation of society to renew yourself. Emotional: You're feeling isolated, lonely, creatively dry or barren, or poor. Storms in the desert indicate emotional issues surfacing that are connected with feeling unloved and neglected. Mental-Spiritual: You're deepening into your spiritual nature, retreating to a place of simplicity, silence, openness, and freedom where you can find clarity. Wandering through a desert indicates a period where you must reexamine what's truly important and possibly give up things you don't need. Finding an oasis means you're connecting with your divine nature, when and where you least expect it.

desk: Physical: Sitting at a desk represents self-exploration and discovery. You're focusing on your work and the technical issues of your life, taking care of business. Emotional: You are protecting your secrets and personal information. How neat the desk is indicates how overwhelmed you feel by details and mundane tasks. If you're at someone else's desk, you lack confidence in your own abilities or are copying someone else's qualities. Mental-Spiritual: You're activating new knowledge and ideas and evaluating problems and opportunities. The kind of desk hints at your sense of personal authority. Desks also represent a place or focus for bringing your creativity to life.

dessert: Physical: You're focusing on the desire to be rewarded for completing a project successfully or doing a good job. You want to enjoy the good things in life, especially if you're eating dessert before the meal. Emotional: You feel unloved and unacknowledged and want to treat yourself, or you need to thank other people for helping you. You're being too hedonistic and self-indulgent and need to focus on being practical. Mental-Spiritual: You're examining ideas concerning what makes you happy, why you celebrate, what tempts you, how you experience being loved, and how you distract yourself from unpleasant situations with rewards. You're beginning to glimpse the love and joy of the spiritual realm and how by evolving into clarity you receive the highest level of your just desserts.

detective: Physical: You're looking into your body to discover any lurking potential health problems. You suspect something is amiss in a project or venture and are sleuthing in the invisible realms to sense what it may be. Someone has lied to you and you're becoming conscious of it. You took a question or problem to bed with you and are looking for answers or ways to solve it. Emotional: You're plumbing the depths of your subconscious, looking for reasons for reactionary emotions and behavior, or making connections between clues that link to a large-scale explanation of your present emotional habits. Mental-Spiritual: You're seeking hidden truths: How does life work? What is the experience of soul? A person you depict as a detective means you associate them with the powers of radar vision, cleverness, and insight into patterns.

detour: Physical: You're looking at a problem with your energy flow or circulation, perhaps focusing on a blockage in your body, an obstacle in a project, or your personal growth process. You aren't ready to deal with something yet and must "go around" or seek a different course of action. Emotional: You're afraid to confront something or someone directly and seeking a way to avoid conflict. You're making excuses to distract yourself from feeling uncomfortable emotions. You're frustrated at being forced to slow down. Mental-Spiritual: You have been going too fast and are learning the direct route isn't always best. You've reached an impasse where a way of thinking isn't getting results, and you must improvise and use your imagination to reinvent yourself or solve the problem. Your soul is moving you in a new, surprise direction that you need.

diamond: Physical: You're focusing on being the best you can be, cleaning up your act, and being totally healthy. Owning and wearing diamonds means you attain honor and recognition. Receiving a diamond from someone means you're forming a committed relationship. Emotional: Finding diamonds means you're about to have good luck, whereas stealing them means you aspire to a higher station in life than you feel worthy of or qualified to have. Losing a diamond means you aren't valuing part of yourself enough. A fake diamond means you or others are pretending to be something you're not, or you feel undervalued. Mental-Spiritual: You're finding clarity in matters that have been clouding you. You're focusing on your own highest, clearest soul consciousness, or clear light. You're looking at core truth, unending love, and what is permanent and enduring.

dictionary: Physical: You need to pay closer attention to the details in your life and to what is truly meaningful. Emotional: You're too dependent on other people's advice and direction. You're examining the building blocks of your reality and what you hold as necessary. Mental-Spiritual: You need to redefine something you've seen as positive/attractive or negative/repulsive. You need to focus and be more precise and articulate in your communications. You're looking for clarity of meaning and definition of your identity, aligning with personal truth and your spiritual purpose. You need to trust your intuition while also listening to other people, realizing they contribute extra nuances of meaning to your life.

dig/dirt: Physical: Dirt represents fertility; you're planting the seeds of a new phase of growth. You need to clean out your body or house or simply be more grounded. Emotional: You want to bury, hide, or deny something. You feel unclean or guilty that you've been acting in an unwholesome or devious way. Mental-Spiritual: You're trying to understand yourself better, looking for root causes, hidden secrets, buried treasure, and basic motives. You're reaching down into the subconscious to unearth answers, information, or talent.

dinosaur: Physical: You're focusing on a problem that seems too big, primal, or powerful to handle. You're remembering a looming issue from your past that you haven't dealt with, which has a negative effect on your health or success. <u>Emotional</u>: You're afraid you're being eclipsed by younger people and becoming outdated, superfluous, and unnecessary. You're frightened by the unknown. You're caught in knee-jerk impulsive reactions. <u>Mental-Spiritual</u>: You're focusing on outdated attitudes and the need to get rid of antiquated habits and ways of doing things. You're dealing with a societal structure or belief system that's unwieldy, antiquated, slow to evolve, and dysfunctional. You're contemplating the transformation from a survival-based reality to a more abundant one.

diploma: <u>Physical</u>: You have achieved a level of success and expertise and are acknowledged by others. <u>Emotional</u>: You are worried about succeeding at a task or job or don't feel qualified to handle a situation. You've completed a difficult time of emotional clearing. It's time to honor yourself for your accomplishments. <u>Mental-Spiritual</u>: You've successfully completed a life lesson or phase of growth and feel natural self-esteem. Let others see what you've accomplished. *(see graduation)*

disease: <u>Physical</u>: Dreaming of illness isn't necessarily literal or precognitive. You may be holding tension and stress in your body, or your energy may be blocked. You need to change a self-defeating lifestyle choice. <u>Emotional</u>: Getting a disease can reflect a fear of the outside world or distrust of your own body and self. If you contract a disease from another person, you feel that person's influence in your life is detrimental. If the disease has a stigma, as with sexually transmitted diseases, you have anxiety about your morality. <u>Mental-Spiritual</u>: You're looking at your lack of faith and where you don't feel the divine, loving presence in yourself and in life.

dive: <u>Physical</u>: You're trying to get to the bottom of a current situation. If you're standing on a diving board, you're preparing for a serious temptation or ordeal that's coming in the near future, and you're summoning your courage. <u>Emotional</u>: You're facing and experiencing deep emotional wounds or seeking to intensify your passion and empathy. <u>Mental-Spiritual</u>: You're delving into your subconscious as well as the greater unknown.

divorce: <u>Physical</u>: This may be a reflection of a real-life experience, or you feel you're being denied a rightful position or an opportunity to work with people you admire. <u>Emotional</u>: You're experiencing stress over a relationship that you're afraid will end or feeling vulnerable and abandoned. You're caught in the blame game. Mental-Spiritual: You feel alienated from yourself and your truth and need to reconnect with your purpose. You need to experience how loved and loving you are, that your self-worth is not dependent on approval from others. *(see ex)*

dock: Physical: You're grounding your creative urges. Seeing a dock from a ship means a positive turn of events and new action. Emotional: You're finding security amid emotional confusion or overwhelming feelings. Sitting alone on a dock means you feel wistful, sad, or dreamy. Mental-Spiritual: You're bringing spiritual insight and visions through your emotion and motivation into fruition in the world, making your dreams real.

doctor/nurse/healer: Physical: You need to attend to your body's condition. Healing has already occurred, is about to occur, or there is a need for healing. If you have an operation in a hospital, you're adjusting the way energy flows through your subtle energy bodies and physical body. You wish for a cure for a problem you're having. Emotional: You need more nurturing, to feel cared for and safe. You feel too deeply probed by someone or are probing into yourself. Mental-Spiritual: You have subliminal insights about the cause of illness in yourself or someone else. You're focusing on the healing authority of your own soul and other knowledgeable souls, making fundamental shifts in the flow of your awareness.

dog: Physical: You're focusing on friendships, new relationships, family values, or masculine energy. You're working like a dog, or dog-tired, and need some rest. Emotional: You're looking at issues of trustworthiness, loyalty, protection, and dogged tenacity, both in yourself and others. Happy dogs and puppies symbolize simple joy in life. Aggressive dogs indicate similar tendencies in you that need appropriate outlets or that you feel defensive about being invaded. Mental-Spiritual: As guardians of the underworld, dogs connect you to the unconscious and often bring important messages. They also teach about openheartedness and positive attitude.

donkey: Physical: You're focusing on your responsibilities and being steady, loyal, dutiful, rugged, and enduring. You're working hard without much reward. Emotional: You need to come down off your high horse, be less self-important, and develop greater humility and practicality. You're stubborn, unyielding, and uncooperative and need to find more fluidity, joy, and heart-based motivation. Mental-Spiritual: If you're successfully riding or leading a donkey, you're focusing on patience, kindness, and good communication and leadership skills. You may be reminding yourself to be an honored, humble servant of the divine, or you're royalty in disguise.

dolphin/whale: Physical: You're focusing on a fluid, easy way of moving through the world, working with your inner senses, especially telepathy and personal vibration. Emotional: You need to trust your friends and colleagues and develop a joyful attitude and beautiful harmonious feelings. You want protection moving into unknown territory or need to feel more trust when exploring emotions. You're developing heightened sensitivity and good communication in relationships. Mental-Spiritual: You're seeking high-level intelligent guidance, or your soul is sending a message to you. Since dolphins and whales are conductors of souls and keepers of ancient wisdom, it's important to listen to what they say. If you're riding a dolphin or whale, you're experiencing optimism, communion, and love for humankind. Dolphins symbolize spiritual excitement while whales link to profound calmness and peace.

door/doorway: Physical: Stepping through a door symbolizes a new endeavor or moving from one phase of life to another. A closed door is an unavailable opportunity, or you must exert effort to open it. A choice of many doors shows a juncture at which a choice must be made. Revolving doors suggest you're moving in circles, going nowhere. Emotional: If doors are locked or obstructed, you're making life difficult for yourself through resistance, or there are repressed, hidden emotions you're avoiding. You need to find the key that allows entry without force. If you can't find the door out of someplace, you're feeling trapped by life circumstances. A door slammed in your face represents opportunities that are denied you, possibly because you feel unwanted. Mental-Spiritual: You're bridging two states of awareness. A small door symbolizes the desire for inner exploration and self-discovery.

dove: Physical: You're seeking greater harmony, love, and commitment in relationships, as well as an end to disagreements. Emotional: You need inner peace, a happy domestic and social life, or you look forward to the return of an old friend. Mental-Spiritual: Doves bring the olive branch of understanding and also represent the Holy Spirit or a connecting link between heaven and humankind. Released from the hands, the dove flies with joy toward the divine. You're seeking communion.

dragon: Physical: You're focusing on protecting or uncovering buried secrets and talents, your heroic nature, and on balancing your internal masculine and feminine energies. Dragons in western culture represent fire and earth. A fire-breathing dragon in a cave means you're freeing your wildness and protective nature. In eastern culture, dragons represent air and water and are good luck. A flying or swimming dragon indicates you're freeing your emotional, mental, and spiritual life. Emotional: Slaying a western dragon means you're overcoming your fears. Riding an eastern dragon means good fortune and wisdom is coming your way. Mental-Spiritual: You're looking at what's hidden deep within the soul — at your true powers and riches.

drawer: Physical: You're looking at parts of yourself that have been stored away or hidden and that you're now ready to use. An open drawer signifies a new opportunity, and if full, you'll have plenty of resources and help. An empty drawer is an invitation to create. Emotional: You're showing yourself your internal state, whether it's disorderly and chaotic or neatly organized with psychological order. A locked drawer suggests obstacles in your path or resistance from someone. Mental-Spiritual: You're reviewing opportunities, resources, and old ideas. If you clean out your drawers, you're making space for a new, more inspired awareness and updated accomplishments.

drift/float: Physical: You need to strengthen personal discipline and reaffirm your goals, or you need some downtime to relax. Emotional: You have lost your motivation, are distracted, or feel unfocused. You're between projects or phases of your life and feeling anxiety about what to do next. Mental-Spiritual: The motion of drifting and floating represents activity in the spiritual realm. You need to let go and simply "be" wherever you are and realign with your higher purpose, letting new direction arise spontaneously.

driving: Physical: You're focusing on taking charge of your life direction and journey. If you can't see the road ahead, you lack a sense of purpose and goals. Driving into oncoming traffic means you're challenging others and making progress difficult for yourself. Emotional: If someone else is driving, you feel passive, powerless, or at the mercy of external influences. If you're speeding or tailgating, you're being too selfish and out of harmony with others. Mental-Spiritual: You're experiencing the process of materializing your life. Driving in reverse or looking in the rearview mirror repeatedly means you're focused on the past or in an illusion and are ignoring important present moment data.

drown: Physical: Your body is bloated and retaining water, or you need to flush out toxins with more water. Emotional: You feel unable to keep your head above water. You're overwhelmed by your life and subliminal emotions or those of others. You feel frightened of being swallowed up by unconscious forces. You're dealing with difficult issues concerning your mother or your birth experience. Seeing someone drown suggests you're too involved in something beyond your control or you've lost your identity. Mental-Spiritual: You're allowing yourself to be reborn, surrender to the unknown, and access deep wisdom and feminine energy.

drugs: Physical: You're focusing on wanting or needing a pharmaceutical substance to help you heal, manage pain, prevent sickness, or maintain health after surgery or during an illness. This points to giving power over to something outside yourself and the idea of being dependent, even though the substance may be a vital part of ongoing health. Emotional: You're connecting certain drugs with creating positive emotions, status, glamor, attractiveness, power, or self-worth. You associate some drugs with rebellion against the status quo, racism, and materialistic values. You connect still other drugs with numbing emotional pain, stress relief, and escapism. You associate drugs with the ability to access and experience new talents and aspects of yourself. Mental-Spiritual: You connect psychoactive drugs with expanded consciousness, intuitive and visionary capacity, heightened imagination, and ability to communicate with nonphysical beings. You long for rapid personal transformation and to be connected consciously to the spiritual realms.

drum: Physical: If you're playing the drums, you're living life on your own terms. Emotional: The kind of drums you play or hear shows the emotional state, and thus the overall tone of your life: It might be jazzy and exciting, militant, wild, or like jungle drums. Mental-Spiritual: To hear a drum symbolizes the rhythm of life, your heartbeat, and the need to keep a steady pace in the pursuit of your goals. There might also be a message in the drumbeat, or someone is calling for help.

drunkenness: *(see alcohol)*

duck: Physical: If you see ducks in a group, you're focusing on the importance of a nurturing family, protection, and ability to be fluid and adaptable. You may need to be more or less sociable. Ducks easily move between water, land, and air. It also reminds you to focus on loyalty, providence, and being the "lucky duck." You can succeed by taking one step at a time. Emotional: You're being reminded to pay intuitive attention to your environment because new opportunities or dangers can be waiting close by. To move forward, you may need to take flight. If you're safe, make progress on land. Focus on your senses, not old emotional habits or beliefs. Mental-Spiritual: You're being guided to live in the moment and enjoy life as it comes. You have the ability to penetrate the subconscious realms, be open and undefended, and take the right path forward. A group of flying ducks means you have help and are making progress on your spiritual journey.

E

eagle/hawk: Physical: You're focusing on your natural authority, nobility, power, courage, fierceness, and pride. You're looking at long-range goals and ambitions, perhaps connected to attaining wealth and influence. Emotional: You're learning to control your emotions and focus attention more neutrally, though you may be aggressive and somewhat ruthless. Mental-Spiritual: You're stretching your mind into the spiritual realms, looking for clear perception, keen discrimination, and larger perspective. These high-flying birds act as messengers from the sun, or soul, from other souls in the highest dimensions, so look for messages and lessons.

ears: (*see deafness*)

earth: Physical: You're working on being fully focused in your body, being practical, and finishing things so you have tangible results. You need to be more loyal, committed, stable, or careful. Issues of fertility are on your mind. Emotional: Under the earth's surface, for example, in caves, tunnels, basements, cellars, and graves, lurk the contents of your subconscious mind, which are often frightening. You're facing your long-buried monsters. Mental-Spiritual: The earth seen as a globe indicates wholeness, the mother principle, and global awareness. The earth also contains buried treasure and ancient wisdom. You're deepening your awareness.

earthquake: Physical: You're experiencing, or are about to experience, a shake-up of your world that threatens your stability and foundations. If you escape from the quake, you overcome the challenges. Emotional: You're caught in feelings of anxiety, insecurity, and helplessness. You can't depend on people you thought were reliable. You're letting go of controlling behavior and old fears. Mental-Spiritual: You're focusing on a total change in the way you view your life — and even reality itself — and on the development of new attitudes and mindsets.

east: Physical: You're focusing on a new beginning, renewal, or birth. You need to dedicate yourself to an area of your life, like your goals, career, family, or personal growth. You're looking for opportunities and adventure. Emotional: You are impulsive and ahead of yourself, overenthusiastic and blind to something. Mental-Spiritual: You're looking for fresh perspective, insight, new intellectual knowledge, and control.

eat/food: Physical: You need a consistent diet of healthy foods, or less or more food. You're seeking gratification based on physical pleasures. Eating with others means harmonious cooperation, personal gain, and joyful undertakings. If someone is taking food away from you, you have trouble with jealous people. Emotional: The food you're eating shows a part of yourself you've been denying that needs to be integrated. You're worrying about something that's "eating at you." If you're eating alone, you feel loss, loneliness, rejection, or depression. You crave companionship and the comfort of being loved. Mental-Spiritual: Eating represents taking in new ideas or trying to find spiritual fulfillment.

eavesdrop: Physical: Others are taking advantage of you, or vice versa. You need to pay closer attention in your waking life to what you're being told. Emotional: You feel left out of the loop and that you must gain advantage by secretive means. You feel insecure because you don't know enough. Mental-Spiritual: You're looking for insight and information you think other people have when what you really need to know is inside yourself. Be more open to hearing the guidance and criticism of others. *(see gossip)*

echo: Physical: You aren't paying attention and need to receive a message that's being given to you repeatedly, perhaps in different ways. You're trying to communicate in a situation where you must repeat yourself to be noticed. Emotional: You feel frustrated that your efforts aren't getting the results you want. You feel alone and that you must do everything without support. Mental-Spiritual: You're focusing on cause and effect, how what you put out into the world creates similar results. You're focusing on being articulate, saying what you mean, and understanding the power of language. You're communicating with beings in higher dimensions or your own soul to seek guidance.

egg: Physical: Develop your inner resources, break out of your shell. You're ready for a new phase of life, and you're focusing on your creative potential. Emotional: You feel nurturing and patient or need this from others. Cracked, broken eggs mean you feel drained, unappreciated, vulnerable, fragile, or like a failure. Mental-Spiritual: You have many unhatched ideas or ideas that need to gestate longer. You're focusing on wholeness and spiritual potential. Broken eggs mean you've spilled your ideas before they were fully cooked.

elbow: Physical: You need to make more space for yourself or push obstacles aside. Emotional: You feel you're fending off people who want too much from you, or you hesitate to take up your own space for fear of being judged. Mental-Spiritual: You're focusing on your ability to translate your heart's desires into form without interference, granting yourself the right to be fully extended into the world.

electric vehicle (EV)/self-driving vehicle (SDV): Physical: EVs in a dream point to the desire and commitment to be innovative and environmentally and socially responsible. You are focusing on living with small sacrifices and moving forward a bit more slowly (recharging yourself more often) to make a habit of good values personally and for the greater good. SDVs point to utopian hopes for greater safety, freedom, spare time, and opportunity for older or disabled people to be able to drive. Emotional: EVs mean you're focusing on patience; having less power and perhaps greater longevity, and being drawn to help others feel more responsible to the planet. You're rejecting dependency on oil or anything that controls you and is bad for the planet. SDVs mean you're contemplating a loss of personal power, skills, and competence. Mental-Spiritual: EVs mean you're focusing on raising your vibration and powering your life from a higher frequency. SDVs point to dystopian thoughts concerning surveillance, loss of privacy, manipulation by artificial intelligence (AI), disconnection from the "real" world, and the morality and ethics of how society might tolerate people dying in SDV-caused accidents. You're focusing on the integration of the physical and nonphysical dimensions and the balance of head with heart.

electricity: Physical: You're focusing on the workings of your nervous system or your charisma and the power to affect other people or be affected by other intense people. A live electrical wire represents the threat of sudden disruption or destruction of your plans. Emotional: Your emotions are too high-strung, or you need a jump-start of excitement. To be shocked by electricity means you need to wake up to a potential danger. Mental-Spiritual: You're taken with new ideas that tend to overwhelm you or push you to the edge of a sudden personality change. You are "rewiring" your internal circuitry, attuning yourself, preparing to run a higher frequency of spiritual energy through your system.

elephant: Physical: You're focusing on laying solid groundwork for prosperity and success through developing a steadfast character, excellent memory and intelligence, gentleness, family values, loyalty, honor, dignity, and the power to perform daunting tasks. Emotional: You feel introverted and in need of greater kindness and sensitivity. If the elephant is wild or untamed, you're looking at rogue or uncontrollable forces and plundering emotions affecting your life. Mental-Spiritual: You're developing your heart to a high degree, merging intelligence with compassion. You're understanding how lucky you are.

elevator/escalator: Physical: You're experiencing many ups and downs in your life, changing status, or moving into different parts of your body to heal yourself. A falling elevator represents a rapid descent from higher dimensions back to the body, often just before you awake. Emotional: If you're going down, you're descending into your subconscious to discover what's blocking you, or you're bringing higher motives to bear in your everyday life. If you're in a falling elevator, you feel out of control or need to surrender. If you're stuck between floors, you need to clarify your intentions and see why you're afraid to move. Mental-Spiritual: Elevators and escalators help you move between levels or dimensions of yourself. If you're moving up, you're addressing important issues, finding a more elevated view, and making progress on your spiritual journey with ease.

elf/fairy: Physical: You need time in nature and exposure to trees, forests, and water. You need to find more magic in life and be more carefree, lighthearted, mischievous, and playful. You want to bring a lighter attitude to your work while still being productive. Emotional: You feel tired, old, bored, depressed, or too serious and need more childlike innocence, humor, and the stuff of fairytales. You need cheerful assistance, more tenderness and affection. Mental-Spiritual: Your thoughts need to turn more toward impish fun, joy, and kindhearted teasing. Someone is tricking you, though perhaps not with cruel intent. You're connecting with a spiritual guide.

emergency room (ER): Physical: If you're being taken to the ER in a hospital, you're focusing on an immediate need to pay attention to something about to go wrong in your body. You're re asking for help, trusting medical staff and information, and allowing yourself to receive what's needed. If you're taking someone to the ER or working in an ER, you're focusing on remaining strong, calm, and clear. Emotional: You're accepting comfort, relief from pain and fear, and focusing on maintaining calm and harmony as the best state of being for expert help and healing to occur. You're activating hope and positive thinking in yourself and others working with you. Mental-Spiritual: You're receiving help and healing from nonphysical spiritual beings and/or realizing the power of your attention, focused at a high loving frequency, to heal yourself or others. If taking someone else to the ER, you're probably part of a team working in the higher dimensions to help heal them. *(also see hospital)*

end of the world: Physical: You're focusing on the dramatic end of a period of your life and a change that's coming that you can barely imagine. Emotional: You feel hopeless and despondent and that your world is out of control and there's nothing you can do to affect it. It may be difficult to imagine what's next. Mental-Spiritual: You may be precognitively aware of the upcoming death of someone. You are attuning to the collective fears of humanity about doomsday prophecies. You're focusing on the idea that the world is a dream, or you're exploring nonphysical spiritual realms of consciousness beyond the physical world.

enemy: *(see adversary)*

epidemic: Physical: You need to cultivate better hygiene and cleanliness habits. You're warning yourself about a health situation that might require a doctor. You're focusing on a large, burdensome problem that seems unconquerable. Emotional: You feel anxious about repressed emotions surfacing and negativity spreading into all areas of your life. You feel infected or plagued by other people's negative beliefs and habits. Mental-Spiritual: You're focusing on broad negative concepts, things like prejudice, religious hatred, genocide, and environmental abuse, held by large groups of people.

escape: Physical: Escape from jail or a confined place signifies your need to move beyond a restrictive situation or attitude. Emotional: You're resisting something you need to face, or you've allowed yourself to become dominated and must take back your authority. Mental-Spiritual: You're taking an escapist attitude, bucking authority, or dissolving barriers and boxes — mental structures — you've been living within. To escape from injury means you're connecting with your natural freedom and well-being.

execution: Physical: You're experiencing the enforced end of something you still want to be involved with — for example, you've been fired, rejected by a lover, excluded from a group, or suspended from driving. You're deeply involved with finishing a project that requires attention to detail. Emotional: You're afraid of being severely punished for something you've done, especially if people have judged you unfairly. You harbor guilt, remorse, or low self-esteem that needs healing. You're drawing attention to times you're critical, vengeful, and retaliatory. You need to forgive someone or yourself. Mental-Spiritual: You're focusing on getting rid of negative thought habits and ways you negate your own creativity and deny your soul.

explosion/bomb: Physical: You're experiencing a sudden release of energy or toxicity in your body or a sudden upheaval and change in your life that might involve loss. Something needs to move, and you need to let go. Finding an unexploded or ticking bomb is a sign that something is about to blow open. Emotional: You're experiencing an emotional catharsis, a release of anger and violence. If you're are blown up into the air or engulfed in flames, you feel the brunt of a betrayal or abuse from others. Mental-Spiritual: You're experiencing a release of *kundalini* (a vital force that lies dormant, but once awakened, leads to enormous spiritual energy) that frees your consciousness to move to higher realms. You're making rapid progress on your spiritual path.

ex: Physical: People you had past relationships with, even old friends, indicate that you're working out lessons that pertained to those relationships. You're integrating a quality the person represented that you have ex-ed out or neglected in yourself. Emotional: You have incomplete emotions from the past that are being triggered by a similar situation in your current life. What you learned from a previous relationship needs to be applied to a present one so you don't repeat a mistake. Mental-Spiritual: You're looking at your inner balance of masculine and feminine energy. You're contemplating the positive traits you want in a new relationship. *(see divorce)*

eyes/eyebrows: Physical: If you see your own eyes, you're focusing on accepting yourself fully or receiving information about the condition of your physical eyes. If someone is winking, you're being let in on a secret or something is being kept from you. If there's something in your eye, there are obstacles in your path. Emotional: You're opening to experience the love that comes through these windows of the soul. Closed eyes mean you're afraid to see the truth, are avoiding intimacy, or need to introvert to find deeper knowledge. Crossed eyes mean you're confused. Eyebrows show emotions like amazement, disbelief, doubt, concern, or disapproval. Mental-Spiritual: You're focusing on your ability to see clearly, how you receive insight, your own visions, and level of enlightenment. If you have one eye, you're refusing to accept other viewpoints. If you have a third eye, you have a clear inner vision of spiritual truth. Floating disembodied eyes are spiritual guides connecting with you.

F

face: Physical: Seeing your face means you're focusing on your self-image or the mask you show others and how much of your real personality shines through. You're experiencing confrontations or heightened visibility in waking life. Emotional: Looking out from another person's face indicates an aspect of yourself you need to accept and express. If your face is scarred, flawed, red, or pimply, you're experiencing erupting emotions, embarrassment, self-consciousness, or slights to your reputation. Interacting with a faceless person indicates you have decided to be impersonal and are not facing emotional discomforts. Mental-Spiritual: Facial expressions convey nuances of attitudes you're unconsciously expressing. A facelift means you want your outer expression to match your inner beauty, clarity, or vitality.

fairy: *(see elf)*

falling: Physical: It's not true that you'll die if you don't wake up before you hit the bottom of a fall in a dream. You need to surrender in an area of your life and have faith. You feel you've lost control or are headed for failure or a fall from grace. Emotional: You're dealing with feelings of insecurity, helplessness, lack of confidence, fear of losing someone, or worry. Falling a long way and landing safely means you can trust your instinct to lead you out of difficulty. Mental-Spiritual: Falling represents the basic downward momentum of consciousness from the higher realms back to the body and can happen just before you awake.

fame/famous people: Physical: You need attention, recognition, freer self-expression, and interaction with others at a larger scale than you presently have. You're focusing on qualities in the celebrity that you'd like to activate or make peace with in yourself. Look for specific character traits and judgments you hold concerning the person. Emotional: You doubt your ability to please others and be loved, or to be as excellent as you can be when scrutinized too closely. Mental-Spiritual: You need to get clear about what success means to you. You're glimpsing what you're capable of when your soul is fully present.

family: Physical: You're focusing on belonging, what your original family's interests, beliefs, and habits mean to you, and why you chose to have this filter for your identity and reality. You're determining whether you still fit with your family pattern or have grown beyond it to a more sophisticated or individualized state. You're looking at whether other people not related by blood are part of your "family." Emotional: You're looking at the emotional interrelationships in the family and how/what you're learning from each person and their connections or disconnections with each other. You want to change the dynamics of your connections with family members, perhaps help or rescue some, or admire and copy others. Is it possible? Is it your responsibility? You're healing emotional pain from an abusive or broken family. Mental-Spiritual: You're looking at your current family's pattern and your role as a leader, teacher, facilitator, nurturer, protector. You're finding how you belong in a soul group or spiritual family, how your ancestors act as guides, and your past lives constitute a different sort of family.

fat: Physical: You need more personal space and insulation from others so you can take up your own space and be yourself without apology. You need to share and release more of your self-expressive energy. Emotional: You're afraid of getting fat and being rejected by others. You feel guilty about something you did. You feel you can't get enough love, and you need to hoard your reserves because loss is always imminent. Mental-Spiritual: You're focusing on the need for gratitude, how you should use what you've already been given, and how big you really are spiritually.

father: Physical: You're examining the way you use power, authority, protectiveness, control, and leadership skills. You need to be more self-reliant. If your father dies in the dream, you need to take a new leadership role in your life. Emotional: You're working out emotional issues you have with your father. Mental-Spiritual: The archetypal father, shown by any male authority figure, represents kingly power, provision, impersonal love, the law, tradition, discipline, and structure. You're looking at your ideas of the Creator.

feather: Physical: You need to let your energy flow easily and lightly, soften yourself, and release tension and contractions. In your work and life, you need to go with the flow. Ornamental feathers mean social advancement, and a feather in your cap means you've done a good job. Emotional: Feathers floating in the air mean you need ease, comfort, greater lightheartedness, playfulness, innocence, and joy. They also connote the aftereffects of a tussle with others where there is a near-escape or loss of dignity ("ruffling someone's feathers," "seeing feathers fly"). Mental-Spiritual: You're focusing on uplifting thoughts. A floating feather means you're looking at higher knowledge and spiritual growth or receiving an insight or spiritual teaching. Finding a feather may be a sign that a dead loved one has visited you. Feathers on spiritual teachers, priests, or shamans represent spiritual authority, wisdom, and the power to materialize visions. Someone holding a large upright feather is a sign of truth being required or revealed.

feces: Physical: You need to cleanse your body, change your diet, or take care with your elimination system. You need to rid your life of toxic people, clutter, and situations that have outlived their usefulness. Emotional: There are aspects of yourself you consider dirty and repulsive. You're in denial or ending a period of denial and self-deception. You have low self-esteem or are caught in too much complaining and negativity. This also pertains to anal retentive behavior. Mental-Spiritual: You're becoming aware of negative habits and getting rid of them or simply letting go of a period of life or ideas that might serve as fertilizer to others.

feet: Physical: You're looking at how you take a stand, achieve grounding, find support and balance, and begin to move forward. You need to be more practical and sensible, or you're ready for more independence and freedom. Emotional: Being barefoot means you're connecting directly with what's real, not putting on false airs. Having no feet means you feel unprepared for what's coming. Mental-Spiritual: You're focusing on foundational thought structures and your sense of understanding. You're contemplating your human connection with the world and how to be more fully present. If you're washing someone's feet, you're respecting that person's spiritual self.

fence: Physical: You're focusing on a limitation you've put on yourself, a challenge or barrier to forward movement, the need for privacy and boundaries, respect for others' boundaries, or the need to pause and reconsider goals. Climbing or jumping over a fence means you're expanding into territory where you may meet with opposition at first. Emotional: You feel ostracized or invaded by others. You're dealing with issues of entitlement. Mental-Spiritual: You're "on the fence" about an issue or decision. You're examining your worldview and its limits, especially if you climb to the top of a fence.

fight: (*see battle*)

files/folders/file cabinet: Physical: You need to keep your facts and information straight. Whether electronic or paper, you're retrieving data and resources you need to function successfully and be yourself. You need to design better systems for your life and work. Emotional: You feel overwhelmed by detail, afraid of falling behind, or insecure because you lack information you need. If a file cabinet is locked, there's something you don't want revealed to others or something is being kept from you. Mental-Spiritual: You're focusing on bodies of knowledge or memories and whether to keep making them real or to let them go. A file cabinet with open drawers means you welcome new viewpoints and ideas.

fire: Physical: Check the "fire element" in your body, often connected to the heart and liver. You need to purify and burn off toxins or get more oxygen. You're ready for a transition that might require total release of the old. If you put out fires, you'll overcome obstacles and succeed, though getting there may seem endless. A bonfire suggests there's a larger goal you hadn't considered. Emotional: Setting fires, seeing an inferno, being burned, or being caught in a fire all indicate that you're angry, full of suppressed rage that threatens to go out of control, and you're afraid of the destructive consequences. You feel passionate, impulsive, desirous, or zealous. Breathing fire means a vicious verbal attack. A fire in a fireplace denotes contentment, safety, and romance. Mental-Spiritual: You're involved in a process of purification, illumination, spiritual transformation, and waking to your positive powers. A firefly means you're receiving bright ideas and insights from your highest self.

fireworks: Physical: You want to celebrate a personal achievement. You'd like to be the center of attention and show off to others. Emotional: You're ready to release pent-up emotion and feel more jubilant. You need more exhilarating activity. Mental-Spiritual: You're entering a period of colorful, uninhibited self-expression where you'll discover exciting new ideas, talents, and levels of creativity. You've broken through to a new level of awareness.

fish/fishing: Physical: Catching a fish, especially a big one, portends success in a venture. Seeing fish means you need to be more adaptable, flexible, and sensitive. Emotional: You're focusing on specific feelings in your subconscious. Catching a fish means dealing with one deep emotional issue. Trying to hold a fish that wriggles away means you're having trouble forming or maintaining a relationship. A dead or dying fish signifies disappointment or hopelessness. You're insecure — "fishing for compliments." Mental-Spiritual: You're dipping into the collective unconscious for creative ideas or messages from the superconscious mind. You're actively pursuing a spiritual quest and transformation.

flag: Physical: You're focusing on your identity as part of a large group or the qualities you hold in common with others. A waved flag warns of dangerous conditions ahead or a new group you're about to encounter, or it signals the end of a process you've been engaged in. Emotional: You're focused on feelings of pride, loyalty, family, and patriotism, and issues of belonging or being an outcast. Mental-Spiritual: You're looking at the goals and beliefs you hold in common with a group.

float: (*see drift*)

flood: Physical: You're experiencing an overwhelming situation, often with tribulations and serious repercussions. Emotional: You feel out of control and overwhelmed by repressed emotions or other people's emotions. You've lost your boundaries. Mental-Spiritual: A gentle flood, leaks in the house, or broken pipes indicate that you're in a process of cleaning yourself up, preparing for a new phase of growth. (*see drown*)

floor: Physical: You're focusing on your support system and the foundations of your life. Repairing, replacing, or shining the floor means you're improving the basic conditions of your home and work life. If the floor is slanted or uneven, you have minor impediments to success that must be patiently remedied. Emotional: You may feel "floored" by emotions that cause you to stop or surrender. Mental-Spiritual: A floor represents a division between the conscious and unconscious minds as well as between various levels of your awareness, as with multistoried buildings. You're shifting your reality if you're moving between floors. The floor you stand on is the reality you're creating.

flower: Physical: You're focusing on the stage of your personal growth process (bud to full flower), your beauty, attractiveness, sexuality, sensuality, and natural self-expression. Emotional: You're activating feelings of peace, gentleness, kindness, pleasure, sweetness, and love. You want to be defenseless. Withered or dead flowers denote disappointment or loss of hope and joy. The flower's color gives clues to the emotion: yellow/joy, white/ sadness and purity, red/romantic love, pink/affection, lavender/ spiritual connection. Receiving a bouquet means you're loved, appreciated, and admired. Mental-Spiritual: You're tuning in to your soul and heart and how perfect, beautiful, and unique you are.

flying: Physical: You're focusing on your dreams, goals, and how far you want to go in life. How you fly represents the way you grow and express your creativity. Flying easily — surveying the landscape — means you're on top of a situation or that you've risen above something that used to be a problem. Running into power lines, trees, mountains, or other obstacles means you're dealing with people, situations, or ideas that block your progress. Emotional: You need more freedom, exhilaration, adventure, and joy. If you feel fear about the inability to control your flight or flying too high, you doubt your power and skill and may dread the possibility of failure. Mental-Spiritual: You're moving up in frequency, expanding your consciousness through the dimensions. You want more spiritual knowledge, the big picture, or a higher perspective on a situation. *(see above)*

fog: Physical: You are invisible to others and aren't making the impact you want. A situation hides some important factors. You aren't facing reality. Others are obscuring the truth. Emotional: If the scene is shrouded in fog, you feel confused, directionless, and lost. Mental-Spiritual: You can't see clearly and need to explore the unconscious, unknown inner realms for answers. If the fog lifts, pay attention to what you see.

food: *(see eat)*

forest: Physical: You need to retreat, achieve calmness, rebuild vitality, soak up the greenness of nature. A forest fire implies that the density of a period in your life is finally clearing. Emotional: You feel overwhelmed by potential dangers, the unknown, or the uncontrollable, especially if you're lost in a forest or traversing one. Mental-Spiritual: You're focusing on your subconscious, secrets, mysteries, memories, and feminine wisdom. You're using your intuition to find answers.

fork in the road: *(see crossroads)*

fortuneteller/psychic: Physical: Your life is about to change. Emotional: You're anxious about your future. You're looking at a tendency to give your authority to others who you think they know more than you. Mental-Spiritual: You have a strong desire to discover the unknown. Soliciting guidance from a spiritually oriented source means a higher part of you is sending an important message.

fossils: Physical: You're focusing on permanence and change and exploring the history of the earth and ancient wisdom. You're curious about longevity, survival, evolution, and what's still buried deep in the earth. Transporting your consciousness to prehistoric time periods gives you a compassionate view of all forms of life and the rise and fall of long and short life cycles. You don't want to look or feel old. Emotional: You wonder if you or what you create will stand the test of time, or will you disappear and no one will remember? Digging up a fossil means you're becoming aware of your old subconscious belief and behavior habits, bringing them to light so you can clear them. Mental-Spiritual: You're focusing on being eternal. You're beginning to remember past lives and knowledge, your soul memory. You're learning to "feel into" the rocks, shells, or bones to feel the original reality and story.

fountain: Physical: You need rejuvenation and fresh energy and to drink more water. You have a thirst for life that needs quenching. You are at the end of a cycle and need to see how effortless a new beginning can be — how new life can spring forth. Emotional: You're focusing on feelings of joy, refreshment, pleasure, and sensuality. You need to be more generous with yourself and others. If you're in the fountain, you are washing away blockages. Mental-Spiritual: You're looking at the unending life force that comes from the source. You're focusing on the abundance of life that gives of itself so generously and unconditionally. Coins in a fountain mean your wishes can come true.

fox: Physical: Someone is acting dishonestly or secretively, or you're acting in a cunning or wily manner. You need to remain silent or speak in favor of diplomacy. Emotional: You feel manipulated or victimized by clever, sly people. You're focusing on a woman who is a "vixen," or "foxy," and whom you don't trust. Mental-Spiritual: You need to sharpen your mental awareness and pay more attention to what's going on around you.

friend: Physical: You're are focusing on personality traits in the friend that you have either rejected, not yet discovered in yourself, or want to activate and integrate into your life. Best friends point to a positive aspect of yourself. Emotional: You're lonely and looking for understanding and companionship. A childhood friend means you're focusing on what you learned with this particular person or at that time or what they represented to you. A dying friend means the qualities they embody are being passed to you to heal, integrate, or express. Mental-Spiritual: You're examining your ideas about what resonates with you, what makes you happy, how you communicate and understand others, and how much you have in common with everyone. You are considering the idea that everyone is special in some way.

frog: Physical: You need renewal, cleansing, or rebirth. You're ready for a major change. Emotional: Because frogs are bringers of rain and messengers of water spirits, they indicate you're clearing your emotions, becoming more sensitive to others, and diving deep into your unconscious to bring truths to the surface. Because frogs live on land and in water, you're focusing on your connection between body and emotion. Mental-Spiritual: You're focusing on metamorphosis; the tadpole becomes the frog, and then the frog becomes the handsome prince. Pay attention to messages from frogs and trust your growth process.

front: Physical: The front part of anything, like a front porch or the front bumper of a car, interfaces with the public and the world. You're focusing on how others see and know you, and how you portray your personality to others. Emotional: You're examining how strong or vulnerable you feel about being a leader, pioneer, or innovator. You feel too visible or unprepared. Sitting in the front row means you're ready to be involved. Mental-Spiritual: You're focusing on what is consciously known. If you are in front of other people, you're teaching or initiating; if others are in front of you, you're learning or following.

fruit: Physical: You need more fresh, highly nutritional food. You're fertile and ready to have a child. You're ripe, full of talent, and ready to express yourself or move into a new phase. Picking ripe fruit or seeing a bowl of fruit is an omen of prosperity and success to come. Emotional: You feel abundant, sensual, sexual, seductive, luscious, and tempting. Bitter, rotten, or wormy fruit symbolizes untruthfulness, lack of trust, or an area of self-expression that troubles you. Mental-Spiritual: You're focusing on positive values, the appropriate span of time for a successful process, and the abundance within.

funeral: Physical: A situation, relationship, or aspect of yourself has ended or needs to end. You're putting something to rest, closing the lid on the past, letting go, and moving into a new life phase. Emotional: You're releasing old feelings you've been clinging to. Attending the funeral of someone who is still alive means you need to separate from restrictions you feel from that person and be more independent. Mental-Spiritual: You're examining lifeless ideas and worldviews that have no relevance for you anymore. You're expanding beyond your known world.

furniture: Physical: You're focusing on the habits, relationships, and the "stuff" of your daily and domestic life. If you're rearranging or moving furniture, you're changing your routine, what you depend on, the way you do things, or the flow of your energy. Emotional: Décor indicates your mood. Dark, formal fabrics and furniture mean depression or seriousness, whereas lighter, contemporary furnishings indicate spontaneity and inventiveness. Mental-Spiritual: Old or worn furniture symbolizes outdated attitudes and old ways of thinking. How you use the furniture shows your mental habits. New furniture means growth and change.

G

games/gambling: Physical: Playing a game suggests you need to relax and stop pressuring yourself. You're looking at your competitive nature and the rules you live by. You're challenging yourself to do better. Winning at gambling means you're likely to have success in an endeavor but not necessarily gambling. Emotional: You're being impulsive, taking risks in an area of your life — either mild, enlivening ones or dramatic, potentially dangerous ones — and looking for reward. You're overlooking clues about how to be successful or want to avoid facing uncomfortable things about yourself. Mental-Spiritual: You need to take more chances and believe you're naturally lucky. You're relying on fate, not taking responsibility for your decisions. You're working out a strategy of a new phase of experience.

garage: Physical: You're looking at your motivation, ability, reserves of energy, and the tools and techniques you use to accomplish your goals. You're in a period of inactivity, getting ready for new direction. Emotional: You're focusing on how stable and safe your life is. The condition (messy, organized) represents the way you store and manage your inner resources. If the garage is crammed with stuff, you feel afraid you won't be prepared for the many demands of the world. Mental-Spiritual: You're focusing on planning, strategizing, goal setting, and maintaining resources, things that allow you to progress. Cleaning out the garage means you're releasing old ideas and techniques that don't work anymore.

garbage: Physical: You need to detoxify or cleanse your body. Rooting through trash indicates you still have use for something you haven't paid attention to in a long time, or you have to do something you don't want to do. Emotional: You feel rejected, tossed aside, unwanted, expendable, or distasteful. Rooting through a stranger's garbage shows your desire for useful, free surprises, new abilities, insights, or creative ideas. Mental-Spiritual: You're ready to discard habits, attitudes, and beliefs that are no longer necessary. You're dealing with ugly, negative thought structures in others that you're seeking to be free from.

garden: Physical: You're focusing on nurturing your body and on new projects you'll cultivate in the future. Weeding and watering suggest the need for organization, tending, clearing of clutter, and renewal of purpose. Emotional: You need new life, beauty, peace, a sense of abundance, nurturing, even magic. Mental-Spiritual: You're focusing on your inner life, on the ideas, habits, and relationships that are growing on you and becoming important. A lush garden indicates your interest and involvement with life, spiritual growth, and healing.

gas: Physical: Smelling gas means you're alerting yourself to a potential danger that isn't immediately visible. It may also mean you are exhausted and need to purify and reenergize your body. Lighting a gas stove or lamp means you need to be extra cautious about situations that could flare up suddenly. Emotional: You feel suffocated by a relationship, responsibilities, or the prospect of an unwanted emotional explosion. Dying in a gas chamber means you feel you have no space or right to be yourself or that you're suffering at the hands of others. Mental-Spiritual: You're attuning to the etheric or subtle energy level of your body and of life. You're focusing on dissolving fixed ideas and beliefs and merging into the collective consciousness. Being put to sleep under anesthesia means you're shifting levels of awareness to higher dimensions.

gas station: Physical: You're focusing on your physical energy and resources, especially your nutrition, and on the reserves you draw on when you're tired and running on empty. Running out of gas means you've worn yourself down and need rest and rejuvenation. Being at a gas station and filling up means you're actively renewing yourself or pushing a project forward. Emotional: You need to put attention on how you nurture yourself and how your emotions fuel your decisions and actions. Running out of gas means you're apathetic, depressed, or too negative; you need to emphasize enthusiasm and generosity. Mental-Spiritual: You're focusing on your own center, where you refuel yourself with love, wisdom, and clear perspective. You're looking at ideas that align with your life purpose and that seem exciting and motivating.

gate: Physical: Going through a gate means you're entering a new phase of life or a transition from the familiar to the unknown. A closed or locked gate indicates you feel blocked or a new opportunity is not timely, appropriate, or safe. Closing a gate means you're protecting what's inside, whether it's ideas, resources, animals, or people. Locking a gate means you're trying to control what's inside. Emotional: Opening a gate and preparing to go through means you're focusing on your courage, sense of adventure, freedom, dread, doubt, or what you'll leave behind. Encountering a locked gate means you're focusing on obstacles and your ability to overcome challenges. Perhaps you aren't ready yet and must find another path forward. Mental-Spiritual: Closed or locked gates mean you are facing a tendency to think negatively, use "yes, buts" to make excuses, or aren't ready to move forward yet. Open gates mean you have access to higher knowledge and truth — that you're qualified and free to reach for it.

geese: Physical: You need freedom or travel and to undertake new actions. You need to communicate and express yourself, especially through stories. A goose laying an egg means a pleasant, valuable surprise. Emotional: You feel you have too much or too little security or loyalty concerning family, marriage, or group affiliations. You need greater perseverance. Mental-Spiritual: You're conforming too much to others or exhibiting silly or gossiping behavior. Migrating geese point to the need to pay attention to instinct and intuition — to going home or centering in the self. You're focusing on your spiritual quest or journeying to other worlds.

gemstones: Physical: You're showing yourself your own or someone else's value and worthiness. Specific characteristics are represented by the type of stone – for example, diamonds or crystals/ clarity and purity; purple stones/spiritual consciousness; green stones/good fortune and healing; red stones/passion, courage, and vitality; yellow stones/intellect, creativity, and optimism. You're validating these qualities in yourself or telling yourself you need to develop more of them. Emotional: You're directing your attention to the feelings, sensations, or emotions you connect to different precious stones. Mental-Spiritual: Receiving a gemstone activates its specific qualities of consciousness in you. Giving a gemstone to another is a message to them that they have these latent abilities and can develop it all to a high degree.

geyser: Physical: You're ready for new action and adventure. Emotional: Your emotions have built to an explosive stage, or you have had a violent outburst of repressed anger and emotion and are looking at how to deal with the repercussions. Mental-Spiritual: There's great enthusiasm in your soul and excitement about life, and new ideas are ready to burst forth.

ghost: Physical: This may be a literal visitation from another being or someone who has died. Look for the purpose behind the appearance. Emotional: You're not occupying yourself fully, or you feel disconnected from your life. You're focused on unresolved memories and repressed feelings or aspects of yourself that you fear. You're afraid of dying. Mental-Spiritual: You're focusing on desires that haven't successfully manifested or part of yourself that has remained in the background, unexpressed. A message from a ghost is from your higher self or a spiritual guide.

giant: Physical: You're facing a great challenge, fear, or authority figure and need to stand up, face it squarely, and move forward in your authenticity. You're showing yourself your own inner strength and intelligence. Giant anything — an animal, tree, insect, or whale — represents the magnified and evolved natural character of the lifeform, which you're reminding yourself that you have as well. Emotional: You're showing yourself how grand you can be when you allow love, joy, kindness, generosity, and gratitude to guide you. And how meanness and aggression don't work in the end, as David and Goliath demonstrated. Mental-Spiritual: If the giant is friendly, it represents a spiritual guide or ally. If it's aggressive, defensive, or warlike, it probably represents qualities of consciousness you have suppressed and must conquer by overcoming or dissolving them with positive thought and emotion. The giant can represent you in your enlightened, higher, inclusive form. If you magnify yourself to that level, what would you be like?

gift: Physical: You're looking at your inner talents, acknowledging and honoring yourself. Receiving a gift brings good luck in fortune and love. Emotional: You feel you need to be appreciated and rewarded. You need to be more open and share yourself with others. You're trying to find a way to carefully express your feelings so you don't hurt or upset others. Mental-Spiritual: You need to focus on your lovable nature, on expressing gratitude to others or to a higher power for what's good in your life.

giraffe: Physical: You need to stick your neck out or extend yourself to succeed or find the right resources. You can reach beyond what others can see or do. Emotional: You have your head in the clouds and need to focus on personal and practical issues. If the giraffe is trying to eat grass awkwardly, you're in danger from sudden attacks. Mental-Spiritual: You have the ability to see different perspectives or both sides of an issue, or you need a broader view of a situation. You need to keep your feet firmly on the ground while viewing the distance clearly.

glass/glasses: Physical: There are invisible barriers between yourself, your goals, others, and the world. Broken glass means something you thought would last will end surprisingly or too soon. Emotional: You feel removed, out of touch with others, or misunderstood. Frosted glass signifies greater feelings of insulation, secrets are present, or you need privacy. Mental-Spiritual: Seeing through clear glass or glasses indicates revelation, insight, or a clear perspective. Dirty glass or glasses means you have limiting beliefs or blind spots in the way. Losing your glasses means trouble judging things correctly. Breaking glass is about shattering illusions to move through barriers.

gloves: Physical: You or someone you know needs to be handled with care. You need to get a better grip on something. Your creativity or ability to touch others is veiled in some way. Gardening or work gloves indicate you're ready to begin a new phase of productivity. Driving gloves mean you're taking control of your life direction. Gloves that are too large mean you took on more than you can handle. Emotional: You're protecting yourself from harm. Throwing down a glove means you're challenging yourself or someone else. Boxing gloves indicate you're ready to confront an opponent or critic, perhaps an inner one. Mental-Spiritual: Putting on gloves means you're preparing mentally for something that requires concentration and effort. Taking gloves off is a sign of completion and friendliness. Dropping a glove means flirtation.

globe: Physical: You're looking for the whole story, wanting to understand everyone's point of view or humanity in general.

You're sensing all the pertinent variables in a situation in your life. You're seeking to expand your business or self-expression globally or internationally. You need adventure, foreign cultures, and travel. Emotional: You're out of touch with personal feelings or the ability to be empathic. You're sensitive to humanitarian concerns and feel overwhelmed that you can't do enough about suffering. You need to stimulate yourself to take more chances and move beyond your comfort zone. Mental-Spiritual: You're zooming out to see the higher and wider perspective on your life. You have eclectic, diverse interests. You're looking for holistic, complete solutions, or you're trying to see and do too much at once.

glue: Physical: You're piecing together aspects of yourself, building a strong, mature personality. You're repairing a situation or relationship that has been fragmented and damaged. Emotional: You're focusing on being committed and loyal, or you're afraid to be stuck in bad relationships and lose your freedom. You feel distrusting. Mental-Spiritual: You're looking for ideas and visions that link parts of your life together and serve a unifying function.

goat: Physical: You are focusing on your determination and stubbornness to reach a goal, especially a difficult one. You're remembering that you're sure-footed and can take a stand for yourself and your ideas. You need to stay focused. You may be showing yourself that you need to be more flexible and open to the flow. You're independent yet need likeminded others to feel happy and calm. Emotional: You're in a situation where you're butting heads with someone or need to face a problem head on. You're experiencing rebelliousness or a desire to be reckless, to kick up your heels and leap about joyfully. You may feel like a "scapegoat," that you're unfairly blamed for someone else's actions or you're blaming someone else for your actions. Mental-Spiritual: You're initiating an ascent to a new, higher level of consciousness. You're focusing on prosperity and joy.

gold: Physical: You're focusing on a treasured part of yourself, something valuable about a situation you should pay attention to, or an inner lesson that will bring success. Emotional: You're working on issues of self-esteem, internal and external abundance, wealth, good luck, and how openhearted you want to be. Mental-Spiritual: You're connecting with high-quality, pure thoughts, wisdom, and spiritual gifts that cannot tarnish. You're in tune to a level of brightness that will attract similar experiences into your life.

gopher: Physical: You need more contact with your body and the earth. You need to get busy and dig in to a project. Someone is invading your territory, leaving holes for you to fall into; look for hidden snafus. Emotional: The pun "gofer" applies here, as you may feel you are doing others' bidding and not what's important to you. Mental-Spiritual: You have strayed too far from common sense. You need silent retreat time to regain mental clarity.

gorilla: Physical: You need to take stronger, more forceful action, or temper your dominating behavior. You're focusing on your wildness and sexual nature. Emotional: You're dealing with your primitive instincts, impulses, and reactionary feelings. You need to feel more pride in yourself. Mental-Spiritual: You're dipping into your primal self and your body's nonverbal wisdom.

gossip: Physical: Overhearing gossip means you're gullible or receiving information that's shallow or inaccurate. If you're gossiping, you're being counterproductive and likely to experience negative repercussions or humiliation later. Emotional: You're afraid to confront someone or share yourself openly. You feel unfairly judged or disrespected. You feel ashamed of the way you treated someone else. Mental-Spiritual: Being gossiped about means you're sorting through negative self-concepts looking for your higher truth or deciding how openhearted you want to be. *(see eavesdropping)*

graduation: Physical: You're acknowledging an achievement and your readiness to move on to new challenges and develop new abilities. Emotional: You need to feel more satisfaction and worthiness. Mental-Spiritual: You've reached a new level of spiritual awareness, an initiation has been completed, and you're entering a new period of inner growth. *(see diploma)*

grandparent/aunt/uncle: Physical: Whether you see a living relative or one who has died, you're focusing on love, security, wisdom, and protection. Emotional: Searching for an older relative means you're revisiting childhood memories and emotional needs. Mental-Spiritual: You're receiving important guidance and wisdom concerning family beliefs and mores.

grapes: Physical: Seeing or eating grapes means you've worked hard, diligently, and patiently and tended to things caringly, and now you're harvesting the abundance. You're wishing for wealth, opulence, and a life of luxury. You're in a position to be a benefactor to others. Emotional: You're caught in too much hedonism, decadence, or self-indulgence and need to reactivate humility, discipline, and common sense. Mental-Spiritual: You have a rich imagination that is overflowing and many creative ideas are yours for the plucking; they can be linked together into larger-scale endeavors. You're focusing on divine feminine qualities like ripeness and fullness, gratitude, and generosity.

grasshopper: Physical: You need to be free to explore and jump from one venture to another. You're synthesizing experience from many diverse observations. You're using up your resources without concern for what might happen in hard times. Emotional: You're anxious and restless and having trouble focusing on one thing, committing to one person or project, or settling down in one place. You feel trapped. You need to trust yourself and life, have courage, and just jump into a new endeavor. Mental-Spiritual: You need to discipline your mind, make clear choices based on your inner truth, and learn to meditate deeply. You feel most comfortable connected to your soul group, traveling with friends who are similar to you.

groups: Physical: You need to work with others without losing yourself. You're looking at ways you can belong to and serve your community. Emotional: You're merging various parts of your character and personality, as well as diverse feelings, to find greater understanding and compassion. Mental-Spiritual: You're focusing on collective consciousness, group mind, and societal beliefs.

green: Physical: You need healing, rest, renewal, or time in nature. You are "green," or lack experience, and need to put in your dues and practice more. You want greater prosperity, money, and abundance. Emotional: You need to feel safe, balanced, calm, peaceful, and harmonious. You need to integrate your male and female energy. Dark green is associated with ambition, greed, and jealousy. Yellow-green can indicate sickness, cowardice, or disgust. Mental-Spiritual: You're freshening up your ideas and growing mentally and spiritually. You're integrating polarized ideas or opposing forces within yourself.

greenhouse: Physical: You're focusing on growing and expanding into a new phase of your life, taking care with the early steps so you'll stay nourished and strong. You're creating a safe environment for yourself or others in which to flourish. Emotional: You need to feel protected and cared for or need to see to your own emotional needs more tenderly. You're involved in a productive time of emotional clearing and growth, with good potential for happy, healthy relationships. You feel you're recovering from a setback and not strong enough to be out in the world too much. Mental-Spiritual: You're attuning to your soul's vibration and awareness, basking in the care and comfort of your deep love and wisdom. You're being introverted now as you regather yourself for the next cycle of growth out in the world.

gun: Physical: You're focusing on personal power with others, especially exerted from a safe distance, and aggressive, sexual male energy. Emotional: You feel pressured by a male person in your life. You need to protect yourself. Shooting yourself or others by accident or on purpose indicates overactive, destructive, or vengeful emotions or a need to assert personal control over a situation. Mental-Spiritual: Firing guns often represents "shooting off your mouth." If you're shot, consider which part of your body has been wounded for clues about the meaning.

guru: (*see priest*)

gym: Physical: You're focusing on the need for more exercise and movement. Being in a gymnasium or health club means you're expressing yourself in a competitive way, either through team sports or competing against yourself to become stronger and more proficient at something. You're building yourself gradually into a healthier, more disciplined person. Emotional: You feel weak and self-conscious, are worried about being rejected because of your body image or fitness level, and are contemplating "shaping up," which can mean you intend to develop your level of emotional maturity. Mental-Spiritual: You're focusing on how to materialize what you want, the limiting beliefs you hold, and the excuses you make to avoid confronting your potential greatness.

H

hail: (*see snow*)

hair: Physical: You're focusing on health, strength, sexuality, sensitivity to the environment, or vanity. Having your hair cut means you're adjusting your self-image and ambitions, you're ready for a major life decision, or someone is censoring you. Smelling someone's hair indicates sexual curiosity and a need for sensual stimulation. Emotional: Being covered in hair means you're confronting your animal nature. If your hair stands on end or turns white overnight, you're experiencing a shock or strong stimulus. Loss of hair signifies vulnerability, anxiety about weakness, and fear of failure or aging. If you're "letting your hair down" or the wind is blowing through your hair, you feel free to express uninhibited feelings. Stroking hair connects to sympathy, protectiveness, and fraternal love. Mental-Spiritual: You're focusing on your attitudes, opinions, and insights. White hair denotes wisdom. Knotted or tangled hair shows uncertainty and confusion. Combing your hair means you're organizing your thoughts, getting your facts straight. Long hair means you're drawing on past history before you act. Touching someone's hair means you're trying to connect on a spiritual or intellectual level.

hallway: Physical: You're making a transition from one life phase to another, beginning a journey into the unknown and further self-exploration. Emotional: If the hall is dimly lit, you feel insecure as you move toward the unknown. Mental-Spiritual: You're about to have an important insight. You're entering a new spiritual or mental rite of passage. The movement of the transition itself is important; notice what is contained in the hallway.

halo/aura: Physical: You're focusing on the quality of your energy and how much you release or radiate into the space around you. You're developing the ability to read auras and energy in people, animals, plants, places, and situations. Emotional: You're noticing how your aura or halo — the frequency of your energy — increases or decreases with different emotions. Mental-Spiritual: If you see someone's face and the space around their head glowing, you're focusing on how spiritual clarity and love move up through the body to create enlightenment. You're noticing people who are guided by the soul and spiritual truth.

hammer: Physical: You're constructing something, actively working to achieve a goal or accomplish a task. You're focusing on qualities like power, strength, assertiveness, physical coordination, and structural know-how. Hitting a nail square on the head and driving it in one stroke means you need to focus — to feel successful and competent. Pulling out a nail means you're repairing old mistakes. Emotional: You're being too forceful and dominating with others, hammering them about an issue to get your way. You need to be less passive or discouraged and rise to the occasion, act, and make your point. Mental-Spiritual: You're using willpower and sharp words to communicate with others, or experiencing this from others is an important lesson. You may be too hard-headed and need to soften your approach to communicating or teaching. You're encountering the universal laws, which can be tough spiritual taskmasters that eventually produce stability and ease.

hands: Physical: You're looking at how you greet and touch others, grasp or take hold, make and create things, and how you give and receive. You need to lend a helping hand to someone or ask for help. Holding hands represents your connection to others and how you connect with the world. Shaking hands with someone means you've reached an agreement, a level of trust, or a new beginning. Emotional: Washing your hands means you're worried or guilty, or you're complete and no longer taking responsibility for something. Rough hands mean a brash or abrasive way of dealing with others. Blood on your hands means you've hurt yourself or others and need to heal the situation. Being in handcuffs means you or something else is holding you back, making you focus on your actions. You're too possessive. Mental-Spiritual: Hands and fingers communicate and convey many messages, often of approval and disapproval. Praying hands mean the left and right sides of your body and brain are balanced and you are in harmony, open to the spiritual realm. Clasped or covered hands mean you're contemplating something or hesitant to agree.

hat: Physical: You're looking at a role you're playing, your desire for power and recognition, or your responsibilities in life. A feather in your hat shows achievement. A top hat denotes formality, elegance, and aspirations for wealth. Emotional: You're concealing or covering up something. You're hiding your opinions and attitudes from others for fear of judgment. Mental-Spiritual: You're focused on the containment of your knowledge, or a body of knowledge. Taking off a hat inside, when bowing, or placing it over your heart, means you are sharing your true self. Putting on a cap or tying a bandana around your head can mean you're putting on your "thinking cap" or getting serious about some mental work.

hawk: (*see eagle*)

head: Physical: You're focusing on accomplishments, self-image, and your perception of the world. You're using your head to solve problems. You need to approach something head-on. A headache means you're headed in the wrong direction. Emotional: You're too hotheaded or headstrong, or you've lost your head about something. You're repressing your common sense and rational thinking, refusing to see the truth, allowing your emotions to be out of control. Mental-Spiritual: You're focusing on knowledge, understanding, intellect, logic, and conscious awareness. You need to be less heady, mental, and analytical.

headphones: Physical: You want to withdraw into your own private world and control what you receive and pay attention to. You are out of touch with what's going on in the world at large. Emotional: You feel isolated and cut off from others or stubbornly refuse to open yourself to be influenced by emotion, either your own or other people's. You are overly sensitive to the chaos in the world and want to protect yourself. Mental-Spiritual: You're paying attention to the messages you receive, to your own perception and what is meaningful to you. You need to be centered and aware of your core, soul, and purpose.

healer: (*see doctor*)

heart/chest: Physical: The heart shows you're focusing on truth, courage, love, romance, and how fully you're living. The chest indicates a focus on pride, generosity, nurturing capacity, and how unprotected and trusting you are. Beating on your chest means you're summoning courage from your heart. Emotional: Problems with the heart, like heartaches or heart attacks, indicate imbalances, loss of love, lack of support and acceptance, or great disappointment. You're looking at how you deal with feelings and express emotion. Hearing a heartbeat suggests you need to recenter into safety and feelings of being nurtured. A racing heartbeat indicates you're anxious, upset, and threatened about something. Mental-Spiritual: You're focusing on integrating your soul's wisdom into your life and understanding who you are, how you give unconditional love, and how courageous you are. You want to get to "the heart of the matter," or the core of a situation, before proceeding.

heel: Physical: You're concerned about something following too closely upon your heels, or you need to improve your appearance (down at the heels, well-heeled). Emotional: You may be too stubborn or rooted (digging your heels in), or you feel extremely vulnerable (Achilles' heel). Mental-Spiritual: You are focusing on limitations of thought that might undermine your purpose and the need for greater practicality of ideas.

helicopter: Physical: You want to lift above the mundane conditions of life to find the big picture or overview. You need to rise above problems, not take them too seriously, and find appropriate solutions. You're are trying to get a new project off the ground, and you want it to happen quickly. You're focusing on being flexible and able to change your plans or point of view on a dime. You need to feel free to come and go as you like. You can zero in on your goals and get right to the point. Emotional: Having your own helicopter means you want to feel highly successful, privileged, and powerful. You need someone or something to rescue you or help you escape from a precarious situation or a feeling of being trapped. You're worried about being out of control, falling straight down from your position or status in life, and crashing dramatically. Mental-Spiritual: The whirling blades mean you need to pay attention to low-level chaotic, destructive thoughts that could hurt you or others. You're reaching new levels of awareness by going straight to the insights you need.

hero/hero's journey: Physical: You're asking yourself to stretch your level of competence, be more courageous and confident, and develop an expanded skill set. Emotional: You're examining your need to rescue others or be rescued. Mental-Spiritual: To make the hero's journey you must first be cut off from your roots and misunderstood, then experience the call to adventure to discover your true self, which comes after a difficult rite of passage where you confront temptation, challenges, demons, villains, handicaps, and unresolved fear. Finally, you experience a spiritual awakening and reach your goal. You must then return to those who misunderstood you and enlighten them. This is the process of spiritual growth we all go through as we evolve. You're reminding yourself that you're living through a stage in the hero's journey, and there is an end eventually. Notice what stage you are focusing on.

hide: Physical: Hiding from someone means you're avoiding an aspect of yourself you've not accepted or integrated. You don't want to face a real situation or issue. Emotional: You need security and protection. Hiding from an authority figure implies feelings of guilt. Hiding an object means you feel it's possible to lose part of your credibility, luck, or power to another person, and thus, you need to protect or hoard it. If someone is hiding from you, you feel frustrated in your desire for intimacy, honesty, or self-expression with others. Mental-Spiritual: You are keeping a secret, withholding information, or denying the truth.

hilltop: Physical: You have reached or want to reach your goal. You're noticing a greater understanding and scope to your perception. You need to get away from the crowd, to spend time alone, to find clarity and a renewed sense of self. You want a place that enables you to see problems or danger coming from any direction. Emotional: You want to rest after a struggle, letting yourself feel how you've earned your reward. You want to reach a hilltop to feel validated. Mental-Spiritual: You seek clarity and helpful advice from a wise person or spiritual guide. You need to raise your vibration to be able to experience spiritual communion, inspiration, and revelation.

hippopotamus: Physical: You're focusing on your hidden strengths, abundance, influence, and power. You're faced with a large, immovable obstacle. Hippos are a symbol of protection in childbirth. Emotional: You feel territorial and easily threatened. You're loyal and protective to those less powerful than you. Mental-Spiritual: You're focusing on the subconscious and collective unconscious, on what lies beneath the surface, attuning yourself to ancient knowledge held in common by many beings.

hitchhike: Physical: You want a free ride. You need to develop more self-reliance. Emotional: You need to lessen your dependency on others. Picking up a hitchhiker means you're carrying others in some way, taking on too much responsibility, with a tendency to become drained. Mental-Spiritual: You're riding on the coattails of others, borrowing their ideas, not doing your own homework. You may be possessed in some way by discarnate beings.

hole: Physical: You're discovering a hidden aspect of yourself or a situation. Falling in a hole means you encounter a subterfuge or feel trapped by something you didn't notice. You have dug yourself into a hole and can't get out without help. Emotional: You feel hollow or empty inside and need fulfillment. You feel open, revealed, and vulnerable. Mental-Spiritual: You're aware of an opening into a new world or dimension of awareness.

hood/veil: Physical: You're hiding behind a false or deceptive identity, or someone is being deceitful with you. Emotional: You're embarrassed to be seen by others. You're protecting your innocence. Mental-Spiritual: There are perceptual differences between you and others that make communicating very difficult. You're open to being seduced or tricked, "having the hood pulled over your eyes."

horizon: <u>Physical</u>: You're focusing on your goals, hopes, dreams, and life plan. You're seeking direction and perspective and orienting yourself for action. You're becoming aware of events that are about to happen. Looking at the sunrise or sunset means you're focusing on new beginnings, completions, insights, or communion with the unseen. <u>Emotional</u>: You need to feel harmonious and balanced — that you are contained comfortably by your life and environment. You're focused on the future, possibly upsetting yourself that your goals and happiness are far away or exciting yourself about the possibility of dreams becoming real. <u>Mental-Spiritual</u>: You're introverted, focusing on hope, universal and global consciousness, and an expanded sense of self. Seeing a 360-degree horizon means you are centered in yourself, in the moment, and understand that you can be as big as you want to be.

horns: (*see antlers*)

horse: <u>Physical</u>: You're focusing on the magnificence of your physical body and on freedom, power, wildness, pride, energy, majesty, courage, and sexuality. The condition of the horse indicates the state of your energy in waking life. You have been "horsing around" and need to get serious. You need to "get off your high horse" and be less arrogant. Galloping or racing horses represent the drive you need to compete and succeed. <u>Emotional</u>: If you're riding a horse that's out of control, you're being carried away by your passions. An armored horse refers to fierceness, aggression, confrontation, or rigidity. Or you're repressing sexual urges. <u>Mental-Spiritual</u>: Horses link to your instinct, intuition, and prophetic ability. White or flying horses (Pegasus) represent purity and good fortune, as well as a strong motivation for spiritual growth. Black or dark horses signify mystery, occult forces, and gambling on the unknown.

hospital: <u>Physical</u>: You need to heal part of yourself, pay attention to your physical health, allow time and space to rest, or ask others for help. <u>Emotional</u>: You feel emotionally drained. You're looking at your need to rescue others or be rescued. <u>Mental-Spiritual</u>: You're correcting misperceptions and attuning to a higher level of awareness. You're healing others in another dimension. (*see doctor*)

hotel: <u>Physical</u>: You need a break from your life, routine, and habits before a new idea or change can occur. You're between stages in your life, preparing for a new identity. Emotional: You feel unsettled or need to temporarily escape from your ordinary life. You need shelter during a confusing time. Mental-Spiritual: You're involved with a collective consciousness, looking at an issue briefly before spending more time with it later. Hotel lobbies represent an environment where ideas are coming and going, and new ideas are being considered.

house: Physical: A house symbolizes your personal self, life situation, current state, and possibly your health. A new house or a bigger house indicates you've entered a new expanded phase. If the house is too small or cluttered, you're finding motivation to begin to change. Emotional: A childhood home represents emotions, attitudes, and behaviors, created when you lived in that residence, that need to be changed now. If the house is empty, you feel insecure and isolated, or you need to develop more independence. A haunted house means unfinished emotional business related to family, dead relatives, or repressed feelings. A burglarized house means you feel vulnerable or violated, or unconscious knowledge is trying to make itself known. Mental-Spiritual: If the house is under construction and not yet complete, or if it needs repair, you're doing inner psychological work, getting ready for a growth spurt. Cleaning house means you're clearing old thoughts and seeking self-improvement. Specific rooms in the house indicate specific aspects of your psyche. *(see architecture)*

hummingbird: Physical: You're searching for the sweetness of life. You may be literally focusing on how to work with flowers or aromatherapy. You're learning to be flexible and adaptable, making the most of new circumstances. Your body is sensitive and intense now, and you're focusing on your fierce appetite for life experience. You need to raise your energy level and have freedom from restriction. Emotional: You are looking for joy and need to spread love and happiness to others. You need to find the beauty and good inside yourself and others, going deep, beyond the outer layers. Mental-Spiritual: You're focusing on how to live in the present moment and maintain inner stillness while in action. Small ideas and concepts possess much power. You're trying to shift away from having flighty thoughts and frivolous ideas. Hummingbird is a magical messenger, bringing special messages from high spiritual levels.

hunger: Physical: You're actually hungry or your blood sugar is low. You're focusing on a food addiction or allergy. You need rejuvenation and healing through diet. You're focusing on an opportunity to prove yourself. You want sex, power, or fame. Emotional: You are hungry for affection, feel unappreciated, and aren't getting what you need. You feel deprived of possessions and material comforts and security. You feel unfulfilled and dissatisfied, and you're starving for recognition, achievement, or wealth. You have an emotional craving for something that will distract you from what you don't want to face. Eating too much means you feel over-stimulated by the world and have taken on other people's emotions. You need better boundaries. You've had enough of some situation or behavior. Mental-Spiritual: You're focusing on a desire to expand your knowledge base or go back to school. You're yearning for spiritual knowledge and growth, unconditional love, or an experience of oneness and enlightenment.

hurricane/tornado/storm: Physical: You're experiencing sudden changes or a clearing of old structures, like changing jobs suddenly or needing to move. Emotional: You feel an emotional upheaval brewing; destructive and powerful emotions, like rage with ensuing chaos and confusion, are beginning to release. Mental-Spiritual: Being in the eye of the storm symbolizes the still, calm center within yourself where you can find insight and strength amidst chaos. If you're swept up in the storm, you are experiencing intensely confusing thoughts and are consumed by overwhelming conditions.

hypnotize/hypnosis: Physical: You're focusing on giving your power to someone else or allowing yourself to be guided or influenced by others. You need to rest and go more deeply into your body consciousness. Emotional: Being hypnotized means you want to escape taking responsibility for your choices, feelings, and actions, or you're beginning an exploration of the emotional blockages in your subconscious realms. You want power over others. Failing to be hypnotized means you need to develop trust and the ability to let go. Mental-Spiritual: You're living shallowly, not examining the deeper meaning of the experiences in your life. You need to be more present, alert, and aware. You're practicing entering altered, or higher, states of consciousness and bringing back important information and guidance.

I

ice/icicles/iceberg: Physical: You're making slow progress, experiencing bleak conditions, or frozen out by unfriendly colleagues or friends. You aren't making use of your full potential. If you're walking on ice, you're taking risks, sensing potential danger or mishaps in a course of action. Emotional: You feel hopeless, emotionally paralyzed or blocked, or unable to express your feelings due to an unsympathetic environment. If you fall through ice, you're about to have an emotional breakthrough where suppressed feelings come to the surface. Melting ice indicates an easing of emotional problems and difficult times. Icicles represent sadness and emotional pain that started to release but became blocked again. An iceberg represents a huge emotional obstacle you need to face, or its hidden aspects might destroy you. Mental-Spiritual: Your ideas and creativity are blocked, or you feel numb and brain-dead.

ID card: Physical: You're examining your identity or life story and whether it's meaningful to you now. You're focusing on becoming more authentic. You're resisting being defined by societal, traditional standards. Emotional: A lost ID card means you're worrying about being able to go and do what you need to do next. You're contemplating who you are without an official identity. You're sensitive to being tracked by government surveillance. You're proud to have an identity that allows you access to privileged information and locations. Mental-Spiritual: Your identity evolves as you advance in life, so getting a new ID card signifies your spiritual growth. As you identify more as your soul, your personal need for official identification lessens.

igloo: Physical: You're focusing on being safe, warm, and connected to family in a difficult situation or environment. Building an igloo of snow and ice means you're sensitive to working in harmony with the environment and weather. Emotional: You're focused on survival and resilience. Entering an igloo means you're stepping into your own authenticity and personal power. Mental-Spiritual: Being in an igloo represents an intuitive space that easily connects you to soul and higher spiritual dimensions.

immigrant: Physical: You're contemplating the loss of home or a threat to your heritage, of being between identities, or living in an unfamiliar reality where others don't understand you.

Emotional: You're calling upon your inner reserves and courage to proceed on a new path into a new reality in spite of doubt, exhaustion, emotional challenges, and fear. **Mental-Spiritual:** You're using every resource you have, working hard, and never taking your mind from your goal of an improved life with greater freedom and safety. You're building character and evolving spiritually into a wise and compassionate person.

infestation/insects: Physical: Something or someone is bugging you or making a pest of itself. You're dealing with minor annoyances and small obstacles that must not be ignored. Emotional: You're worrying excessively or feel irritated. If the insects bite or sting, you're afraid of being wounded by sharp words. Infestations, whether by people, animals, insects, bacteria, or clutter, represent feeling invaded, overwhelmed, overrun, and undermined. Strengthen your boundaries. Look to the location of the infestation for the area of life it's affecting. Be more assertive and take up your own space. Mental-Spiritual: You're neglecting important information because of an obsession with one thing. You need to organize your thoughts and sort through your priorities. Insects represent precision and are often divine messengers.

infinity sign: Physical: You're focusing on continuous motion with smooth transitions, eliminating conflict and polarizing blockages. You think you're in an unending cycle of thought, behavior, or outcomes. You're focusing on the continuous journey of growth and healing. Emotional: You're contemplating how it feels to be interconnected to others and life. You're intimidated by the idea of the already known or the unknown going on forever. Mental-Spiritual: You're focusing on whether a love can be everlasting or the concept of infinite, evolving love. You're beginning to experience the ever-expanding nature of the divine, of eternity, or the repeating cycle of life, death, and rebirth.

inheritance: (*see treasure*)

ink: Physical: You're focusing on impurities in your system. You're looking at opening a line of communication with someone, or with yourself. You're beginning to work out a solution to a problem. Spilled ink means you're dealing with a smear to your reputation or a setback on a project. Writing something in ink means the statement is permanent and binding. Emotional: You're looking at repressed emotions or what's hidden in the recesses of your subconscious. Red ink means you're receiving a warning and must fix something or face a loss or serious consequences. Smeared or spilled ink means you are going too fast or are ahead of yourself. Mental-Spiritual: You have the means for expressing your innermost thoughts. You're exploring a new way of looking at things or new avenues of creativity. You may be considering writing as self-expression or a new career.

internet: Physical: You need to pay attention to your circulatory systems and the balance of what you take into yourself and what you release. You're focused on networking, marketing, communicating about yourself, or expanding your self-expression. Emotional: You feel pressured to access and integrate more information than is comfortable, or you're stuck in "fear of missing out." You feel lonely and want increased connection with others. You're looking at your dependence on superficial relationships or an avoidance of intimacy. Mental-Spiritual: You're hungry to learn and grow intellectually. You need to pay more attention to detail. You need to focus more on connecting with your inner self. You're merging into an awareness of global, collective consciousness and spiritual unity.

intruder/thief: Physical: Someone is trying to control or influence you surreptitiously or to take something valuable from you, like your authority, reputation, credit for something you did, or actual property. You're experiencing unwanted sexual attention or envy. Emotional: You feel victimized and vulnerable, compromised, disrespected, taken advantage of, or manipulated. You feel guilty for invading someone else's territory or having success you don't feel you deserve. Mental-Spiritual: Disturbing thoughts are breaking into your peace of mind. Someone, or your own inner victim, is trying to bring you down with negative thinking.

invention: Physical: You want to increase your ability to find innovative ideas that can help advance society and human development. You want to materialize new ideas into tools and utensils that people need. You want to overcome limitation, expand your capacities, and overcome ordinary habitual processes that are outmoded. Emotional: You're frustrated by what is old, boring, ineffective, or ugly. You want to find joy in practical creativity. Mental-Spiritual: You're focusing on your ability to solve problems, access intuition and imagination, and create something brilliant, new, and useful. You want to use your consciousness to stretch into higher realms and the future to bring spiritually appropriate forms into existence.

investments: Physical: You're focusing on building security for the future and on your current foundation in life. You're looking at how much you invest in your own abilities, how much confidence you have, and how good you are at gambling. Emotional: You're afraid of being poor and helpless. Your self-worth is tied to financial success and gain. You need to balance overoptimism with caution and common sense. Trading stocks frequently means you're impatient to improve your life situation without putting in your dues and doing the work. Mental-Spiritual: What you invest in represents a quality of you that you need to believe in. You're focusing on developing intuition and awareness of what makes winners and losers. You're looking at broad societal trends and the psychology of the masses.

invisibility: Physical: You're focusing on a loss, a person or opportunity that has become unavailable, a desire to escape responsibilities, or the need for greater recognition. Emotional: You feel unfairly overlooked and misunderstood. You feel embarrassed and want to disappear or avoid an unpleasant experience. Mental-Spiritual: If an object disappears, you're focusing on its importance in your life and the knowledge you gain by having or not having it. If you become invisible, you're seeking secret knowledge about others and life. You're looking into the true nature of things.

iron: Physical: Iron objects like garden tools, construction tools and materials, kitchen utensils, or even railroad tracks mean you're focusing on having the physical strength or willpower to begin and complete something difficult or challenging. Emotional: You're looking at your ability to hold your own, have good boundaries, and face life courageously. You're focusing on how controlling or inflexible you are. Mental-Spiritual: You're focusing on the balance of inner strength and lack of confidence. You're examining universal laws and principles. You may be focused on dissolving fixed structures to experience more trust and freedom.

ironing: Physical: You're trying to smooth out the wrinkles in a situation or relationship. You're trying to improve the image you project publicly. Emotional: You feel anxiety about being too informal and unkempt. You're focusing on domestic comfort and orderliness. Mental-Spiritual: You're looking for a crisp, true, perhaps somewhat formal, worldview. You're learning to communicate clearly to others.

island: Physical: You want to escape from a problem, rest, and relax. You need solitude. You have a strong sense of individuality, boundaries, and integrity. If you're stranded on an island, you're at an impasse in your life, wondering where to go next. Emotional: You feel separate and isolated from others and life. You feel deprived. You need to acknowledge the presence and power of emotion or the unconscious in your life. Mental-Spiritual: You're retreating into yourself, focusing on what's deeply true and real.

itch: Physical: Your body is talking to you. You're experiencing a minor irritation or frustration or "itching" to do something new. Emotional: You're having strong sexual urges. You feel anxiety about having to do something or start over from scratch. Mental-Spiritual: You're beginning to grasp a new concept or understand how a new direction will unfold. You're having a strong, allergic reaction to someone or something, indicating there is incompatibility with your life purpose.

ivy: Physical: You're focusing on being resilient, vigorous, and able to thrive in challenging environments and situations. You create strong bonds with the world you encounter. Emotional: You want to be joyful and exuberant, as well as steadfast and enduring. You're stubborn and will always find a way. You're too clingy or attached to a relationship, situation, goal, or definition of yourself. You're drawn to a cozy mood of hospitality and nourishment. Mental-Spiritual: You're realizing you have achieved more spiritual strength, connection to the divine, and fidelity to ongoing spiritual development. You have an evergreen nature with strong tendrils that hold fast and allow you to survive and find eternal life.

J

jaguar: Physical: You can tackle large projects or challenges with success, especially using your powers of observation, intelligence, strategy, surprise, precision, and patience. You're working on your senses of timing and foresight. You have the strength and power to accomplish whatever you want and need without brute force. Emotional: You need to learn to move more quietly and intentionally, not too impulsively so you can hear your inner voice and discern the right time for crucial action. Mental-Spiritual: You can disengage from ordinary reality and find the "treetop" view of your terrain and situation. And you can swim confidently in the instinctive, intuitive, telepathic, and clairvoyant realms. Make sure to use all your faculties to keep yourself connected to the wisdom of your soul.

janitor: Physical: You're focusing on having to clean up your own or other people's messes. You want someone to help you clean up a mess you've created. You've taken on extra responsibilities that seem simplistic, distasteful, or boring. You're looking at whether you want to work alone. Emotional: You feel unappreciated and overlooked — even disrespected and scorned. You need to be more responsible for the impact you have on others and the environment. You need to tend to your own needs. You need to serve others lovingly. Mental-Spiritual: You're focusing on the art of tending or attending — being mindful of beauty, order, and cleanliness and honoring each thing in the material world as a divine creation.

jaw: Physical: You need more willpower, determination, or forcefulness in some situation. You're too stubborn and need to be a little more "slack-jawed." Emotional: If your jaw is tight, you feel it's not safe to speak your truth, are withholding anger, or feel extremely nervous about an outcome. Mental-Spiritual: If you're in the jaws of an animal, you're threatened by the rash judgments and actions of others, or you have attacked someone unfairly. If your jaw is broken or dislocated, you're not fully aligned with your own beliefs and principles, or you need to develop greater faith and flexibility.

jewels/jewelry: Physical: Your health is improving. You feel strong, protected, and energized physically. Specific jewels are indicative of different kinds of healing and specific qualities you need to activate in yourself. Emotional: Jewelry you own symbolizes particular relationships. You feel good about yourself, pleased with life's possibilities, and can value and cherish others easily. Broken jewelry means your happiness is challenged. You're decorating yourself to impress others with superficial adornments. Mental-Spiritual: You're focusing on your wealth of knowledge, what you hold precious, and your psychological riches and self-worth. You're attuning to your soul qualities and gifts, the light within, and spiritual ideas. Finding or being given jewels signifies rapid spiritual growth.

jigsaw puzzle: Physical: You're focusing on completing a complex project or bringing your body back to full health, looking for all the pieces or ingredients you need. Emotional: You feel fragmented and frustrated by too many details. You feel overwhelmed by the amount of time something is going to take and need to develop more patience. Mental-Spiritual: You're facing a mental challenge or problem you need to solve. You're putting ideas together in different ways so you can see a larger picture or worldview.

job: Physical: You're looking at how well your current work suits you and how satisfied you are with your life direction. You're solving problems from your actual work environment. A task must be accomplished. Being fired from a job means you need to be more engaged with everything you do, or you're ready to end a relationship. Emotional: If you're job hunting, you feel unfulfilled and frustrated. If you fall asleep or are absent from work, you feel you're in a dead-end situation that doesn't nurture you. Mental-Spiritual: Getting a new job or promotion means you're expanding your self-expression and spiritual growth. How excited you are about your job represents how aligned you are with your life work and soul's purpose.

joints: Physical: You're focusing on how you bridge energy and information from one area, or focus, to another, and how you make connections. Having joint problems indicates you're experiencing difficulties in a process coming together as you want. Emotional: You're looking at how rigid or flexible you are emotionally. A broken joint means energy is leaking from a weakness you haven't faced. Mental-Spiritual: You're focusing on how well you give and receive from others, and how well you transmit awareness between the different levels of yourself.

journey: Physical: You're focusing on your life path, transitions between phases of life experience, and developing new personality traits. Along the way, you face challenges, discover new things about yourself and life. A short journey means change. Emotional: Traveling with a companion or interacting with strangers shows how you feel about intimacy and how well you cooperate and cocreate. Mental-Spiritual: Your destination symbolizes a goal you haven't fully realized. The scenery you see gives insight into current circumstances. You're on a spiritual quest.

judge/jury/trial: <u>Physical</u>: You're focusing on authority, morality, justice, and order. You're actually dealing with legal issues. <u>Emotional</u>: You feel pressure to be perfect. You are examining an aspect of your behavior that's been out of line, judging others, or feel others are judging you. You feel guilty about something, and your conscience is urging you to do the right thing. You feel something or someone is unfair. You're threatened with embarrassment from false statements and accusations, or your reputation is at stake due to your actions. <u>Mental–Spiritual</u>: You need to decide about something based on your own mores. You're focusing on universal laws and principles.

juggler: <u>Physical</u>: You're focusing on your physical coordination or ability to multitask. You feel exhausted or overwhelmed with too much to do. You're showing yourself that you enjoy performing. <u>Emotional</u>: You're anxious about what might happen if you drop the ball(s). You're stalling, keeping all the balls in the air, and need to get down to work. You're apprehensive about being cheated or tricked. <u>Mental–Spiritual</u>: You're showing yourself how you keep things separate instead of merging them into a single coordinated flow. You're focusing on a certain number of areas of your life and may not allow new ones to occur.

jump: <u>Physical</u>: Leaping hurdles and jumping over things means you're experiencing success and strong forward motion. Jumping rope shows you can coordinate your actions well. You're jumping at the chance to do something or jumping in with both feet. <u>Emotional</u>: You're impatient and leaping from one thing to another. You're too impulsive or too controlled. You need to take a leap of faith or look before you leap. You're jumping the gun, jumping through hoops to please others, or jumping ship to avoid consequences. If you're afraid to jump, you don't like change or fear you can't complete a task. You're jumping down someone's throat, expressing sudden criticalness. <u>Mental–Spiritual</u>: You're jumping to conclusions, or you're encountering a quantum leap or transformation. You need to let go and surrender to the unknown. Jumping up indicates joy and readiness to shift levels of awareness into higher realms.

jungle: <u>Physical</u>: You're exploring your instincts, wild side, passions, and untamed nature. You feel entangled in a situation, and you can't find your way out. <u>Emotional</u>: You're afraid of being out of control and messy. You're freeing yourself from inhibitions. You feel lost or trapped by a chaotic, unpredictable, dark situation. Negative feelings are hindering your progress; you must cut through with greater mental clarity. Mental-Spiritual: You're traveling through the deep part of your unconscious or subconscious mind, facing exotic, dangerous creatures that represent creative ideas, new motivations, and untapped abilities.

junk/junkyard: Physical: You're focusing on the need to cleanse your body inside and out. You have unfinished business that's cluttering your life and stalling progress. You're telling yourself to literally clean up clutter and create some open space so a new period or project can begin. You have to do something that's distasteful or beneath you. Emotional: You feel rejected, unwanted, unneeded, useless, or expendable. You're exploring subconscious feelings that are outdated, ugly, dysfunctional, or actually belong to someone else. You feel second-rate and disappointed because you're getting someone else's rejects. Mental-Spiritual: You need to discard old habits and ways of thinking. You're discovering treasures in an old, undervalued way of thinking, or in another person's "trashed" philosophy. You are finding the "gifts in the garbage," the soul's lesson in a difficult experience.

K

kaleidoscope: Physical: You're focusing on the wondrously diverse aspects of your own personality, other people, and life itself. You're exploring potential paths of action that lie open to you, as well as your many talents and goals. Your life is changing rapidly from one focus to another, offering surprises that may be exciting. Emotional: You need to accept the fragmented parts of yourself and see how they all fit together. You feel confused and crazy, overwhelmed by the stimulation of everything around you. Mental-Spiritual: You're examining patterns, fractals, holographic interrelated realities, and the connections among all forms of life. You need to find your center so the multitudinous possibilities of life can settle into a beautiful harmonious pattern, and you can see yourself as a more expansive, colorful individual. You're learning to be hugely entertained by the sheer complexity of life.

kangaroo: Physical: You're focusing on enthusiasm, leaping ahead, and making quick progress, as well as endurance, strength, mobility, and freedom to move. You're about to go on an unexpected, exciting journey. Emotional: You need to protect yourself by kicking something out of the way. You are protecting a vulnerable part of yourself or focused on an overprotective female figure or on mothering itself. You're jumping over obstacles, like fears and limitations. Mental-Spiritual: You're jumping from one idea to another and need to develop greater concentration skills. You need to use more intuition. You've set yourself up as a kangaroo court, being judge and jury, possibly directed at yourself. You're connecting with family in a larger sense and with ideas like caretaking and sharing.

keyboard: Physical: You're focusing on combining letters, symbols, or musical notes into a meaningful order; you're shaping your thoughts: writing, designing, composing music, working with mathematics, or organizing data as part of a project you're creating in daily life or in the higher realms. You're finding you inner voice. Emotional: If the keyboard is dirty, jams, or doesn't function properly, you're alerting yourself to old emotional patterns you need to clear, a blockage to the flow of your self-expression or creativity, or a feeling of distraction or boredom. Mental-Spiritual: You're accessing intuition and higher consciousness as you express yourself and create. You're experiencing direct knowing, channeling inspiration into form. Playing a musical keyboard means you're bringing divine harmony into your life and sharing it with others.

keys: Physical: You're accessing new opportunities, unlocking secrets, or opening doors to a new phase of creativity. You're looking at issues of power and authority, being able to go where others cannot, and reach goals easily. Handing a key to someone else means relinquishing responsibility to others. Emotional: You're locking away or protecting things, ideas, or parts of yourself. You're excited or nervous, keyed up. Keys that don't fit a lock indicate frustrated desires or feeling shut out of a relationship or opportunity. Losing your keys indicates you aren't ready for a new opportunity, are out of control, or are blocking yourself through doubt. Mental-Spiritual: You're at a turning point, about to find a solution or obtain guidance. If you find a key, you're looking for an answer to a question you didn't know you were asking, decoding information, or searching for new potential within yourself or in relationship to others. You're attuning to methods for attaining wisdom, higher spiritual knowledge, and enlightenment.

kick: Physical: To kick something or someone means you're rebel-ling, reacting against repression or constraints, trying to move something forward forcefully, venting frustration and anger, or struggling with a dominating force in your life. Being kicked or kicked out means you feel threatened, powerless, ashamed, or overwhelmed. Emotional: Kicking up your heels means you're full of joy and want to express it exuberantly. Kicking down a door means you feel trapped, need to move ahead toward freedom or involvement immediately, or want an obstacle out of your way. Mental-Spiritual: Kicking a ball, especially toward a target, shows you have self-control, focus, and the ability to reach your goal. "Getting a kick out of something" means you're activating joy and appreciation. Being "kicked in the pants" can mean you're asking yourself to wake up and make more progress on your spir-itual path.

kidnap: Physical: An area of your life has taken you hostage by being too emphasized. You need a chance to get away from the entanglements of your daily routine to start fresh. Emotional: You feel victimized, trapped, or carried away by the desires and plans of others. You feel forced to do something against your will, or you're taking advantage of someone else. You've given your power away. Mental-Spiritual: The part of yourself that has kid-napped you needs attention and recognition. You're developing a strategy to evolve beyond limiting conditions.

kill: Physical: You're addressing or trying to get rid of an unwanted part of yourself or an issue that's causing great dis-tress. You want to make someone go away. Killing small animals can refer to abortion. You're stalled or "killing time." Emotional: You're experiencing intense feelings of anger, frustration, or even hatred. Killing in self-defense means you're standing up for yourself and developing confidence. Killing someone you know means you're worried that you've hurt the person through actions you've taken. Mental-Spiritual: Your motivation has been killed by some idea or has simply died. You're experiencing ego death and loss of identity. You're removing fixed ideas that interfere with spiritual progress.

killer: Physical: A killer pursuing you or someone else means you feel you're in a dangerous situation and need help to avoid damage or failure. As when dealing with monsters in dreams, you might introduce another character to the dream to change the balance of power, then turn, face the enemy, and with help, kill it, him, or her. This is not literal but symbolically allows you to take your power back. Emotional: You want to rid yourself of a bothersome person or situation. You're dealing with someone who kills your ideas, joy, and spirit; it's up to you to change your reactions. Mental-Spiritual: You're blocking the love and genius of your own soul — in effect "killing" your life force.

kiss: Physical: You're focusing on bonding, sharing, and making connections with others, especially in intimate relationships. You want to be more sexual. Emotional: You need affection, approval, appreciation, romance, love, intimacy, and passion. Watching others kiss means you're participating in others' lives too closely or focusing on infidelity, jealousy, or voyeurism. You feel betrayed (kiss of death), rejected (kissed off), or are detaching from something (kissing it goodbye). Mental-Spiritual: You're opening your heart, finding similarities between yourself and others, and learning to experience communion.

kitchen: Physical: You need better quality food and nutrition. You're in a creative process, cooking something up. Emotional: The state of the kitchen reflects how you experience your well-being, abundance, nourishment, and emotional warmth. You're focusing on how nurtured you feel and how you nurture others. Mental-Spiritual: You're focusing on receiving spiritual nourishment. If you're cooking a meal for yourself and/or others, you're actively engaging in the process of healing and opening to love.

kite: Physical: You need to be free, expansive, and break loose from too much practicality. Emotional: You feel out of control, at the whim of circumstances. You feel giddy. Mental-Spiritual: Without care and attention, you could crash or fail suddenly. You need to pay attention to managing your life and maintaining a good balance of activities. You're looking for higher perspective on situations and on yourself.

knee/kneel: Physical: You're focusing on your ability to be adaptable or humble (to kneel). Emotional: You're caught in too much pride, stubbornness, emotional inflexibility, and refusal to change. You feel subservient, submissive, inferior, or dominated. You feel defensive, with "knee-jerk" reactions to situations. Mental-Spiritual: You're focusing on the need to experience awe and reverence. You need to be more fully engaged with life instead of having "knee-deep" involvements.

knife/sword: Physical: You're focusing on male aggression and sexuality, as well as protection and readiness to take decisive action. You're creating by carving something from scratch. You're achieving easily (a knife through butter). Emotional: You feel attacked, betrayed, and emotionally injured (knife in the back). As a phallic symbol, a knife can represent sexual assault. You feel you're at war. You're injuring yourself or want to hurt someone else. Mental-Spiritual: You're developing your intellect and the ability to think clearly, analyze, cut through, or penetrate into your subconscious mind. *(see cut)*

knitting: Physical: You're focusing on healing your body, as in tissue or bone knitting together or the skin repairing itself. You're focusing on making a new creation out of a stream of insights and small actions over a sustained period of time. You need to slow down, relax, and let yourself do something peaceful that promotes renewal of your energy. Knitting that comes unraveled means you experience temporary setbacks and frustrations where efforts must be repeated — patiently. Emotional: You're knitting a relationship together after wounds have been inflicted. You want to feel cozy and protected, domestic and nurtured. Mental-Spiritual: You're looking for the connecting thread in a series of seemingly disparate experiences. You're examining how things grow and evolve, the positive use of repetition, and the patterns you want to design into your life pattern. *(also see weave)*

knock: Physical: Hearing a knock on a door, wall, window, or table means "pay attention" — you're about to meet someone or have a new opportunity that's important. You want to start a new endeavor and need the support or invitation of others to begin. You're pregnant (knocked up). You need to stop doing something (knock it off). Emotional: You want greater intimacy and social connection with others. You feel frustrated, exhausted, like a victim (school of hard knocks, knocking your head against the wall). Mental-Spiritual: Something needs your attention or a clear choice. This is a "wake-up call"; a warning, guidance, or neglected part of you is breaking through to your conscious mind. You're criticizing something or someone (knocking it, knocking them down a peg) or are experiencing it yourself. You're experiencing something amazing and stunning (a knockout). You're feeling superstitious (knock on wood). *(see alarm)*

knot: Physical: Something is restricting you, or you're trying to control something or prevent loss. Emotional: You're experiencing anxiety and worry (being tied in knots). You're making a commitment and focusing on security, as in marriage (tying the knot). Mental-Spiritual: You're working on a complex problem that needs to be solved. You're untangling a confusing situation.

knuckles: Physical: You're coming to grips with something in your life. You are focusing on working hard or "knuckling down." You're knocking on a door to gain entrance to a new relationship, experience, or period of your life. You are preparing to fight for something, to use "brass knuckles," or give someone a "knuckle sandwich." Emotional: You feel intimated by someone and are "knuckling under" to pressure. You're experiencing extreme anxiety and anticipation of something terrible with "white knuckles." Rapping on the knuckles means you're reprimanding yourself for a misdemeanor. Mental-Spiritual: Knuckles resting on the ground is a sign of passive, apelike behavior and low intelligence. You're focusing on thoughts that pertain to defense and assertiveness. Knuckles made into a fist and raised in the air means you're raising your personal power for the higher good. Cracking your knuckles means you need to release tension about doing, greeting the new, or reaching out to others.

koala: Physical: You're focusing on being deliberate, selective, and purposeful in everything you do. You're building surely toward the results you want. You're focusing on feminine energy. Emotional: You need to feel more secure, calm, nurtured, and kind. You'd like to avoid responsibilities and go back to the innocence of childhood. You want to feel luckier and more fortunate in your dealings with other people and increase your gentleness and ability to love. You're being too dependent or placid and need to stand up for yourself more. You need to look deeply for the fierceness to defend yourself (the peaceful koala squirts skunklike urine on intruders). Mental-Spiritual: You're making great progress in developing your intuition and accessing inner guidance. You're exploring your rich inner life.

L

ladder: Physical: You're concerned with career aspirations, achievement, increasing material prosperity, or climbing the social ladder to greater status. You're making progress via hard work. Climbing down a ladder means you're avoiding responsibilities.

Falling from a ladder means you encounter hardships and setbacks. You're concerned with the health of your spine. Emotional: Holding a ladder for someone else means you're being unselfish and generous — helping to support and stabilize that person's growth — or receiving such help yourself. A broken ladder or missing rungs indicates fear of failure, challenges, or a handicap due to missing life experiences. Mental-Spiritual: You're climbing to a new level of understanding and spiritual awareness, actively pursuing your spiritual path. You're looking for a different perspective. You need to meditate and pray.

ladybug: Physical: A ladybug walking on you means good luck, love, and blessings. You're being shown that you can move quietly, methodically, and intentionally and have a successful life. Ladybugs are helpful in gardens and farms, providing natural pest control, pollination, and ecosystem balance. These are qualities/ abilities they bring to your societal life: the ability to facilitate a positive, functional environment. Emotional: A ladybug reminds you to be gentle and innocent and to show your beauty to the world. It teaches children not to be afraid of other forms of life. Mental-Spiritual: A ladybug represents a positive transformation from larva to adult; you're showing yourself you can shift into a new, beautiful being by being one with the natural flow. Ladybugs fly as well as crawl, and they gather in colonies or community. They're comfortable in the physical, mental, and spiritual realms and have both individual and collective consciousness.

lake: Physical: You're looking at the settings and situations of your life. If you're floating on, swimming in, or boating on a calm lake, you're experiencing peace, freedom from limitations, and ease. Emotional: If the lake is disturbed and wavy, you are going through emotional turmoil, are being overwhelmed or shaken up by situations, and may experience losses. Mental-Spiritual: You're exploring the unknown, wanting to penetrate into the mysteries, especially if you're diving or swimming under water.

lamb: Physical: You're focusing on innocence, purity, and gentleness. You're ready to have children or good, trustworthy friends. Emotional: You feel you've had to sacrifice a precious part of yourself, or you give too much of yourself to others. You need to be more assertive. You're opening your heart to romance. Mental-Spiritual: You're working with humility, sweetness, and letting go of stubborn resistance to make progress spiritually.

laptop: (*see computer*)

laryngitis: Physical: You're focusing on the importance of what you need to say to others. Losing your voice indicates you need to think twice about speaking up right now. Emotional: You feel overpowered by other, more forceful or glib people, as though your contribution isn't worthwhile or you aren't strong enough. You feel misinterpreted. Mental-Spiritual: You need a period of silence and contemplation to let your truth arise naturally. You need time to carefully craft your message.

laser: Physical: You need to focus narrowly and specifically on an issue and do one task at a time. Laser beams guarding an entrance means you must be in tune with the truth to move into a new phase of life. Using a laser sword or laser beam as a weapon means you're wielding the force of truth — possibly using it destructively — or mistaking your own prejudices for the truth. You're burning off impurities or blemishes. Emotional: You're hiding from the truth or someone who can see through you. You're being too critical of others or life. Mental-Spiritual: You're looking for clarity, cutting through what's superficial to get to the core. You're learning to focus on truth and the power of light.

late: Physical: Being late for an appointment means you're reminding yourself not to miss opportunities. You're experiencing anxiety over being behind on a project. You don't want to be controlled by outside circumstances. Emotional: You feel ambivalent toward a situation or passive-aggressive toward an authority, are neglecting a responsibility, or would like to avoid a commitment. You feel disrespected or insulted by someone. Mental-Spiritual: You realize you want to learn more, grow more, be more involved in life, contribute, and live fully in the present moment.

laughter: Physical: You need to release pent-up energy that's been held back by worry, negative thinking, fear, or too much sedentary activity. You need lighthearted social activity with like-minded others. You need more experience trusting, bonding, and having the sense of solidarity within a group. Emotional: If you or someone is laughing uncomfortably, you're focusing on feelings of overwhelm, shock, discomfort, or nervous energy. If you or someone is laughing at another person or situation, you're focusing on behaviors motivated by derision, superiority, manipulation, or cruelty. You're experiencing relief. Mental-Spiritual: Spontaneous laughter and playfulness mean you're focusing on joy and spiritual openness. You're moving beyond normal logical thinking into higher realms of perception. You're seeing life's restrictions as the cosmic joke.

lava: (*see volcano*)

lawn: Physical: Your attention is on keeping your body and domestic life orderly, healthy, peaceful, and beautiful. Mowing or watering a lawn means you're sustaining the positive, abundant flow in your life. A neglected, dead, weedy, or brown lawn means you aren't involved enough in nurturing the world around you; you're preoccupied with success in the world at large, or you've withdrawn into an introspective space. Emotional: You're dissatisfied with your home life. You're looking for contentment, and to feel a deep sense of well-being, pleasure, and satisfaction. A dead lawn means you're depressed or apathetic. Mental-Spiritual: You're concerned about what others think of you. A lush green lawn means you're actively fertilizing your mind with creative thoughts and inquiry.

lawyer: Physical: You're focusing on rival, or on a conflict or potential conflict in which you need someone on your side. Emotional: You feel misunderstood, betrayed, defamed, taken advantage of, or unfairly ganged up on by clever, manipulating people. You feel antagonistic, defensive, or victimized. You're giving your authority away to others and need to stand up for yourself and have clearer boundaries. You need to ask for help. Mental-Spiritual: You're concerned with injustices at a personal, societal, or global level. You're focusing on what constitutes morality. You're caught in dualistic, right-wrong, black-and-white thinking, the blame game, or victimization thoughts. You're attuning to universal principles and the natural order of life, which is totally harmonious and fair.

leaf: Physical: The condition of the leaf or leaves indicates the condition of your body's nutritional balance and overall health. You're focusing on a new phase of growth where you're likely to attain success, abundance, good health, and happiness. There's an improvement occurring in your life. Falling leaves at the end of the season mean you're withdrawing into an introspective period or you're letting go of relationships, possessions, or activities. Emotional: Brown, withered, or diseased leaves mean you're suffering from self-doubt, criticism, lack of nurturing, depression, hopelessness, or overwhelming negative conditions. Mental-Spiritual: You're opening to take in increased light, knowledge, nurturing, and life force. Fallen leaves mean there's a need for rest and letting go of pushing forward for a time.

leak: Physical: You're wasting energy on fruitless endeavors. You're experiencing the slow loss of resources. Emotional: You're giving too much of yourself away to others without being appreciated. You feel the loss of something. Repressed feelings are slowly emerging from your subconscious. Mental-Spiritual: You're giving your ideas away. New insights are seeping into your consciousness, one bit at a time.

left: Physical: The left side of the body symbolizes receptivity, creativity, going with the flow, and nontraditional ways of doing things. You need to receive the qualities symbolized by someone or something to your left. You need to work more with your inner-directed, feminine/yin energy and pay attention to the women in your life. Emotional: You're activating repressed feelings, artistic sensitivity, and intuition. You feel too passive or negative. Mental-Spiritual: You need to take a break from your intellectual orientation. You're exploring mysteries, what's dangerous, destructive, and irrational. If you're left-handed, the meanings for left and right may be reversed.

legs: Physical: You're looking at how steadfast you are, how you take a stand, step or move forward, and support yourself by making money. You're examining your pace and how fast or slowly you're moving ahead. Emotional: A broken, injured, weak, or deformed leg suggests you're hesitating (or preparing) to take initiative, you feel emotionally vulnerable, or you're stubbornly refusing to change. You lack balance, autonomy, or independence and rely on various crutches to get by. Mental-Spiritual: Focusing on someone else's legs means you want to adopt their successful ideas and methods. If one leg is shorter than the other, you're emphasizing one idea at the expense of others. *(see feet)*

letter/postcard/e-mail: Physical: Receiving a letter indicates you're focusing on a new opportunity or challenge, or a quality represented by the writer of the letter. Sending a letter means you need to communicate and express yourself more. Emotional: An unconscious aspect of yourself or a repressed emotion is trying to surface and make itself known. Mental-Spiritual: You're receiving guidance from your inner self. An unopened letter or unread email indicates you aren't using your intuition or are deliberately ignoring certain information. If you receive or send a postcard, look for meaning in the picture side.

library: Physical: You're seeking new meaning or new skills. You need to study and evaluate a situation before acting. Emotional: If the library is disorganized, too much information is coming at you at once; you feel overwhelmed by information and details and are having trouble sorting through it all. Mental-Spiritual: You're focusing on knowledge you've accumulated over the years and what is crucial to your success now. You're hungry to learn. You're tapping into the collective consciousness and the *akashic records* (memory banks of the planet) to explore your own and planetary history as well as your life vision.

light/lighthouse: Physical: You're lightening up and letting go of density, clutter, or physical weight. A light bulb turning on means you're ready to face reality. Emotional: You're lightening up your emotions and becoming more humorous, joyful, and untroubled. Mental-Spiritual: Your awareness is moving into clarity, truth, understanding, wisdom, and enlightenment. You've found an answer and seen the way through a problem. Small, pointed lights like candles, flashlights, or light bulbs represent insights or guidance. Broad, diffused light represents an atmosphere of understanding. Lights turning off means you need to face something in your subconscious or let your mind be quiet. Lighthouses and beacons symbolize an inner source of guidance you must follow to be safe.

lightning: Physical: You are likely to have a stroke of good luck. You must act on something immediately. Emotional: You're experiencing a shocking turn of events. If you're struck by lightning, a transformation or irreversible change is occurring in your life. You feel afraid you're being punished by the wrath of God. Mental-Spiritual: You're opening to sudden awareness, illumination, and purification. Something is being pointed out to you by divine intelligence, possibly a warning.

lightworker: Physical: Dreaming of a radiant person or being means you're opening to a higher level of consciousness. This might be a religious figure, an intergalactic being, a beloved relative, a special animal, or a person who is a wise teacher, healer, or counselor. You're showing yourself that you're becoming a lightworker, that you have much to offer others to assist their evolution. Emotional: You need more meaningful connection with people/beings of higher consciousness and are either joyful or slightly nervous about interacting with them. Mental-Spiritual: You're ready for a leap in consciousness and abilities that once were called supernatural but now are becoming much more normal. You're being readied for a revelation.

lion: Physical: You're focusing on courage, power, aggression, fierceness, and protectiveness, especially of those you consider family. As king of beasts, the lion symbolizes strength of character and quiet strength, dignity, dominion, majesty, pride, and leadership skill. A lioness means you're hunting for opportunities and will find what you need. You're looking for honesty in those around you. You're too laid back or lazy. Emotional: You want to control or rule others and have greater influence. You want to be the center of attention, are showing off, or are being arrogant. You need to exercise more restraint in your ambitions. Being attacked by a lion indicates a huge obstacle coming, or you're acting in a self-destructive way. Mental-Spiritual: As spiritual guides, lions glow with golden sunlight, leading you safely to your destination. You're becoming a spiritual leader.

lips: Physical: You're focusing on a need to speak and communicate, eat, or kiss someone to find romance, affection, and sex. Emotional: The expression the lips were making indicate feelings you need to experience and understand better: pleased, scornful, approving, aloof, indifferent, seductive. You're hungry emotionally or dealing with feelings of greed, lust, or gluttony. Mental-Spiritual: You're opening to greater tenderness and intimacy and thus to a spirit of communion. To buy, see, or wear lipstick suggests you're not being truthful.

lizard: Physical: You're focusing on primal instincts and desires for food, sex, and safety. You want to bask in the sun. You're involved in a process of creativity, renewal, and revitalization. Emotional: You're focusing on someone you consider to be cold-blooded or thick-skinned, or you're too much this way. Mental-Spiritual: You're developing better powers of perceptiveness as well as a quicker response time. The lizard is considered a protective spirit and brings fertility and tranquility in the home.

locusts: Physical: You're underfed or malnourished. You're focusing on attaining great amounts of material assets and resources. Greedy people are seeking to destroy what you've created, or you're being plagued by constant annoyances, grievances, and obstacles. Emotional: Your emotional needs are voracious, or you're dealing with someone who's devouring you emotionally. You feel you may be on the edge of true scarcity. You feel a need to exact retribution or repent about something you've done. Mental-Spiritual: You're focusing on a collective consciousness that's marked by self-serving needs or the desire to dominate. You're focusing on long-term cycles and personal transformation. You're focusing on how times of loss can bring new life.

loss/lost: Physical: Losing something means you're focusing on lost opportunities, past relationships, or forgotten aspects of yourself. You're warning yourself of a potential real loss. You need to clean out and reorganize your life. Emotional: You're worrying about not having enough and need to release an attachment to what the lost item symbolizes. You feel insecure about the path you're taking. If someone else is lost, you have unresolved issues regarding the person. Mental-Spiritual: If you're lost, you need to experience your center, orient yourself to a new direction, or get rid of confusing situations. You've lost sight of your goals. You're experiencing ego death or loss of identity, a step toward awareness of a spiritual reality.

lottery: Physical: You're gambling on a path of action or possible outcome. You're relying too much on fate instead of taking responsibility for your own actions. You want to escape the pressures of everyday life and have unrealistic expectations about how you will pay the bills. Winning means you're likely to have success in an endeavor, not necessarily at the lottery. Emotional: You're focusing on what it means to feel loved and blessed, or on what you feel you have to do to be worthy and deserving. You're anxious about losing your freedom or uniqueness by going along with the crowd. You're being impulsive, taking risks in an area of your life, looking for reward. You're overlooking clues about how to be successful or want to avoid facing uncomfortable things about yourself. Mental-Spiritual: You're working out a strategy for a new phase of experience where you're in tune with the flow of abundance. You are learning about materializing realities via attention.

luggage: Physical: You're holding on to too much and are weighed down by clutter, unfinished business, responsibilities, and possessions. It's time to pack up and move on, take a break, determine what's important to keep, and what you can leave behind. Emotional: You need to reduce problems, create better emotional boundaries, and alleviate pressure and worries. If someone is carrying your bags, you're about to experience some supportive relationships. Mental-Spiritual: Heavy bags or excess baggage means you need to throw out old ideas and prejudices. A new set of luggage means a new set of priorities and movement into a new reality.

lungs: Physical: You're focusing on taking a breath of fresh air, finding a new start, reorganizing your life. You need renewed creativity, inspiration, and motivation. You're warning yourself about an actual respiratory problem. Emotional: You're involved in a situation or relationship in which you feel stressed and suffocated. You're dealing with issues of grief, sadness, isolation, or suffering. Mental-Spiritual: You're opening to a more expansive worldview and a greater connection to the world.

M

magic/magical powers: Physical: You want something to work miraculously, or you want to avoid going through all the normal steps. If you have a magical power, you can make your dreams come true. Performing magic suggests you need to approach problems from a new angle, or an issue or task is trickier than you anticipated. Riding a magic carpet means you're overcoming obstacles and physical limitations. Emotional: Black magic means you feel manipulated or controlled or are doing this to others. You feel deceived and exposed to evil and treachery. You've attained your goals in an underhanded way. Mental-Spiritual: You're disillusioned or fooling yourself or someone into believing a lie. If you have magical powers, you can serve others in a grand way.

magnet: Physical: You're focusing on your innate physical attractiveness and ability to influence others with your presence. You're being attracted or repelled by a circumstance, opportunity, or person. You're asserting your personal power and charisma to attract people and resources. You need healing or energetic balancing when magnets are placed on your body. Emotional: You feel a lack of self-esteem that can be repellant to others. You feel powerless to say no to charming, seductive people. Mental-Spiritual: You're examining concepts and things you find attractive and repulsive. You're looking at the way you're naturally drawn to circumstances and ideas that match your own vibration and level of development.

maid: Physical: You're focusing on the need to clean up a messy, or you must clean away clutter in your life. You're relying too much on other people to support you and do the tasks you don't want to tackle, or you're overwhelmed with work and need help. You've taken on extra responsibilities that seem simplistic, distasteful, or boring. Emotional: You feel unappreciated, inferior, overlooked, disrespected, or scorned, or you're treating someone else this way. You need to take care of yourself. You need to serve others lovingly and not put your own needs first. Mental-Spiritual: You're focusing on the art of tending or attending — being mindful of beauty, order, and cleanliness and honoring each thing as a divine creation. You want to experience joyful service instead of sacrificial service.

makeup/mask: Physical: You're covering up your true identity, putting on a false face for the public due to shame. You're putting your best face forward. If others are wearing masks, a situation is not as it seems, you have trouble identifying people's true nature, or you struggle with lies, deceit, or jealousy. Putting on makeup reflects concern about appearance and social presentation. Emotional: You lack confidence in yourself. You're trying to please others. Difficulty applying makeup suggests anxiety about an important social event. Smeared makeup shows failed attempts at presentation. Mental-Spiritual: The reality you're dealing with is symbolic of another, deeper reality. You're experimenting with playing new roles. Removing makeup shows a need to see yourself more clearly. *(see face)*

mandala: Physical: Seeing a mandala means you're contemplating the harmony in your life and the developmental process you're going through, step by step, layer by layer. You're focusing on your sense of wholeness. Emotional: You're seeking to calm yourself and integrate various aspects of your personality, especially at times when you're upset or fragmented. Mental-Spiritual: You're psychically reorganizing yourself to be in alignment with spirit. You're entering the sacred circle or square to journey to higher states of consciousness, realizing how you're connected with the universe itself. You're on a spiritual path to transformation and enlightenment.

map: <u>Physical</u>: You're beginning a journey, searching for a new path, studying the variables inherent in a change of direction and what the ensuing experience will bring. You're looking for alternate routes to accomplish your goals. <u>Emotional</u>: You feel lost and panic-stricken. <u>Mental-Spiritual</u>: You're soliciting guidance from higher parts of yourself, looking at your destiny and its most natural unfolding.

market: <u>Physical</u>: You want to fill a lack or physical need, or you're bored and need a growth spurt. You need the stimulation of new possessions, nurturance of fresh food, and support of new tools and resources. The specific items you're shopping for symbolize your inner needs. <u>Emotional</u>: You want to feel good by having the good things of life. An empty market means you feel a void within, you feel hopeless and depressed, or you've missed opportunities. <u>Mental-Spiritual</u>: You're shopping for possibilities, decisions, or variety. You need to exchange with the hustle-bustle world, business, and commercial ventures. You're tuning in to healthy ideas of an industrious, cooperative, prosperous society. If the market is clean, busy, and well-stocked, you're ready to experience abundance and greater involvement in the world. *(see buy)*

marriage: <u>Physical</u>: You have a literal desire to marry. You want to join forces with a person or entity, as in a new business partnership. The characteristics of the person you're marrying are the qualities you need to incorporate within yourself. <u>Emotional</u>: You need to harmonize your feminine and masculine energies or unify other separate aspects of yourself. Marrying your ex means you've learned from past mistakes or need to learn the lessons now, or a current relationship is parallel to the old one. <u>Mental-Spiritual</u>: You're in a transition period, focusing on greater commitment, harmony, communication skills, diplomacy, generosity, cocreativity, and loyalty.

martyr: <u>Physical</u>: You're focusing on the depth of your commitment to something, whether you're willing to sacrifice something to reach a goal or have been misunderstood, betrayed, or treated unfairly. You're looking at your own courage to stand up for a deeply held belief or what is ethical or spiritually correct. <u>Emotional</u>: You're looking at feelings of profound disappointment, sacrifice for no reason, or loss that made you feel like a victim. Is playing the victim helpful to anyone, or are you using it to control others and life? You feel righteous about something.

Does that help people understand the issue or does it push them away? The extremism of martyrdom needs to be carefully considered. Mental-Spiritual: Are you letting a belief interfere with the greater wisdom in the flow of life? What's worth making a dramatic point about, and what holds back your spiritual growth?

matches: Physical: Striking a match means you're preparing to be creative, productive, and dynamic. Blowing out a match means you've completed an important task or phase. Emotional: You need to ignite your passion and enthusiasm and overcome dark emotions that hold you back in the past or in fear. You're focusing on feelings of helplessness or apathy and your need to rekindle your motivations, positive expectations, and love of yourself and others. Mental-Spiritual: You're focusing on a specific insights or revelations that you need to shed light on a path of action. You're opening into your true self one step at a time, one bit of light leading to the next amount of light, and the next.

mathematics: *(see numbers/mathematics/numerology)*

maze: Physical: You feel lost or confused in an area of your life and may need to just pick a direction and see where it goes, knowing there are twists and turns along the way. You're reminding yourself that it's natural to make mistakes. Emotional: You're making a situation harder than it really is, blocking your progress by complaining or protesting. Mental-Spiritual: You're on a spiritual path, a quest for meaning and truth. You need to work intensively with your intuition. You're being blocked by fixed beliefs, fear-based ideas, and lack of faith.

medicine/pill: Physical: You're focusing on healing yourself. Your troubles are temporary. You're looking at the actions you need to take to improve a situation. Emotional: If you suspect the medication is incorrectly prescribed, you distrust your support people and caretakers. Someone is lying to you or trying to manipulate you, or you're operating in an underhanded way. You feel poisoned by an outside influence that you took too personally. Mental-Spiritual: You're adjusting your awareness to a healthier level that's conducive to the expression of your vitality and soul. You're correcting misperceptions that have caused you to make mistakes.

men: Physical: Any male figure represents your animus or the way you use and understand masculine energy. You need to express more — or less — power, compartmentalization, assertiveness, or initiative. Emotional: You're facing unresolved issues with your father or male relatives. Mental-Spiritual: How the men are dressed provides a clue about the area of your life that needs more yang energy. You're focusing on will, logic, and intellect.

menu: Physical: You're looking at your choices in life — what to create, what you need to get the job done, where to go, when to leave, who to partner with. Your life is too narrow, and you need more options. A restaurant menu means you're focusing on abundance and the many ways you can nurture yourself and others. Emotional: You're overwhelmed by the variety of life and feel paralyzed or hyperactive and jittery. You're ambivalent or apathetic and need to reconnect with enthusiasm so a direction becomes clear. Mental-Spiritual: You're searching for information and understanding so you can discriminate your choices more clearly. A drop-down computer menu means you're following a chain of tasks and knowledge to complete a task. You're opening to unlimited possibilities.

mermaid: Physical: You're focusing on your mysterious, secretive female aspect, or anima. You're unable to fully participate in a love relationship or can't give your all in a situation. Emotional: You're facing emotional traumas, learning to be comfortable with feelings. You're linking your primitive and conscious nature. For a man, the mermaid can represent fear of seduction and sex or being drowned by the feminine aspect of his psyche. For a woman, the mermaid can mean doubt about femininity or sexuality. Mermaids are often associated with transgender identity confusion. Mental-Spiritual: You're bringing beauty and wisdom up from your unconscious. You're facing temptations, exploring the depths, overcoming obstacles with superhuman skills and strength in the inner realms first.

merry-go-round: Physical: You're going in circles or stagnating. You're in the beginning stages of romantic love. Emotional: You're expressing anxiety about the transition into adulthood or to greater responsibilities. You want to retreat to childlike joys. You're afraid of remembering and reliving parts of your childhood. Mental-Spiritual: You're aware of the cycles of life and creativity and focusing on the restfulness and rejuvenation of playing and flowing easily.

metal: Physical: You're focusing on qualities of neutrality and strength of character. Emotional: You feel someone is too cold, hard, overly technological, or inhuman, or you're being this way. Mental-Spiritual: Since metal is cold and hard yet malleable and can melt, it represents an attitude that's rigid but not brittle, yet capable of conducting great heat or passion. You're focusing on spiritual or superconscious information and truths.

microscope: Physical: You're traveling down into your body, focusing on your cells and particles. You need to take a closer look at a particular situation or bring an aspect of your life into focus. You're examining the causes of a problem or the underlying blueprint of a situation so you can help things unfold without snags. Emotional: You've been too impersonal and disengaged, and you need to be more involved with people, feelings, and life. You're looking at the roots of your emotional pain with an eye to clearing blockages. Mental-Spiritual: You want to understand the deeper dynamics of your life, why it unfolds as it does, and what the influencing factors are. Your focus is too narrow; you're missing the big picture.

milk: Physical: You're focusing on wholesomeness, domestic bliss, deep inner nourishment, maternal instincts, motherly love, and human kindness. To spill milk means a loss of faith, precious resources, opportunity, and trust. Emotional: You need to receive or give love and care. You need to strengthen ties with others. Sour milk means you feel deprived of nurturing, or you experience problems instead of successes. Choking on milk means you feel overprotected. Mental-Spiritual: Warm milk means you're relaxing and centering yourself.

mine: Physical: Entering or being inside a mine indicates you're penetrating to the core of an issue, looking for deeply buried riches, resources, and secrets. You're focusing on the inner workings of your body. Emotional: A collapsed mine shaft means you need to work harder to free emotional issues that are blocked. You may be claiming what is "mine." Mental-Spiritual: Bringing the contents of a mine to the surface means that issues from your subconscious are becoming conscious. If you're buried by a cave-in, you need to be quiet and grounded, absorb wisdom from the earth, and attune to the divine feminine awareness. *(see cave)*

minister *(see priest)*

miracle: Physical: You're focusing on accomplishing something big and pushing your boundaries beyond what you think is normal.

You need a spectacular amount of help to succeed in a project you've undertaken. You're working too hard for other people who expect miracles without understanding the process. Emotional: You're exhausted from struggling, or you're feeling alone or that no one cares about you. You need to release the emotional pressure to please others or to act only in culturally approved ways. You need to allow yourself to be helped. Mental-Spiritual: You're focusing on having more trust and faith, as well as a more real experience of the divine. Seeing a miracle means you're reminding yourself that there's an easy way to do things when you work with the flow and the invisible forces. You're examining how the unified field functions and how the power of love accomplishes what many think is impossible.

mirror: Physical: You're examining yourself and your image. The way you appear indicates the way you think you look to others, or something you need to admit to yourself. The image in the mirror represents your secret, inner self. Emotional: A fogged mirror means a hazy self-concept and questions about goals, identity, and purpose. A cracked or broken mirror means a fragmented personality, a disturbed and distorted sense of self. Breaking a mirror means you're shattering an old image of yourself or ending an old habit. If you're being watched by others through a two-way mirror, you feel criticized or scrutinized unfairly, or you're highlighting a behavior in yourself that you want to change. Mental-Spiritual: You're focusing on your imagination and the link between your conscious mind and subconscious. Seeing images reflected in a mirror is a safe way to work with information from your subconscious. If you're looking through a two-way mirror, you're seeing the hidden dynamics of an issue that concerns you.

money: Physical: You're focusing on your intrinsic value, inner abundance, confidence, self-worth, and success. You're looking at your energy level. Winning money means that success and prosperity can easily manifest for you. Losing money indicates depleted inner resources, temporary setbacks, or the need to be more detached concerning outcomes. Investing money in the stock market means you have faith in your own talent and potential. Emotional: Having inadequate money denotes fear of losing status or being unprepared, weak, passive, out of control, and powerless. To be underpaid or not rewarded monetarily means you feel ignored, neglected, undervalued, and unloved. Hoarding money means you're focusing on what you don't have; you're worrying about debt, unemployment, or negative cash flow in waking life. Stealing money or having money stolen means you need to let go and trust that you'll have what you need. You feel envy toward fortunate people, as though you're being unfairly deprived. You need to reach toward the things you value and feel entitled. Mental-Spiritual: You're experiencing inner richness and values concerning provision, deservedness, and influence. You're looking at attitudes about love and matters of the heart. Giving money away means you're giving love and support to yourself and others. Finding money means you need to express gratitude for what you have and expect improved circumstances.

monitor: (*see screen*)

monk: Physical: You need to go on a retreat or take time by yourself to renew your energy, find your center, and reconnect with nature and the divine. You need to detach from worldly concerns and desires. You need more discipline in thought, motivation, and action. You want to focus on your faith and heart. Emotional: You feel too isolated and need nurturing activity with friends or family. You feel uninspired and need to find fun and enthusiastic motivation. You need to be a little more unruly and spontaneous, or you've been too much that way and need to deepen your felt sense of life. Mental-Spiritual: You're seeking spiritual or religious guidance from a wise person. You're telling yourself to meditate more, be simpler, and be more mindful about your spiritual practice. You're contemplating being of service to people who could use upliftment, counsel, healing, respect, or clarity.

monkey: Physical: You need to be more playful, humorous, mischievous, or even silly. You're acting immature or playing tricks on other people who don't appreciate it. You need to develop greater agility and flexibility. You need to develop better communication skills. You're dealing with repressed sexuality. Emotional: You don't want to be controlled, or you're trying to control someone else. You're experiencing deceit or deceiving others. You want more companionship and community. Mental-Spiritual: You need to develop a more serious, focused attitude and stop "monkeying around," jumping from thing to thing. You need to be more ingenious and inventive. You're giving in to worry, doubt, fear, excuses, distractions, the chattering "monkey mind," and you need to find stillness through meditation.

monster: Physical: You need to acknowledge your untapped power and capacity to have a positive impact in the world. Slaying monsters means you successfully deal with rivals and advance to a higher position. Emotional: You're afraid of inner rage, hatred, hungers, or desire for control. You feel threatened or are plagued by negative or obsessive thoughts. You're facing repressed fears, a trauma, or qualities you've judged negatively and haven't accepted in yourself. Mental-Spiritual: Killing a monster means you're absorbing the power of that particular thought form into your totality, thus achieving psychological completion and wholeness.

moon: Physical: You're interested in traveling, cycles of growth and self-expression, and anything that fluctuates constantly. You're focusing on feminine energy and what's hidden. A new moon means new beginnings, potential, gestation, waiting, and resting. Emotional: You're focusing on your changeable emotional or irrational nature, feelings of lunacy, drama, and manic-depressive self-expression. A full moon shows a need for full self-expression, magic, romance, nurturing, reaping rewards, and completion. Mental-Spiritual: Your thoughts need to be more mystical, intuitive, and fluid. A lunar eclipse signifies that your feminine side is being overshadowed or blocked temporarily.

mother: Physical: You're focusing on unconditional love, shelter, comfort, life, guidance, and protection. You're caretaking others or part of yourself. Emotional: You need nurturing and to feel your own caring, receptivity, sexuality, pleasure, seduction, attractiveness, and fertility. You're working out unfinished business with your mother and whether you feel abandoned or smothered. Mental-Spiritual: A generous, nurturing mother figure represents creativity, growth, and abundance. Mothers are wise guardians and guides who bring important messages. So if you hear your mother call you, listen well.

mountain: Physical: You're facing obstacles, challenges, and the desire to reach a difficult goal or decision. Climbing a mountain means you need to develop ambition, determination, and stamina. How you climb depicts your inner and outer process of achievement. Reaching the summit means you have accomplished your goals, are successful, and now have a new view of your life. Emotional: You're avoiding hard work and want to take the easy way and escape from demanding situations. Mental-Spiritual: Being on a mountaintop means you're actively pursuing spiritual evolution, involvement with a sacred process, or a higher realm of consciousness, knowledge, and truth. If you fall off a mountain, you're in a hurry to succeed without thoroughly thinking about or honoring your path.

mouse: Physical: You're experiencing minor irritations and annoyances, or problems with insincere, sneaky friends. Something is pestering you, gnawing away at you, or something you value is being eroded slowly through other people's jealousy or greed. If you kill a mouse, you're overcoming disturbances and petty problems. Emotional: You're focusing on your lack of assertiveness, fear, meekness, and feelings of inadequacy. Mental-Spiritual: You're curious, looking into everything, and hungry for answers. Focusing on small ideas and details can bring rewards.

mouth: Physical: You're focusing on physical and nonphysical hunger and self-nurturing through eating. Emotional: You're looking at tendencies toward gluttony, greed, and sexual desire, as well as emotions like disgust, approval, awe, generosity, or stinginess. Mental-Spiritual: You need to communicate, to talk about an issue that's bothering you, or share ideas. Perhaps you've said too much and need to keep your mouth shut. *(see lips)*

movie: Physical: You're observing your own life to understand it or watching life pass you by, living vicariously through others. Starring in a movie means you need more attention, to express yourself more colorfully, or have a greater impact. The role you play or character you're drawn to represents an element of life you're preparing to embody. Emotional: You want to escape from the reality of your own life or protect yourself from painful emotions. Mental-Spiritual: Movies often symbolize the process of dreaming itself. Being in a movie and watching it simultaneously can provide the trigger for a lucid dream. You're looking at your life purpose and plan. *(see DVD)*

mud: Physical: You're involved in a messy, confusing situation, problem, or relationship. You need to cleanse your body internally. If your face or clothes are muddy, your reputation is being questioned or damaged by too much "mudslinging." Emotional: Mud is water (emotion) and earth (the physical) and symbolizes stirred-up emotions that affect your success. You feel weighed down or depressed. You're too perfectionistic and need to be more uninhibited and down to earth. Mental-Spiritual: If you're stuck in the mud, there's difficulty making progress due to mental resistance, negative thinking, and unconscious habits. A mudslide means a sudden release of negative beliefs and ideas of failure.

museum: <u>Physical</u>: You're looking for artifacts and treasures (memories, talents, skills, creations) you have stored away from the past. You're reviewing and reflecting on the things you value. You need a breath of fresh air, more movement, and vitality. <u>Emotional</u>: You need to break free of tradition and old habits and take some risks. Memories bring emotional issues you have to deal with. You feel removed from the experiences of your life. <u>Mental-Spiritual</u>: You're visiting the higher dimensions looking at the records of your past and the planetary history.

music/musical instruments: <u>Physical</u>: Hearing harmonious, soothing music means you're focusing on balance, beauty, high-level self-expression, pleasure, and healing. You're removing blocks to better energy flow. If you're playing or composing music, you're expressing your creative talents, communicating effectively, and engaging with the flow of life. Musical instruments represent different parts of your nature, from your sexuality to spirituality. <u>Emotional</u>: Hearing discordant or sad music links to painful inner issues, while wild, erratic music connects to your animal nature. You're accessing memories. <u>Mental-Spiritual</u>: Hearing or composing music means you're moving through the higher mental and spiritual realms, reorganizing patterns in your awareness to incorporate increased harmony, joy, and sensitivity. You're using your intuition.

mustache: (*see beard*)

N

naked: <u>Physical</u>: You're awkward or out of place in your social setting. If you're uninhibited being nude, you feel comfortable in your own skin and are entitling yourself to full, carefree self-expression and to be seen for who you really are. You're tired of maintaining a facade. You're trying to be something you're not. <u>Emotional</u>: If you're uncomfortable being nude or in a state of undress in public, you feel ridiculed, disgraced, caught off guard, unprepared, exposed, or anxious about how others see you. You feel shame or guilt about your shortcomings being shown to the world. <u>Mental-Spiritual</u>: You're examining your inner truth and bringing forth new aspects of your character you've been unaware of or hiding. You're defenseless and focusing on your innocence.

navel: Physical: You're focusing on your originality, your connection to your mother and nurturing, or to your birth or rebirth. You need to center and find middle ground. Emotional: You're too self-absorbed. You're looking at unconscious codependency issues or how you feel drained by people who want to control you by taking care of you. If you pierce your navel, you're asserting your need to feel unique. Mental-Spiritual: You're connecting with universal divine feminine energy. If you're contemplating your navel, you're reaching down into the unknown, focusing on your divine origin, and remembering your soul.

neck/throat: Physical: You're focusing on how you connect your mind and body, head and heart, or any two significant things. You're experiencing a slowdown or bottleneck. You're examining how confidently you express yourself and how willful you are. Emotional: You feel vulnerable about speaking your truth and sharing your ideas or are restricting your feelings. You're afraid to "stick your neck out" and put yourself at risk. You may find an idea "hard to swallow" or in more extreme cases, you may be choking on an idea or potential reality. A thick or stiff neck means a stubborn, prideful, quarrelsome nature. A beautiful neck indicates a graceful, sensitive nature. Mental-Spiritual: You're focusing on finding your voice, communicating easily, and having faith in yourself and others. You're looking at your capacity for inspired creativity, so if this area is constricted or strangled, you feel stifled about using imagination, or your intuition is cut off. Having your throat cut means you're surrendering personal will to divine will.

needle: Physical: You're focusing on mending a misunderstanding or repairing a tear or breach in a situation. You're creating something beautiful and practical, patiently taking small steps. Threading a needle means you're concentrating on accomplishing a very precise goal. Being punctured by a syringe needle means you're focusing on being penetrated or invaded by foreign substances or energies, which can be helpful or harmful. Emotional: You're stitching an emotional wound to help it heal. Someone or some situation is "needling you" making you feel irritated. You're "on pins and needles" waiting nervously for something to happen. A syringe links to anxiety about medical problems, hospitals, doctor and dentist visits, and drug addiction. <u>Mental-Spiritual</u>: A sewing needle means you're connecting ideas together into a holistic understanding, vision, or plan. "Poking holes in something" means you're looking for lies and truth. Your awareness is traveling through the surface of things to discover deeper layers of knowledge.

nest: <u>Physical</u>: You're looking at building or moving to a new home or renovating and redecorating the place you have. You're preparing to have a child and thinking about family. You're focusing on the health of the feminine organs. You're focusing on a new opportunity or project that promises to be successful and prosperous. Eggs in a nest means you're focusing on being lucky and protective. Feathering a nest means you're making money for yourself, perhaps at the expense of others. <u>Emotional</u>: You want more warmth, coziness, mothering, comfort, safety, or freedom. An empty nest means you feel sad about children leaving home, a lost friendship, or a lack of new ideas or opportunities. You're focusing on problems and issues that arose in childhood. A single "nest egg" means you want security for uncertain times. Broken eggs in a nest mean disappointment about plans or dashed hopes. <u>Mental-Spiritual</u>: You're getting ready to birth and focus your creativity, or you're reforming your worldview. You're preparing for and welcoming new knowledge and spiritual growth into your life.

net: <u>Physical</u>: You need to expand out into the world and gather in greater resources. You need to follow leads to meet new, helpful people. <u>Emotional</u>: You feel caught in a net of confusion, intrigue, or limitation. You're entangled in a complicated life situation. <u>Mental-Spiritual</u>: You're focusing on the global grid of energy, the internet of information, or your network of personal contacts.

newspaper: <u>Physical</u>: You're focusing on current or breaking information you need to operate effectively. You feel out of touch or behind and are trying to bring yourself up to speed. You're looking at promoting yourself or your business or "spreading the news" about something. You're focusing on the power of media and a need to communicate effectively or see through biased reports. <u>Emotional</u>: You feel other people know too much, or not enough, about you, or they're misunderstanding or slandering you. You're shocked by upsetting, sudden news. <u>Mental-Spiritual</u>: You are receiving precognitive information or knowledge from other dimensions. You're becoming aware of something important.

night: Physical: A nighttime dream setting indicates something is still unconscious and seeking to be known. You're focusing on discovering secrets or mysteries. Emotional: You're dealing with subjects about which you feel fearful, uncertain, or directionless. You feel anxiety about being in the dark or alone. You're experiencing stealthy motives, sneakiness, or feelings of a dark or questionable nature. You're hiding something. Mental-Spiritual: You're introverted and contemplative. You're relaxing into a softer, intimate awareness that isn't action-oriented, where you feel freedom from social conventions.

noose/lasso: Physical: A noose hanging from a tree means you're focusing on being trapped, restricted, restrained, and unable to express yourself freely. Or you're focusing on roping or obtaining a new opportunity. Emotional: You're experiencing anxiety about someone trapping you or punishing you for speaking your mind or about being powerless against people bent on rejecting or getting rid of you. You want to throttle or silence someone else who's interfering with your self-expression. You need to experience greater humility and trust. Throwing a lasso to catch an animal means you're trying to keep your emotions and wild urges under control. Mental-Spiritual: You're learning to be articulate, precise, and beautiful in your speech. You're focusing on the breath of life, on valuing inspiration, and using silence as well as words and language.

north: Physical: You're seeking to correct your life direction. You're attuning to ancient wisdom, the elders, and a neutral point of view. You're experiencing frozen conditions and lack of momentum. Emotional: You feel coldness and lack of intimacy. Mental-Spiritual: You're aligning to "true north" or magnetic north, where you will find universal truth and clear inner guidance.

nose: Physical: You're being curious or perhaps too "nosy," meddlesome, interfering, or pushy. Emotional: If your nose is stuffed up, broken, out of joint, or bleeding, you've invaded someone else's reality and been rebuffed, or you haven't been trusting your intuition and higher sensitivity. Mental-Spiritual: You need to "follow your nose," and pay attention to intuition and instinct to avoid danger and find your way. You need to "sniff out" or detect new or hidden information or learn more about a situation at hand.

numbers/mathematics/numerology: Physical: You're evaluating in detail a situation in your waking life. You're solving a problem or finding a new approach. You're focusing on multiplicity, relative size, or a multifaceted process. Specific numbers represent different kinds of energy and consciousness, as well as aspects of your personality, ways of doing things, and stages of your growth process. You're giving yourself encoded guidance about how to proceed. A date on a calendar, street address, phone number, number of objects, or a number superimposed over a scene all indicate important clues. Emotional: You need to be careful about being overly emotional or, conversely, too rational. You have emotional associations with the numbers you see: a year of your life, date of an important event, how many children you have, or a lucky number. Mental–Spiritual: You're attuning to spiritual understanding, large patterns of consciousness, and archetypal human qualities. In complex numbers, examine each of the digits and add them together until you have one digit. This core number reveals deeper insights. Look for the qualities of the numbers as listed here to find hidden meanings:

>> **0:** *(see zero)*

>> **1:** Individuality, authenticity, autonomy, personal will, courage, assertiveness, self-determination, self-reliance, inner strength, leadership, dictatorship, pioneering spirit, impulsiveness, impatience, beginnings, entrepreneurial ability, originality, independence, risk-taking behavior, authority, self-absorption, ego lessons, definition of personality

>> **2:** Cooperation, harmony, balance, receptivity, giving, mirroring, diplomacy, peacemaking, comparison, merging and dissolving boundaries, sharing, cocreation, relationships, partners, approval, agreements, linking and bridging, teaching, counseling, negotiating, indecision, oscillation, conflict, sensitivity, empathy, patience, female energy, marriage/divorce

>> **3:** Self-expression, creativity, open-mindedness, drama, social activity, popularity, communication, release, ease, flow, humor, outgoingness, spontaneity, imagination, verbal skill, promotion, sales, public speaking, singing, teaching, writing, performing, indecision, naturalness

>> **4:** Structure, personal discipline, work, effort, tangible results, responsibility, tradition, construction/building, the body, methodical, patience, determination, practical action, endurance, loyalty, limitation, attachments, business skill,

three-dimensional design and art, seriousness, stubbornness, real estate/housing, focus, commitment, karma, overcoming obstacles, strength

>> **5:** Freedom, movement, change, travel, new experience and ideas, sensory stimulation, curiosity, restlessness, versatility, flexibility, cleverness, agility, mathematical and verbal ability, impatience, dancing, adventure, superficiality, temptation, communication, creativity, foreign cultures and languages, creativity, promotion, confusion, lack of security, paralysis

>> **6:** Service, nurturing, balance, adjustment, creation of divine harmony, beauty, settling down, idealism, romance, healing, wellness, art, counseling, teaching, events and gatherings, nutrition and food, cosmic parent, home and family, intimate groups, centers, openheartedness, sympathy, martyrdom

>> **7:** Truth, universal laws and metaphysics, love of knowledge, study, academia, research, perfectionism, privacy, introspection, objectivity, abstract/ conceptual thinking, analysis, refinement, precision, silence, meditation, music, investigation, behind the scenes, mathematics, science, technology and computers, alignment of personal and divine will, aloofness, planning, retreats, spiritual pilgrimages, ego death, revelation of the spiritual

>> **8:** Manifestation, authority, power, competence, business and executive ability, organization, administration/management, systems, strategy, money, success, achievement, drive, ambition, materialism, professionalism, value system, superstructures, justice, the higher order of things

>> **9:** Universal awareness, compassion, altruism, humanitarian service, collective consciousness, idealism, romance, dreams/ visions, big thinking, social and political action, personal loss or disappointment, invisibility, nonphysicality, mysticism, impersonalness, inspiration, generosity, completion, surrender, philosophy, imagination, sympathy, broad outlook, feeling overwhelmed, spaciousness, death and the other side

>> **10:** Wholeness, completeness, a new beginning at a higher level of consciousness and responsibility, spiritual self-discovery

>> **11:** Revelation, inspiration, communion, spiritually based relationships/soulmates, public outreach, intuition, high sensitivity, integration of opposites, spiritually motivated artists, teachers, counselors, ministers

>> **12:** Cosmic cycles, divine order, harmony, completeness, divisibility into harmonious units, conscious governance

>> **13:** Transformation, divine feminine energy, lunar cycles, productive growth; only superstitiously connected with bad luck

>> **22:** Sacred structure, enlightened effort, practical mystic, material master/builder, ritual and ceremony, societal organization, focusing abstract, conceptual structures

>> **33:** Universal service, enlightened healer, martyr, family of mankind, soul group consciousness

>> **1111:** Spiritual awakening, enlightenment, the merger of spirit/matter, divine partnership, alignment with higher purpose, positive thoughts, ability to materialize via individuality, soulmates connecting

nurse: (*see doctor*)

nut: Physical: You're looking for the core, meat, or kernel of truth inside an idea, person, situation, or yourself. If you consider nuts as a pun for testicles, you're focusing on the physical health of this body part or on sexuality. If you're eating nuts, you feel prosperous and confident about attaining your desires. Emotional: You're focusing on craziness, confusion, or "nutty" behavior. You feel "nuts" for someone or something, or someone is "driving you nuts." Mental-Spiritual: You're focusing on valuable ideas, latent talents that can be developed, or other seeds of new creativity and growth. (*see acorn, seed*)

O

oar: Physical: You're focusing on your ability to move yourself forward, steer a steady course, or change directions on a dime. You're struggling against circumstances. If you're paddling with one oar, you need to work with others to stabilize your momentum. A broken oar means a handicap or setback. Emotional: You're exerting control over your emotions. You feel a lack of support. If you've lost your oars, you feel powerless and at the effect of circumstances. Mental-Spiritual: If you're rowing with a team of people, in unison, you're focusing on ideas of collaboration and cocreation and moving through the collective consciousness.

oasis: Physical: You're dehydrated and need more fluids. You need a rest or a vacation. You're focusing on the need to reach a stopping point after an overwhelming endeavor. You need a safe haven where you can replenish yourself. You're about to receive the rewards from some hard work. Emotional: You're focusing on coming out of a long dry spell where you've been starved for affection and support. You need to feel soothed. Mental-Spiritual: You're focusing on the need for, and experience of, meditating. You need to quiet your mind, eliminate chatter and mental clutter, and connect with the wellspring and deep nurturing of your own soul.

obelisk: Physical: You're focusing on your own uprightness, ethics, strength, and alignment with truth. You want to shine out and reach out to many people as an authority. You are focusing on achievement through hard work, discipline, and high standards. You're looking for someone or something to inspire awe in you. Emotional: You need more stability and trust in your life. You're caught in victim-dominator roles and behaviors. Mental-Spiritual: You need greater ability to recognize authentic authorities versus people with big egos. You're focusing on your ability to be a connecting link between physical and spiritual consciousness. You're learning to communicate with beings in nonphysical realms. Climbing to the top of an obelisk indicates you're ready to receive a new ability, level of consciousness and power, or direct connection with enlightened teachers.

obesity: Physical: You need more personal space and insulation from others to be your full self without apology. You need to share and release more of your self-expressive energy. Emotional: You're focusing on being judged and rejected or doing that to others. You're focusing on being guilty about something or a misfit or rebel. You're focusing on underlying feelings of apathy, cynicism, or anger. Mental-Spiritual: You're looking at the idea that you can't get enough or that you must hoard reserves because loss is always possible. You're focusing on the need for gratitude and generosity, how you can use what you've already been given, how big you really are spiritually, and how little you really need to be happy being yourself.

ocean: Physical: You're looking at deeper patterns concerning creativity, fertility, birth and death, and human origins. You're contemplating how unlimited you are and how much you're capable of expressing. You're harmonizing yourself with the tides and currents of life. Emotional: You're examining deep emotions (oceanic grief or terror), secrets, and fears of vastness or nature's annihilating power. If you're in stormy seas, you probably have chaos in your life. If you're being pulled under or facing a tsunami, you're struggling against overwhelming conditions in waking life. Mental-Spiritual: You're focusing on reaching limitless mind, the source of life, the collective consciousness, the deep history of the planet, and exploring issues shared by your culture or humanity. Swimming deep in the ocean means you're traveling in the spiritual realms, free from limitations, in touch with ancient wisdom. A calm ocean means inner peace and spiritual revelation.

octopus: Physical: You're involved with many different things or changing your self-expression or colors like a chameleon. You're successful at getting what you want. Emotional: You feel clingy or possessive or emotionally engrossed and smothered by entanglements. You fear being dragged down by your desires or other people's emotional needs. You've experienced or perpetrated sexual harassment. You're tuning in to spirits of the underworld. Mental-Spiritual: You have a brilliant intelligence, many ideas simultaneously, a rich imagination, a hunger for life, and the capacity to take in and synthesize huge amounts of information.

old age: Physical: You're focusing on your life experience and internal ageless wisdom that may have been written off by others or by part of your own mind. You're entering a pleasurable stage of life. Emotional: You are afraid of the aging process, frailty, or of letting go and allowing yourself to be cared for. You have ambivalent feelings about your lineage and ancestors. You're afraid you'll be seen as old-fashioned and ineffective. You need to be flexible and open-minded. Mental-Spiritual: You need to honor maturity. An old lesson has a new application. You're learning to be more philosophical, forgiving, innocent, and at peace. You need to review and reconcile your life. *(see grandparent)*

onion: Physical: You're examining your personal growth process, or you need to see how a situation in your life is multilayered. You're peeling back the layers of yourself to get to the root of a problem. Emotional: You feel sad or need to cry about something. You're warding off an evil influence or something you sense is detrimental to you. Mental-Spiritual: You're expanding your wisdom, growing in stages, patiently. You're full of an almost magical power to protect what's good.

orange: <u>Physical</u>: You need to be more stimulated, invigorated, enthusiastic, expansive, happy, determined, encouraged, and assertive. Orange represents purification, creative urges, ambition, appetites, and boldness. You like getting attention and being visible. <u>Emotional</u>: Rusty orange is linked to autumn and an experience of harvest, winding down, and giving a last show of lively color before deeply resting. You feel warm, sunny, sociable, excited but not overly passionate or aggressive. <u>Mental-Spiritual</u>: You're stimulated mentally. Orange monks' robes mean purification of negative desires and release of clinging tendencies.

orchestra: <u>Physical</u>: You're focusing on the overall health of your body and how all your systems and organs are working together in harmony. You're organizing and synchronizing resources, timing, action, and events for a successful final outcome. You need to be involved with music and sound. <u>Emotional</u>: An orchestra tuning up means you're coming out of a fragmented, discordant state into integration and an attunement to your own highest feelings. <u>Mental-Spiritual</u>: You're arranging and coordinating the many parts of yourself, your many interests, and your life lessons into a harmonious whole that will allow you a much grander sort of self-expression.

orgasm: <u>Physical</u>: You're experiencing a sexual or physical release of some kind, or you have pent-up energy and need to let it flow. A situation in your life has built to a nearly unbearable point where tension needs to be released and a conflict resolved. <u>Emotional</u>: You're focusing on having an emotional breakthrough or emotional fulfillment and joy. <u>Mental-Spiritual</u>: A frustrated or blocked orgasm means you're overly tense, distracted, "in your head," or ahead of yourself. You're focusing on opening to a much larger worldview by trusting the process of letting go of your ego and fixed identity. You're going through a spiritual initiation into a higher level of consciousness.

orphan: <u>Physical</u>: You're focusing on being independent and successful on your own, as well as looking for where and with whom you truly belong. <u>Emotional</u>: You feel unloved, rejected, lonely, unwanted, invisible, needy, insecure, or misunderstood. You fear abandonment or isolation or can't find your place. <u>Mental-Spiritual</u>: You're looking at the importance of your parents, what you need to receive from parents, how to be a good parent, and what family means in the broader sense. If you're helping orphans, you're opening your heart to serve in some way.

ostrich: Physical: You're in your own private world and not fac-ing reality, unwilling to accept the truth, or avoiding or deny-ing responsibility or uncomfortable experiences. You need to be more practical, alert, and courageous. Emotional: You're avoid-ing repressed emotions or are caught in delusions. You feel you don't fit with your peers, like this largest bird that cannot fly. Mental-Spiritual: You need to hone your perceptual skills, handle problems immediately, and discover something that's right in front of you. Ostriches represent people who appear religious but don't act holy.

otter: Physical: You need to develop greater playfulness, light-heartedness, and joy. You're focusing on happiness, good fortune, cleverness, fluidity of motion, and cleanliness. Emotional: You're making friends with your emotions, learning to swim through tough spots, let go of resistance, and be more flexible in your habits. You need to express tenderness with friends and loved ones. Mental-Spiritual: You have the skill to intuitively see what's below the surface of things and the ability to find nourishment in the hidden depths of spirit. The otter is particularly connected with women and precognition.

outlaw: (*see criminal*)

oven: Physical: You're focusing on the womb, getting pregnant, or being pregnant. You're looking at gestating or incubating a concept or project. You're actively creating and looking at the "heat" or enthusiasm you're capable of generating. You're mak-ing yourself aware of something or someone who is "half-baked" or not fully cooked, and thus not strong and reliable. Emotional: You need emotional warmth and care from those around you. You need to tend to and nurture others. Warm and hot ovens mean you're focusing on your enthusiasm and the need for loving and passionate involvement with life. A cold oven means you feel aloof, protected, out of touch with feelings and passion, useless, or empty and depressed. Mental-Spiritual: You're shaping infor-mation or communications into an appetizing, digestible form. You're actively growing and expanding, transforming from one way of being to another.

owl: Physical: You're about to experience change or an impor-tant transition, or you're practicing shapeshifting. You need more, or less, solitude. You need to move swiftly, purposefully, and silently. Emotional: You're afraid of the dark, death, or your subconscious mind. Owls bring messages and secrets from the other side or the unconscious, which may trigger anxiety or growth. You're caught in deception or illusion. You're brooding or too introspective. You're comfortable with your shadow self. Mental-Spiritual: You're considering higher education or increasing your intellectual knowledge. You need to use better judgment. You need to hone your intuition and keen observational skills. You can penetrate into the darkness to see what others can't. You have the potential to be clairvoyant, see behind masks into the soul. You're ready to experience a death and rebirth or spiritual initiation to a new level of awareness. Owls are particularly connected to the moon and magic.

oyster: Physical: You're looking for the prize pearl, the experience of being rewarded handsomely for your efforts. You're working hard to make something beautiful from humble beginnings. You feel lucky, as though "the world is my oyster." You want more sexual activity and eroticism. Emotional: You're shutting others out with a defensive attitude, or you feel enclosed in a hard, protective shell. You feel others want to take advantage of your natural gifts and beauty. You're afraid of new experiences. Mental-Spiritual: You're focusing on thoughts of beauty, ripening and growing yourself spiritually gradually over time, transforming from a grain of sand to a precious jewel. You're creating a fertile, safe environment or context in which you can develop optimally.

P

pain: Physical: Experiencing pain in a dream can link to real pain or the memory of pain from the near or distant past. It can be a warning to pay attention to a specific area of the body and can mean you're tired. Someone in your life is acting as a pain in the neck or causing you pain. Emotional: You're experiencing emotional pain that is connected to the meaning of the body part where you experienced the physical pain. You feel loss, humiliation, or rejection. Mental-Spiritual: You're experiencing an empathic connection to another person's, or society's, pain.

painting/photograph/portrait: Physical: You're looking at visions you hold about life, how a process will unfold, or what you can become. You're focusing on beauty, inside and out. Take your artistic abilities more seriously. Emotional: The mood of the image, its color, crispness, realism, size, and texture all give clues about how you feel about yourself and your future. You're picturing the worst or seeing how you want things to turn out. Mental-Spiritual: You're becoming aware of false images, ideas, or hopes. You're using your imagination to create your reality. You're showing yourself a snapshot of something important that requires attention.

parachute: Physical: You're focusing on taking a great risk or on escaping from a situation in which you feel trapped. You're coming down to earth to face reality. Emotional: You are concerned about survival and fear being out of control or crashing and failing. You have protection and security during a time of turmoil. If your parachute doesn't open, you feel abandoned or betrayed by supporters. Mental-Spiritual: You're designing an escape plan. You're encouraging yourself to have faith and let go.

parade: Physical: You want to publicly display your various talents and character traits in a celebratory, upbeat way. You need more variety, color, music, social activity, and cooperation with others. Emotional: Watching a parade means you need to get more involved in life and not just look on shyly from the sidelines. You feel blocked about showing your true colors. Mental-Spiritual: You're going through a specific rite of passage or remembering one from your past. You're aligning your ideas and life direction with the people around you.

paralysis: Physical: You feel helpless about a situation in your life. You need to be totally still and attend to something or just do nothing for a while. You feel frozen and unable to act. You're experiencing part of the dream cycle itself, where during REM (rapid eye movement) sleep the body becomes "paralyzed" and doesn't move. Emotional: You feel dominated, powerless, depressed, unable to express yourself freely or make your own decisions, possibly due to unconscious fear. If you associate paralysis with aliens or evil forces from the underworld, it means you feel vulnerable and need to strengthen your core sense of self and your boundaries. Mental-Spiritual: You've reached an impasse where your beliefs and worldview no longer serve your growth. You need to attune to the still, small voice within to find new direction.

paramedics: (*see ambulance*)

parrot: Physical: You're speaking without understanding what you're talking about. You need to pay attention to what you really mean, to using the right words, and being original, not just "parroting" what other people say. Emotional: You're upset by others gossiping or not understanding you. Mental-Spiritual: You're reminding yourself about your core intelligence and cleverness. You're learning to be more fluid in your communication skills.

party: Physical: You need more social activity, celebration, relaxation, and exchange with others. Emotional: A birthday or surprise party means you need recognition, to feel greater self-worth, and to be grateful for your life. A dinner party means you're focusing on the nurturing, support, and love you give and receive with a close circle of friends or colleagues. Mental-Spiritual: You're processing a recent interaction with others. You need to develop greater comfort with shallow conversation, or you need more introversion or extraversion.

passport: Physical: You're focusing on your identity and ability to make transitions between phases and situations. You need freedom of movement and to be welcome in new groups, associations, endeavors, or places. You need to have permission from an authority figure to do something. Emotional: If you lose your passport, you feel like an outsider or that you're trapped, or you have anxiety about authorities. Mental-Spiritual: You're in a process of finding yourself and discovering who you are. You're preparing to explore many parts of your identity and knowledge or embark on a spiritual quest.

peacock: Physical: You want to express yourself more dramatically, without reservation. You're looking for greater prestige, confidence, pride, or the ability to celebrate. Emotional: You're covering over feelings of being plain or shy with color, showiness, vanity, bragging, or an attitude of superiority. Mental-Spiritual: Peacocks are connected to the phoenix and represent the soul. You see with the many eyes contained in the peacock's plumes, or you are shedding your plumage, identity, and growing it anew. You are transforming from plain to magnificent.

pelican: Physical: You're taking on and carrying more than you need or is healthy for you. You have a greater capacity than you think. Emotional: You need nurturing and care or you want to give support. You need to focus on your selfless, charitable nature. Mental-Spiritual: You're full of knowledge and resources. The pelican symbolizes piety and Jesus in Christian legend.

penguin: Physical: You're focusing on qualities of hardiness, endurance, humor, playfulness, and quirkiness. Your problems aren't overly serious; you need to be steady and coolheaded. Emotional: You're looking at how couples work patiently together to support each other, how nurturing fathers can be, how loyal and protective parents need to be. You're focusing on fluid movement through difficult emotional times. Mental-Spiritual: You're attuning to survival of the spirit amid dire circumstances — the power of great love, intuition, and the group mind. You're aware of polarized, black-and-white perception.

perfume/cologne: Physical: You're focusing on making yourself attractive and sensual. You want more pleasure and sexuality. You're following the scent of something, hunting for answers or outcomes. You're learning to trust your instinct. Emotional: Smelling perfume that pleases you means you're healing yourself emotionally, changing a dark mood to a lighter, higher, more peaceful one. You are trying to cover up something you don't like about yourself or hide your feelings. A scent that makes you gag means you're attuning to a part of yourself that you have rejected, or there are people in your life who are toxic for you. Overperfuming means you don't want other people to come too close or be intimate with you. Mental-Spiritual: You're focusing on making decisions based on scent: fishy, sweaty, sour, sweet, fresh, or uplifting, for example. You are looking at how becoming intoxicated or repelled by situations compromises your clarity. You're shifting awareness to higher, more spiritual states.

periscope: Physical: You have a problem related to your neck or eyes. You need to stretch out and rise above a current situation to find a clear view. Emotional: You're moving past emotional confusion and murkiness by finding a more neutral point of view. Mental-Spiritual: You're maintaining contact with the collective consciousness, and your feelings while ascending to a higher level to gather important data and perspective.

pets: Physical: You're focusing on an aspect of yourself that you need to love, especially if the symbol is a personal pet. The pet is teaching you a lesson, like being more compassionate, trusting, playful, or independent. You're dealing with a person similar to the animal. Emotional: You need to develop more vulnerability, loyalty, and responsibility for others. You want more attention, affection, and unconditional love and to be able to demonstrate your own love more openly. You want a better home and family life. Mental-Spiritual: You're focusing on informal, personal connections to others and the world and on opening your heart.

phoenix: Physical: You're ready for a new phase of life, dramatic change, and deep renewal. You're releasing something that's holding you back, perhaps an old definition of yourself. Emotional: You're experiencing anxiety about loss and change. You feel like destroying part of a life you've built without understanding why. Mental-Spiritual: You want to believe that anything is possible, and you have the power to change things for the better. It's time to have faith in your soul so you can transform into your most radiant self. You can regenerate, no matter how bad things look.

pie: Physical: Seeing a whole pie represents the sense of reward and abundance or that something is as "easy as pie" to create. You're focusing on a project or endeavor that is complete. You're focusing on what your share of the pie might be. Emotional: A piece of pie can indicate that you're focusing on your fair share of something divided among others. You're focusing on a sense of comfort, belonging, hospitality, or welcome if you are served or are serving it at a social gathering. You're associating someone with the idea of affection, as in "sweetie pie" or "cutie pie." Mental-Spiritual: A pie divided into various sized servings can mean you're focusing on organizing and balancing the areas of your life to create harmony and functionality, as in a "pie chart."

pig: Physical: You're experiencing your various appetites. You're hoarding or "hogging" something, the limelight, someone's time, or money. You're too messy, dirty, smelly, fat, or unkempt. Emotional: You're focusing on gluttony, greed, stubbornness, or feeling dirty, especially concerning sexual desires. You need to clean up your act and express your sweet nature. Mental-Spiritual: You're focusing on being intelligent, clever, instinctual, and prosperous.

pill: (*see medicine*)

pillar/column: Physical: You're taking a firm stance. You're proving your strength of character and stability. You're supporting other people, or you need to support yourself. You're focusing on male sexuality. Emotional: You're dealing with emotions that are too rigid and based on fear. You need to hold steady and not run away. Mental-Spiritual: You're focusing your thoughts vertically to connect with the heavens or to be a bridge between nonphysical realms and earth. You're relying on or trying to embody higher teachings that you see as absolutely truthful and incorruptible.

pirate: Physical: You need some adventure and wildness in your life. You want freedom and to defy dominating authority figures. Someone is stealing from you or "taking you hostage" with charming or self-centered behavior. Emotional: You feel like an outcast. You're dealing with chaotic emotions or a person who's running rampant over your feelings or pretending to be your friend. You want to indulge your wild rebel side. You're confusing stealing and taking with abundance. Mental-Spiritual: You're focusing on freedom and the need to be yourself without compromise. You're learning that you deserve respect, love, and unconditional support.

planets: Physical: You're focusing on needing new perspective on your reality; the specific planet can offer insight (see the list of planets). Planets represent different aspects of your consciousness, way of doing things, needs, and integrated experience. Emotional: Traveling to another planet means you want to explore the unknown and new ways to feel. A distant planet represents a need for escape from the mundane. Mental-Spiritual: You're focusing on how your personality is composed of energies and consciousness from all the celestial bodies in our solar system and from many we don't know about yet. Visiting a specific planet means you have abilities relating to that "plane" of consciousness or need more of that energy. Seeing an issue from the point of view of different planetary energies helps you gain neutrality and clarity. Look to the astrological qualities of each planetary body listed below to find insights to apply to your own growth, creative process, or problem-solving. You may need more, or less, of the various aspects. *(see astrology, earth, moon, numbers, sun)*

>> **Mercury:** This planet pertains to everything mercurial: communication, public speaking, languages, travel, mental clarity and fluidity, teaching, rapid change, and interdimensional messages. It facilitates change, adaptability, and transformation. You may change your mind often, be too curious, not finish things, or not go too deeply into things. You may be curious and hungry for new knowledge and attracted to busy, urban environments. Mercury is

connected with alchemy and the ability to find wisdom and goodness in any situation. Being quiet, intuitive, and meditative are helpful here.

» **Venus:** You're focusing on beauty, harmony, relationships, divine feminine energy, pleasure, personal desires, artistic sensitivity, music, attractiveness, love and affection, self-love, and soul embodiment. Venus extends the earthly consciousness of these things into higher frequencies of divine understanding. Being authentic, realistic, and self-confident are helpful here.

» **Mars:** You're focusing on being strong, direct, impulsive, assertive, motivated, driven, passionate, courageous, competitive, and needing energy release through physical action. Taken too far, this planet's essence can make you reckless, aggressive, quick to become angered, extremist, violent, and warlike. Balance, patience, and seeing the other's point of view are helpful here.

» **Jupiter:** You're focusing on freedom, optimism, expansion, good luck, higher learning, philosophy, exploration, travel, anything foreign, sports and challenging physical activity, more rural or wilderness environments, prosperity, generosity, universal law and justice, spirituality and religion, spiritual guidance. Being introverted, alone, and peaceful are helpful here.

» **Saturn:** You're focusing on structure, discipline, patience, endurance, responsibility, working with limitation, and overcoming obstacles. You need to be aware of time, aging, repeating cycles, karma, delayed gratification, development of earned wisdom, and lessons learned by facing difficult truths and the shadow side of your personality. You have it within you to become a truthful, influential spiritual teacher. Playfulness, rest, beauty, and time in nature are helpful here.

» **Uranus:** You're focusing on freedom to explore and be unique, rebellion against old habits and thinking, sudden change, disruption, innovation, "electrical" experience, and the ability to adapt to unforeseen situations. You respect revolutionary, unconventional thought and new possibilities, largescale societal evolution toward spirituality, and personal cosmic consciousness breakthroughs. Focusing on music, water, gardening, or poetry are helpful here.

>> **Neptune:** You're focusing on subconscious and supercon-scious/spiritual awareness, intuition, psychic and so-called "supernatural" abilities, communion and compassion, collective consciousness, visions and imagination, transcen-dence, and the depths and heights of your inner self. You want to be connected, even merged with, the divine and not be limited by material concerns. You resist and dissolve boundaries and thus feel the world as yourself, often want escape from the suffering you feel, and are drawn to surrender to the unknown. Creativity, artwork, music, dance, and tangible forms of service are helpful here.

>> **Pluto:** You're focusing on cycles of birth/ death/rebirth and personal phoenixlike transformation, uncovering hidden secrets and truths, releasing what's old and false, regenera-tion, and using personal power wisely for the good of self, others, and the planet. There are immediate repercussions from unaligned thought and action. There is great intensity and ability to penetrate deeply with attention. Everything is aimed at facilitating transformation. Playfulness, humor, simplicity, and trust in the flow and people's souls is helpful here.

plumbing: <u>Physical</u>: You're focusing on the circulation and elim-ination systems of your body. You are looking at how the energy and communication is flowing in a project or endeavor. Clogged pipes mean you have an energy blockage. Calling a plumber means you're actively working on solving the problem. <u>Emo-tional</u>: You're focusing on the flow of your emotions. Backed-up pipes mean you're facing repressed or pent-up feelings that need to be released. <u>Mental-Spiritual</u>: You're looking at the ideas you don't need anymore and how to eliminate them. You're looking at the supply of new visions, ideas, and understanding that is avail-able to be tapped.

pocket: <u>Physical</u>: You're focusing on a part of yourself you're not aware of or a place inside where you hide precious parts of yourself: memories, secrets, or inner resources. You have a physi-cal health issue where too much, too little, or almost no energy is flowing. You're focusing on the need to hide something. Put-ting something in a pocket means you want to possess, protect, or personally use what the item represents. Pockets sewed shut means you must use your valuables, share them, or give them away. <u>Emotional</u>: You're concealing something that's indicated by the hidden object. Pockets turned inside out means openness and sincerity. Hands in pockets means you're waiting for the right time to act or showing others you aren't aggressive or interfering, or you feel helpless. Mental-Spiritual: Finding something in a pocket indicates an ability or new knowledge coming to light or aid coming to you. A hole in your pocket means you're unconsciously "leaking" energy or resources.

poison: Physical: There is a condition in your life that's physically or emotionally toxic to your well-being. Something is weakening your life force. Emotional: You have bitter feelings or are trying to free yourself from a hurtful condition or emotionally toxic atmosphere. Someone is secretly sabotaging you, or you're in pain due to bad chemistry with someone. Mental-Spiritual: You're operating from a worldview that doesn't fit your character and life purpose. You must rid yourself of negativity.

polar bear: Physical: You're focusing on being powerful and resourceful in spite of difficult conditions. You blend in with your surroundings. You need more solitude. Emotional: You feel isolated and want affectionate companions who understand you. You feel highly protective of family and friends. You're trying to be warmhearted in the midst of fearful people. You're breaking through emotional barriers and frozen feelings. Mental-Spiritual: What you have is precious. You have a connection to higher dimensions and deep space.

police: Physical: You're exploring issues of authority and control (external and internal) and reminding yourself to be conscientious, keep your word, live a balanced life, or avoid reckless behavior. You're looking at the value of conventionality, rules, social mores, and order in your life. Emotional: You feel chaotic and full of commotion and need to settle down. You feel violated, powerless, and need rescue, protection, and security. You feel threatened by an authority or feel guilty. Mental-Spiritual: You're breaking rules, crossing boundaries into forbidden territory, and creating disorder in your mind, and you need to live in alignment with universal laws. Your spiritual guides are directing you.

pollution: Physical: You're focusing on the state of your physical energy and body; you need to cleanse yourself. You're living in a mess created by the thoughtlessness or laziness of others or yourself. It's damaging your vitality and life. Emotional: The state of the global environment and the future is causing you anxiety.

You're exploring your subconscious mind, or the collective subconscious mind, and feeling overwhelmed by the volume of fear-based emotions that need to be cleared. You're noticing how other people's negative behaviors and beliefs have affected you. Mental-Spiritual: You need to clean up your words and thoughts. You're receiving contaminated, biased communications from the media or others. Someone is digging up dirt about you. You're littering your mind with ugly cluttering thoughts that distract you from what's true. You need to meditate on core truth and loving-kindness.

pool: Physical: You are focusing on a need to relax and have some recreation, exercise, and a greater energy flow. Floating or swimming in a pool means you seek peace, a feeling of luxury, or a release of daily worries and responsibilities. You want greater freedom, fluidity, and magical movement. Emotional: You're becoming comfortable with your emotions. Being pulled under the water represents overwhelming circumstances in your waking life. Other people in the pool indicate social relationships and how you join in or miss out on nurturing experiences. Mental-Spiritual: You're developing intuition and empathy. Being in the deep end means you're entering the collective consciousness and exploring your spiritual origins. *(see swim)*

porcupine: Physical: You're dealing with a delicate situation or touchy people where you must be careful not to overstep your boundaries or offend anyone. You're being too prickly and disapproving and need to develop greater tolerance and patience. Emotional: You feel vulnerable or threatened and need to protect yourself from being wounded psychologically and emotionally. You're emphasizing trust, gentleness, and openness. You're being too aloof and edgy repelling people around you. Mental-Spiritual: Your thoughts and communications are marked by criticism and sharp words. You need more privacy to collect yourself and find your center.

portal: *(see stargate)*

postcard: *(see letter)*

pregnancy: Physical: You're exploring the idea of becoming pregnant, or you are pregnant. You're taking responsibility for another person or animal. Something new is gestating and about to emerge in your life. Miscarriages and aborted pregnancies mean you aren't ready for a new phase of creativity or lack the energy to complete a project. You're ready for an increase in your income. Emotional: You feel anxiety about being alone or about being crowded and responsible for others. You feel stuck and impatient, waiting for something to happen. Mental-Spiritual: You're focusing on what's original about yourself, what you want to create, and what ideas are becoming interesting to you. *(see baby, birth)*

priest/minister/guru: Physical: You're examining your experience with religion and religious leaders and how you connect with the spiritual part of yourself and life. You're looking at how you give your power away to experts. Emotional: You feel confused or lost and need inner guidance, comfort, and reassurance. You're relieving a guilty conscience. Mental-Spiritual: You're connecting with spiritual teachings, developing greater virtue in yourself, and revealing your own spiritual qualities, strengths, and abilities. You're moving beyond your personal self and ego into higher dimensions.

prison: Physical: You're looking at the limits you impose on yourself or allow others to impose on you, and the way you stifle your creativity. You can't escape from rules, restrictions, and responsibilities. Emotional: There are parts of yourself, or subconscious fears, you have locked away and want to examine and release. You're dealing with authority problems, feelings of guilt, punishment, being trapped or restrained, or excluded or shut out. Mental-Spiritual: You're living inside a box of limited thinking and fixed beliefs, narrowing your possibilities. You need to be still, remove distractions, and focus on your core self.

prostitute: Physical: You want more sexual freedom and exploration, sexual power, and less inhibition. You want to enjoy someone without committing to a formal relationship. You're paying a price for being involved with someone. You're being pressured to do things you don't want to avoid losing a relationship or job. Emotional: You're sorting through feelings concerning the connection between love and sexuality. You need to stop pleasing people to survive or making people "pay" to love you. You feel guilty or dirty concerning your sexual desires and actions. You feel sex is a "job" rather than an expression of love and respect.

You want to feel more attractive and desirable. You or someone you know is acting deceptively in a relationship. Mental-Spiritual: You aren't speaking your truth to powerful people. You're avoiding the divine because you feel shame. You need to realign with your soul's life purpose and focus on what you really want to be and what you love to do.

psychic: (*see fortuneteller*)

public speaking: Physical: You're focusing on your ability to speak your truth, convey your message, and express yourself confidently and joyfully. Emotional: You're examining feelings of being scrutinized or judged by others, weighing the quality of what you offer, and assessing your comfort level with being visible. You're exposing your own weaknesses. Mental-Spiritual: The topic of your talk shows what issues you're concerned about and what your message is, while the setting for the talk shows where you feel people are receptive or not receptive to you.

purple: Physical: You need to experience more richness in life, a greater feeling of royalty, rank, and deservedness, as well as distinction and dignity. You have mixed feelings about the church, priesthoods, and pomp and ceremony. Emotional: You need to surrender, have faith, let go of negative emotions, and feel protected by unseen forces. You're feeling romantic or nostalgic. Mental-Spiritual: You're stimulating your spiritual life and universal understanding and your awareness of unity, spiritual healing, miracles, mystery, magic, transformation, and transmutation.

purse: (*see wallet*)

pyramid: Physical: You're focusing on your largest, highest goals and deepest yearnings. You've accomplished a goal, especially if your dream includes the apex. You need to visit a holy place. Emotional: You're finding insight and understanding about your deepest feelings, experiencing a release from suffering and pain by bringing the hidden into the light. You feel anxiety about an ordeal you must go through to prove yourself. Mental-Spiritual: You're searching for ancient wisdom, esoteric knowledge, secrets, and higher energy. You need to remember that life is sacred. You're transforming your personal, materialistic, human experience into its spiritual counterpart. (*see mountain*)

Q

quail: Physical: You are uncertain about a situation, person, action, or decision. You're shrinking away from a path of action or losing heart. A covey of quail means you are fortunate, have abundance, and good relationships with coworkers, friends, and family. You need to focus on cooperating with others and working interdependently. Emotional: You need to develop better self-reliance, groundedness, and steadiness. You want to avoid danger before you've investigated what's really happening. You're dealing with issues that cause you to lose courage. Mental-Spiritual: You're easily diverted and distracted. You're focusing on superficial thoughts without much substance. You're focusing on ideas like loyalty, commitment, and trust of your close friends but distrust of the world outside. Spiritually, you're focusing on the collective consciousness.

quarantine: Physical: You're focusing on being forced to limit your self-expression due to circumstances you can't control. You need to pause or even stop to realign yourself with your inner purpose. You need protection from threats or negative influences around you. You're exhausted and need rejuvenation. Emotional: You feel trapped, punished, unfairly restricted as though you're in prison. You need to take time alone to feel what causes you to feel pressured, bored, upset, or dissatisfied with your work and life. You feel lonely, sad, and unable to find and connect with people on your wavelength. You need space to process disorienting trauma. Mental-Spiritual: You're learning to see that what restricts you is a gift, not a punishment. By being still, you can achieve more than by pushing ahead with willpower. You have the opportunity to grow spiritually through patient, mundane work, and you have the power to animate seemingly "boring" tasks by using your imagination.

quarry: Physical: You're focusing on penetrating, hard work, and making slow but steady progress toward a goal. You're digging down through layers of family history and your own past to find places where energy became stuck or solid. You're excavating, searching for inner resources and hidden talents. You need to create a stable foundation. Emotional: You're discovering long-buried emotional wounds to understand and clear them. The quarry itself represents generosity in spite of unconscious or unkind treatment. Mental-Spiritual: You're extracting new or forgotten knowledge and skills to build a successful life. As you dig down into the earth, secrets are revealed. You're curious about ancient history and the evolution of the earth and humanity. You're looking at your motives: Are you being greedy for the raw material you're taking from the earth or are you respectful of all that has come before?

quarterback: Physical: You're focusing on the power of your individual self, leadership skills, charisma, coordination, physical health, and strength. You want to direct the flow of a project or feel you're being successful in running your own life or business. You need to learn to work cooperatively with others and gain their admiration. Emotional: You need recognition and to stand out among others. You feel performance anxiety about being in the right place at the right time and being fully connected to, and involved with, your environment and key people. Mental-Spiritual: You're in a position to pass advice, knowledge, or teachings on to others. You're focusing on strategies, plans, systems, and methods for expressing yourself and attaining your goals. You're looking at your ability to inspire others.

quicksand: Physical: Your energy is being drained. You are on unstable ground or have been tricked or trapped by something that at first seemed solid and safe. You need to be patient, change your tactics and perspective (such as, lying on your back in quicksand will free you), and call on inner resources or outside help to unstick yourself. Emotional: You feel overwhelmed and dragged down into your subconscious by heavy emotional issues. The more you struggle, the more exhausted you become. You feel unsupported and powerless. Mental-Spiritual: You're out of touch with your true self, caught in too much materialism and resistance. You need to stop fighting, strip yourself of excess weight and baggage, and work with the universal forces. You need to remember you're lighter than the entrapping situation and by filling with your own essence, and taking it easy, you will rise to freedom. *(see paralysis)*

quilt: Physical: A patchwork quilt represents many aspects of yourself and your life that you're seeing as interrelated and forming a beautiful, harmonious pattern. You're recycling old experiences into new endeavors. Emotional: You want a warm, comforting, protective, emotional environment. Mental-Spiritual: You want to know and use all of yourself. You're integrating many ideas and experiences into yourself, allowing yourself to be complex and colorful, yet orderly. *(see blanket)*

R

rabbit: <u>Physical</u>: You're focusing on fertility, sexuality, the proliferation of work or self-expression, or increasing your abundance. A rabbit in the garden means you're experiencing the subtle destruction of your efforts and resources or a setback in personal growth. You're running from problems. <u>Emotional</u>: You need to be less soft and docile, passive, and naive. You need greater humility and vulnerability. You feel you are the victim of predators or have been wounded by life's basic insensitivity. You feel criticized, hunted down, or hounded. You want to be petted or cared for. <u>Mental-Spiritual</u>: You're unwisely idealistic. You believe in luck. You're sacrificing yourself or something precious for the good of others. Going down the rabbit hole means you're looking inside to find your deepest self and the origins of the universe. A white rabbit means magic and spiritual awakening.

raccoon: <u>Physical</u>: You're focusing on people who are making mischief, deceive you, or steal from you. You're disguising your true motives or masking an element of your personality you don't want others to know about, or someone else is presenting a false face. You need to be more industrious and able to adapt to a variety of environments and conditions. <u>Emotional</u>: You're being secretive and unavailable and need to come out in the open and join with others. You're anxious about the danger of uncleanliness and germs, or don't care enough to pay attention to your hygiene. <u>Mental-Spiritual</u>: You want to develop your wit and cleverness, resourcefulness, inquisitiveness, leadership in groups, and ability to empower others. You're learning to be inventive, stick with something, and try repeatedly until you succeed.

radar: <u>Physical</u>: You're focusing on the subtle messages under the surface of the physical reality, especially on things that might go wrong with your health, people who might not be who they seem, or decisions that are likely to produce more problems. You sense that others are invading your space energetically. <u>Emotional</u>: You're highly sensitive and picking up feelings that belong to other people, or you're reacting more strongly than necessary because you feel overwhelmed by the vibrational chaos around you. Mental-Spiritual: You're honing your intuitive abilities to read others, situations, and trends, as well as to use your inner senses of hearing and touch (clairaudience and clairsentience) to communicate and navigate through life. You're developing precognition and psychic abilities.

radio: Physical: You're focusing on receiving information from your body and discriminating the true messages from the static caused by bad diet and tension. Being on the radio means you're entering a time where you will express yourself more expansively. Emotional: You're focusing on listening to the messages from your subconscious mind. You've been talking too much, covering up feelings of vulnerability or seeking more attention. You need to share your feelings with others. Mental-Spiritual: You're aware of the level of static interference in the world. You're focusing on hearing your inner voice and intuitive insights, working telepathically with others, or even communicating with nonphysical beings. You're tuning in to the voice of the collective consciousness or "soul of the world."

radioactive: Physical: You're activating a more intense, flowing state of energy in your physical body, perhaps after a period of dormancy. Emotional: You're moving into a manic state where your emotions are hyperactive and perhaps erratic. You're fired up and influential, full of yourself, and overflowing. You're negatively impacted by other people's zealous or delusional behavior. Mental-Spiritual: Your ideas are highly charged and contagious, spreading rapidly to others. You're being infected by negative thinking based on prejudice, self-destructive motives, fear, or jealousy. You're receiving a strong influx of energy, light, and consciousness from higher realms and undergoing a transformation or enlightenment process.

rain: Physical: You're washing away old structures, cleansing yourself, fertilizing, replenishing, and nurturing a new period of growth and expansion. If the rain is gentle, you're about to experience a peaceful, productive time. If the rain is heavy, you can expect an increase in opportunities and abundance. Emotional: A heavy rain means feeling overwhelmed by dark, gloomy, depressing emotions, often accompanied by tears. Subconscious issues and emotions are entering your conscious mind. Too much unwanted rain means you feel you have bad luck or are being punished. Mental-Spiritual: You need to trust in providence. You're looking for the silver lining inside the dark clouds, attuning to the heart, the feminine, and nurturing.

rainbow: Physical: You've weathered difficulties and better, happier times are on the horizon. Emotional: You need to feel more optimistic and lucky. Mental-Spiritual: You're dreaming of better things, getting in touch with your destiny. You're bridging worlds, connecting your earthly experience to the divine. You're reminding yourself to be joyful, imaginative, and even magical. The pot of gold at the end of the rainbow means the revelation of your soul and your true nature as light and spirit.

ram: (*see sheep*)

rat: Physical: You're worried about contamination, germs, filth, physical sickness or disease; you're feeling ratty and rundown. You "smell a rat" or discover people acting in underhanded, stealthy, thieving, or sabotaging ways. Someone has "ratted" on you, betrayed, or lied about you. You need to stop, rest, and get out of the "rat race." You're an adaptable survivor, though perhaps without morals. Emotional: You feel apprehensive, worried, disgusted, or repulsed. Something is gnawing at you, undermining your peace of mind or confidence. You're experiencing frightening instincts, urges, or distasteful parts of yourself. Someone is using sex for material gain or is deserting ship when difficulties arise. Mental-Spiritual: You're inquisitive, sniffing out answers and new experiences. You're clever, resourceful, and instinctive. White rats mean protection from beneficent forces.

razor: Physical: Shaving with a razor means you're focusing on putting forth a clean, neat, focused image to others and that you're acting in a way that's marked by openness, precision, and close attention to detail. A sharply honed razor means you can cut through irrelevant issues quickly to find what's most important. Being on the razor's edge means you're walking a fine line and must be extremely alert to the tiniest mistake. Emotional: A razor used as a weapon means you're dealing with sharp rage and criticalness born of resentment and hatred. You've been cut by other people's tactless, cruel actions. Mental-Spiritual: Your mind is edgy and brilliant, and you can use it to reveal truth or hurt people with unkind remarks. You're on a spiritual path that's narrow and highly focused, especially on ethics and clarity.

recipe: Physical: You're focusing on the steps in a process for creating something new. You're entering a new phase of life and seeking guidance. You feel dependent on having a plan that you can follow, or you need to let go of the method and use intuition and imagination to achieve results. You're free to modify the "recipe" whenever you want. Emotional: You're looking at the foods you habitually eat and what goes into them; is it nourishing? You're processing deep emotional patterns. A recipe passed on through generations of family represents integration or dissolution of inherited behaviors. Mental-Spiritual: If you can't follow a recipe, or the result comes out differently than you envisioned, you may feel out of your element, uninterested, or frustrated in daily life. Making traditional food versus something new and unusual points to your need for security versus the desire for freedom and exploration. Taking great care when following a recipe and loving the ingredients means you're integrating spiritual guidance to attain a higher level of consciousness and presence.

red: Physical: You're focusing on your physical vitality and energy, heart, blood, blood pressure, metabolism, respiration rate, a birth or breakthrough, or survival. You're involved in something dangerous, exciting, impulsive, passionate, intense, willful, violent, or explosive. You need to develop more courage, high visibility, and leadership skills. You're warning yourself to be careful about accidents, to slow down or stop, or deal with an emergency. Emotional: You feel hot, frustrated, angry, warlike, and vengeful. You need greater stimulation, eroticism, and romantic love. Mental-Spiritual: You're focused on beginnings, basic life force, the power of the deep earth, and making quick decisions. You need to find balance between passion and safety. You need to pay attention.

refrigerator: Physical: You need plenty of resources and provisions on hand to accomplish what you want to do. Emotional: You're hoarding something because you're afraid you won't have enough. You've put your ignored feelings on ice. You need nurturing or are responsible for caretaking others. You want to feel abundant. Mental-Spiritual: You're preserving important thoughts or secrets for use late, or keeping yourself fresh, pure, and ready for action. *(see food)*

reincarnation: Physical: Seeing a past life, or a specific experience from a past life, can be a literal memory, while it may also represent an aspect of your current personality or a potential you're activating. You're alerting yourself to a latent talent or a habit to be cleared. Emotional: You're alerting yourself to unresolved emotions or the need to heal and learn from a repeating experience. A past life dream often has special weight and a vibration you recognize as different from a normal dream. Mental-Spiritual: You're expanding your notion of how much you know, how experienced you are, how universal you are, and how much you have in common with others. The memory is surfacing so you can reactivate old wisdom more easily, heal a wound that's been waiting to be seen from a higher perspective, or feel encouraged to enter a new phase of growth.

renovation: Physical: Renovating a house or building means you're reorganizing and reinventing yourself and your life. Emotional: You feel old or outdated and are afraid you'll lose value to others. Mental-Spiritual: You're changing the way you see and act in the world. You're replacing old ideas with a new worldview and new knowledge.

resort/spa: (*see vacation*)

restaurant: Physical: You need physical nourishment. A fast-food restaurant means you're not letting yourself integrate the full value of what you receive, or you're ignoring your social needs. The restaurant's ambiance symbolizes how close you'd like to be in your relationships with other people. Emotional: You want greater emotional intimacy or a more romantic or colorful mood. A bad meal or poor service means you don't feel important or worthy, or you aren't giving others enough value. Mental-Spiritual: You need intellectual stimulation and exchange of ideas with others. Cafeterias mean abundant variety and a wealth of ideas. You're ready to receive nurturing in an "all you can eat" fashion.

rhinoceros: Physical: You have great determination and follow-through. You need to work toward your goals and not let anything get in your way or sidetrack you. You're focusing on male sexuality. Emotional: You're provoked easily and react with forcefulness and blind rage. You're protected, shielded, and thick-skinned, avoiding your feelings. You need to develop greater vulnerability and tone down your warlike nature. Mental-Spiritual: You're developing instinct and intuition, opening your third eye. You're maintaining clear boundaries concerning your identity.

ride: <u>Physical</u>: Riding in a vehicle means you're seeking a new destination, letting someone else help you get there. You're resting from being responsible for a while. Riding a horse or other animal means you're accessing your instinctual nature to help you move forward. <u>Emotional</u>: Someone else is controlling you, and you feel helpless, passive, or that you are "just along for the ride," with no say in things. <u>Mental-Spiritual</u>: You're contemplating, observing, and gestating, waiting for the right vision, enthusiasm, and moment to guide your life in a new direction.

right: <u>Physical</u>: The right side of the body, and anything to the right, symbolizes action, forward motion, personal power to accomplish, masculine or yang energy, and cultural standards. <u>Emotional</u>: You're afraid to vary from the norm, be out of control, or to be wrong. You need to break some habits and be open to your feelings. <u>Mental-Spiritual</u>: You're focusing on logic, analysis, goals, will, and movement toward the conscious, outer-directed part of yourself. If you're left-handed, your meanings for left and right may be reversed.

ring: <u>Physical</u>: You're focusing on commitment, belonging, completion, and wholeness. You're contemplating marriage, or divorce. You're part of a group or cause to which you've pledged loyalty. <u>Emotional</u>: Losing a ring means you're looking at your commitment or love for the person, group, or ideals it stands for. <u>Mental-Spiritual</u>: Rings connect you to universal knowledge. Receiving a ring means you're connecting to specific qualities and ideas represented by the giver of the ring, your grandmother's courage, your father's love, or you're taking on an identity — like the prestige of your alma mater.

river: <u>Physical</u>: You're looking at the flow of your energy, your life path, or the passage of time. Crossing a river means you're intentionally entering a new phase, facing emotional issues to do it. Watching a river from its banks means you need to be more involved in creating your life. <u>Emotional</u>: You're focusing on your emotional processes and whether they're peaceful and progressing slowly or flooded and in turmoil, with rapids and snagged debris (complex emotional issues). Being in a boat or swimming in a river means you're immediately involved in an emotional process. How much you steer or guide yourself shows how proactive you are in your life. The condition of the water — clear, muddy, turbulent, stagnant — shows the state of your emotions. <u>Mental-Spiritual</u>: Flowing with the river represents peace or surrender to a higher power. You're linking yourself to, and moving toward, a greater source of inspiration and wisdom. Trying to go upstream means you're out of harmony with your purpose.

road: Physical: You're focusing on the journey of life, your direction, and how you reach your goals. The kind of road indicates your current process. A straight, flat, well-marked road means you're going in the right direction, moving directly to your goals. A twisty, bumpy, muddy, unpaved, impassable, or steep road means you're struggling or uncertain. If you're on a superhighway, you're going fast (or too fast). Emotional: A roadblock means you feel stuck, held back, or checked up on by someone in authority. Being stranded means you feel unsupported and isolated. Running off the road means you must pay attention and be more responsible for your success. Mental-Spiritual: You're focusing on your destination or life purpose and on how you make the journey. You need to pay attention to the quality and details of the process as well as end results.

robin: Physical: You're focusing on the coming of spring, a new beginning, opportunity, or birth. You're starting first and can expect success. "The early bird gets the worm." Emotional: You feel fresh and ready to tackle any emotional challenge. Mental-Spiritual: You're experiencing a burst of new ideas, optimism, and spiritual renewal.

rocket: Physical: You're focusing on rapid progress and bettering the circumstances of your life. Your plans are taking off. You are in too much of a hurry and aren't paying enough attention to doing things properly and carefully. Your sex drive is strong and perhaps distracting you from other things. Emotional: A repressed emotional pattern is surfacing suddenly and rapidly, exploding into your life with uncontrollable consequences. You're totally obsessed with one thing. Mental-Spiritual: References to rocket science mean you're looking at your assessment of your own intelligence level or making excuses for not comprehending complex information. You're learning quickly and aggressively, seeking advanced degrees, or moving into spiritual dimensions rapidly (or too fast).

rodeo: Physical: You're freeing your wild side and need to move more, have more excitement, challenge yourself to do riskier things, and learn to channel your raw energy into productive outlets. You're focusing on your ability to ride out difficult times or rope in the elusive resources you need. Emotional: You're experiencing emotional chaos, as many old memories surface and clash. You're dealing with your animal nature and rebellion concerning societal norms. You're looking at controlling the flow of life or surrendering to it. Mental-Spiritual: You're freeing your imagination and synthesizing a variety of elements to feed your creative process. You're learning to tolerate and enjoy the wild, undomesticated forces in life, seeing everything as a path to wisdom and spiritual fulfillment.

rollercoaster: Physical: You're focusing on the crazy, yet exciting, ups and downs of life. You're examining how you grow in cycles with peaks and troughs and how there's a continuous flow all along the way. Emotional: You're looking at being out of control or in turmoil. Do you feel thrilled, frightened, or trapped? You're feeling childlike joy and the release of worry. Mental-Spiritual: You want life to be more predictable, or you want it to be more stimulating and surprising. You're connecting with the moments when the wave turns, when energy begins to rise then shifts to the fall. You're smoothing out your spiritual path by trusting what the flow brings and seeing how each cycle brings more perspective and clarity.

roof: Physical: You need protection, shelter, and material comforts. Emotional: You feel vulnerable in the world at large and want a smaller focus to operate within. You're afraid of being exposed. Mental-Spiritual: There's a barrier between your daily awareness and the higher realms, which can be your ideology, philosophy, ideals, and worldview. A leaky roof means new information or spiritual awareness is becoming conscious. If the roof is caving in, you must recommit to your ideals, or you can't live up to your own high expectations. *(see ceiling)*

room: Physical: You're looking at your various talents, aspects, and life activities. Discovering rooms you didn't know were there means you're discovering new capacities or roles. Moving from one room to another means you're changing focus and shifting your mode of self-expression. Emotional: A basement or attic space indicates you're contacting your subconscious mind and fears, blockages, or old memories. The décor and mood of the room indicate emotional issues. Mental-Spiritual: You're focusing on a specific set of ideas or entering a specific reality to explore an aspect of yourself.

rooster: (*see chicken*)

roots: Physical: You need to be grounded or committed to a place, activity, or person. You're exploring the origins of your life and family. You need to get back to basics. Emotional: You've been too wishy-washy or flighty and need to "set down some roots" and stop avoiding uncomfortable feelings. Mental-Spiritual: Roots symbolize the need to connect deeply with the collective consciousness or subconscious mind. You're on the verge of a revelation. Roots growing into your house or water pipes indicate deep wisdom surfacing for you.

rope: Physical: You're examining how you connect to things you see as separate from you, what you're grasping at, how you secure things, and how entangled or tied up you are by situations in your life. Uncoiling a rope means the beginning of a new phase, while coiling a rope means a successful completion of a difficult task. Someone throwing you a rope is a promise of assistance and rescue. Climbing a rope means you're determined to succeed and overcome adversity. Emotional: Being tied up means you feel criticized, restricted, and helpless in your self-expression. Climbing down a rope means you feel disappointed and incapable and have given up, or you're coming back to earth safely without falling or failing. Mental-Spiritual: Walking a tightrope means you're concentrating on your path, paying attention to the nuances of what keeps you safe and on purpose.

rose: Physical: You're focusing on love, romance, respect, honor, beauty, innocence, and appreciation for a great performance or job well done. You're looking at femininity and female sexuality. Emotional: You want to feel sweet, beautiful, and loved. The openness of the flower indicates your level of emotional openness and self-expression. A bud means you're closed and afraid, while a wide-open, flat, spent rose means you're exhausted. A single rose means gratitude. Mental-Spiritual: You have a complex, elegant self-expression and spiritual awareness. You are unfolding gracefully. Note the color of the rose: white, innocence/purity; pink, romance/love; red, passion; yellow, friendship and caring; black, illness or death.

rot/rottenness: Physical: You're allowing failures to transform into useful raw material for new creations. You're evaluating your life — what stays, what to release. Things are going "wrong" in your life, but you're learning to see why and the value for your growth. It's time to fully let go of something you've been clinging to because it's outlived its usefulness. Emotional: Eating decaying or rotten food means there are problems you've been putting up with for too long and they're draining and possibly depressing you. You're focusing on regret or missed opportunities. Something is toxic or unhealthy for you. Mental-Spiritual: You need to clean up negative reactions, beliefs, speech, and behavior. You're focusing on not wasting your potential, on being neglectful, or on allowing fear and negativity to block the expression of your soul. You're releasing all past actions, blessing them, forgiving yourself for mistakes, learning from everything, and remembering who you really are.

ruins: Physical: You're focusing on the possible destruction or failure of a project in your life. You're aware a phase is coming to an end and offers no more benefit. Your life is in ruins, or your security has collapsed. Emotional: You feel the loss of a relationship, a part of your identity, or a goal. You feel depressed and defeated. Mental-Spiritual: You're about to begin again and to experience rebirth. Ancient ruins indicate you're discovering or remembering deep parts of yourself and secrets from your distant past. You're uncovering the ancient wisdom of the collective consciousness or piecing together your history throughout time.

running: Physical: Running for exercise means you're looking at your energy level, strength, exuberance, discipline, and the force you have to move through life. You need to speed up, slow down, or pace yourself. Emotional: Running away from something means you need to face an issue, you feel trapped or pressured, or you're not taking responsibility for your actions. Running in slow motion or where your feet won't move as you intend them to means you lack confidence or self-esteem, or you're ambivalent about a goal. Mental-Spiritual: Competitive running means you're focusing on how to achieve your purpose, how much you need to use personal will, why you feel ambitious and motivated, and what's behind your current challenges and rivalries. *(see competition)*

rust: Physical: Seeing rusted metal means you're focusing on the aging process or on a project or possession that's beginning to fall apart and self-destruct. You're warning yourself about a deterioration of your health. You've neglected an aspect of yourself or life and need to take better care with tending and maintaining yourself. Emotional: You're focusing on fear of declining luck, fading friendships, or depressing conditions that might debilitate you.

You need to cleanse and rejuvenate yourself emotionally, abandon negative attitudes, and refurbish your positive motivations. Mental-Spiritual: You haven't used your mental faculties or some specific consciousness skill, like intuition or memory, for a long time, and you need to reactivate it and build it back up.

S

saint/spiritual guide: Physical: You're focusing on the amount of good you contribute to the world, whether it be through actions or philanthropy. You're experiencing difficulties and must not lose heart; you can make it through. You need to shift your focus from material concerns to the quality of your inner life. Emotional: You feel uneasy or guilty about current choices and behaviors. You need to make amends for something you did. You're sacrificing yourself for others or are suffering. Mental-Spiritual: You're focusing on a high ideal. You're questioning your spiritual path or considering another that may result in others disapproving of you. You're receiving spiritual guidance from a higher level of your own self. *(see angel, animals)*

school: Physical: You're focusing on what you can learn from your circumstances. You need to pay attention to new information or points of view. You're learning about yourself and improving your life. You're learning the hard way. Emotional: You're remembering your school years, especially the time when you went to the kind of school in the dream, when you felt insecure about making the grade, were unpopular, had authority problems, or surprising success. You have performance anxiety and are afraid of failing. Mental-Spiritual: You're examining how you learn. You're exploring higher realms, bringing knowledge back to your daily life from the collective consciousness. You're learning a spiritual lesson. *(see test)*

scientist: Physical: You need to be more careful about details and proof. You need to experiment more and focus on invention and practicality. Emotional: You feel that people are judging you for being too eccentric or mental; you need to feel more and allow emotions to enrich your life. You need to celebrate. Mental-Spiritual: You need to be inspired and remember your higher purpose. You need to be guided by intuition and beauty. You're focusing on patterns of mathematics and knowledge in higher dimensions.

scissors: Physical: You need to take control or get rid of something in your life. You need to cut away excess that's weighing you down. Emotional: You feel cut off from others or cut out of or denied opportunities. You're angry and tempted to attack someone. You dread a coming separation or loss of a loved one. Men may fear emotional castration. Mental-Spiritual: You need to cut through to the heart of the matter or be decisive. You're experiencing sarcasm or criticism from others. Cutting something out of paper or fabric means you're carefully defining an idea or plan. *(see cut, knife)*

scorpion: Physical: You're focusing on a situation where you got stung by glossing over possible dangers. You're being vigilant for false friends. You're focusing on generating intensity, vigilance, and the ability for concealment to succeed in an endeavor. You're experiencing the end of a cycle and the beginning of something new — death and rebirth. Emotional: Someone has hurt you with caustic, stinging remarks or criticism, or you've struck out at others defensively or destructively. You're dealing with bitterness, self-destructive feelings and behaviors, or intense negative drama. Mental-Spiritual: You're warning yourself about self-defeating thoughts and habits. You're transforming spiritually, refining your lower nature into higher awareness.

search: Physical: You're looking for something that's missing or needed in your life, possibly a part of yourself, or you're becoming aware that you need more than you have. Emotional: You're trying to remember something from your subconscious that's blocked. Your identity is threatened by the loss of something; the object gives clues to the characteristic you need to re-own and integrate. Mental-Spiritual: You're working out a solution to a problem. If you're searching the internet, you're moving through the collective consciousness aligning with your higher purpose.

seed: Physical: You're focusing on the beginning of something, creating the first steps carefully so the end result will unfold well. You need "seed money" to start a new venture. You're looking at concepts like vitality, fertilization, germination, and the continuity of life. You've "gone to seed," or stopped taking care of yourself. Emotional: You feel anxious about your potential and ability to initiate new things. Mental-Spiritual: You're focusing on your heritage, the human psyche, and soul. Seeds of new ideas have been sown in your mind, and you're helping new experiences develop from them. *(see acorn, nut)*

self-driving vehicle (SDV): *(see electric vehicle)*

sex/sex organs: <u>Physical</u>: You want more physical intimacy, sexual relations, or emotional love. You're activating or merging with new aspects of yourself and life represented by your dream partner. You're focusing on your balance of yin and yang energy. <u>Emotional</u>: If your partner is famous, you're telling yourself you're as good or talented as that person is. You're examining vulnerability and intimacy issues, sexual problems, and past abuse experiences. You're anxious about being alone, want someone to rescue you, or want to be distracted from problems. You're looking at how receptive and aggressive you are. <u>Mental-Spiritual</u>: You're experiencing longings of a spiritual nature — a desire for communion.

shadow: <u>Physical</u>: You're focusing on parts of yourself you've rejected, hidden, or defined as weak, evil, or ugly. You're tired, weak, or out of practice, "a shadow of your former self." <u>Emotional</u>: You're dealing with uncomfortable negative emotions like jealousy, rage, greed, shame, or panic. You feel insecure, passive, depressed, or paranoid because you're "living in someone's shadow" or in the shadow of an event you can't forget. You're nervous and jumpy — "afraid of your own shadow." <u>Mental-Spiritual</u>: You have doubts based on your insecurities, or you're certain, knowing something "beyond the shadow of a doubt."

shark: <u>Physical</u>: You're focusing on a person who's greedy, unscrupulous, selfish, and aggressive, with no regard for others. You have legal or money problems and are dealing with lawyers and creditors. You need to be more direct in pursuing a goal or have more stamina. <u>Emotional</u>: You're focusing on frightening emotions you believe can destroy or devour you. Sharks in a feeding frenzy means you're looking at collective negative emotions like violence or hatred. You feel threatened by something you can't reason with or control. <u>Mental-Spiritual</u>: You need to be less distracted by superficial ideas and focus on what's most important. You're accessing ancient wisdom about how to survive.

sheep: <u>Physical</u>: You're focusing on developing self-confidence, individuality, and initiative, especially if you dream of a ram. <u>Emotional</u>: You're easygoing and readily influenced by others. You feel like one of the flock, without personal power or influence, conforming or going along with the flow. You feel like an outcast, "the black sheep of the family." You feel panic and skittishness about some issue in your life. You're rushing headlong into situations and being hotheaded. Mental-Spiritual: You hesitate to express your ideas openly, or are shy, apologetic, or sheepish about being yourself.

shell: Physical: You're focusing on safety and feeling protected. You need to be strong and able to endure as you deal with challenges. You're thinking of the legacy you will leave behind or the way others will see your accomplishments. A broken shell represents cracks in your own foundation or a wound that hasn't healed. Emotional: Shells can represent good luck, how beautiful you are, or the amazing variety of ingenious ways to express yourself. The radiant scallop shell that resembles the sun's rays represents safety on spiritual pilgrimages. Mental-Spiritual: Certain shells allow you to hear the sound of the universe or Music of the Spheres. Some can be played to produce sacred calls to action. You're focusing on connecting and merging your physical/emotional life with your spiritual soul-self. You're following the spiral journey to enlightenment.

shield: Physical: You're focusing on a need for self-protection, presence, confidence, and readiness to hold your own in a chaotic, often hostile, environment. It symbolizes the grace of higher powers to keep you safe and moving forward. You may need to create clear boundaries with certain people who tend to dominate and control others. Emotional: You're focusing on strengthening your faith, courage, and trust in the flow. You're overcoming fear. Mental-Spiritual: You're learning to stand your ground against temptations or threats. You're discovering that your own pure soul presence, radiating around you in all directions, is the only "shield" you need; in fact, you don't need a shield at all when you experience your interconnectedness with all forms of life.

shoes: Physical: You're looking at the way you connect to reality and live your life. Changing your shoes means you're changing roles, taking a new approach, or evaluating your goals. Worn, tattered shoes mean you need to focus on being grounded and in touch with details. High heels mean you want to accentuate your sexuality. Boots mean you're working seriously or dealing with trying conditions where you need a good footing. Emotional: You need to feel protected as you move forward. Slippers mean you need to relax and feel comforted and homey. Mental-Spiritual: Ill-fitting shoes that hurt your feet mean you lack energy or confidence in your path and purpose. Losing a heel means your basic assumptions about life are incorrect or unstable. Outdated shoes mean your convictions and ideas need updating.

silver: Physical: You're focusing on wealth, what you receive and give, your investments, or savings. Emotional: You need to feel soothed, cooled, more feminine, or introverted. You're focusing on an emotional or sentimental treasure. Mental-Spiritual: You need to have a neutral attitude. You're connecting with the moon, the silver lining inside dark clouds, positive thinking, intuition and psychic ability, and magic.

size: Physical: You're looking at the importance you attach to people or things or the power and authority others have over you. Emotional: You feel dwarfed by someone's dramatic or dominant self-expression, or you're belittling others. A towering object means you want to feel invulnerable and strong. Mental-Spiritual: Tiny objects mean you need to pay attention in a much closer way.

skeleton/spine: *(see bones)*

skin: Physical: You're looking at how sensitive you are to the environment or others and how you represent yourself to the world. You need to penetrate further into an issue or situation. Emotional: Skin problems or rashes mean you feel irritated, self-conscious, self-critical, ashamed, too visible, or uncomfortable about how you appear to others. You're being too superficial or shallow. Covering your skin with clothes means you feel vulnerable and are shielding your inner self. "Baring lots of skin" means you invite intimacy. Being "thick-skinned" means you're unaffected by criticism. Mental-Spiritual: You're focusing on your personal self, separate from the unified field of energy in the universe. You're looking at beauty that isn't only skin deep.

skunk: Physical: You're driving people away with a negative attitude or repellent language, or there's someone who's fouling your environment with bad behavior. "Something stinks" in your life. You're leaking vital energy or sexual energy, dumping woes and responsibilities onto others. Emotional: You have suppressed anger that's on the verge of exploding. You feel defensive. You've been walked on and want some respect. You need to assert yourself and dare to be outrageous. Mental-Spiritual: You need to examine the kind of people who are attracted to you and why they are. Look at the kind of reputation you have and what you contribute to the world.

sky: (*see air*)

slow motion/speeding: <u>Physical</u>: You're giving yourself impor-tant feedback about your pace in waking reality. Moving in slow motion, like wading through deep water, snow, or mud, is akin to paralysis; you're experiencing stress, frustration, and obstacles in a real situation. You also may be experiencing part of the natu-ral dream state where the body stops moving. You're moving too fast in a relationship or project. <u>Emotional</u>: You feel anxious about meeting a deadline, driven to complete a goal, and are pushing yourself or others too hard. <u>Mental-Spiritual</u>: You're experienc-ing the different frequency rates connected to various dimensions and states of awareness. (*see paralysis*)

slum: <u>Physical</u>: Your body is rundown, and you need rest and rejuvenation. You're focusing on something in your life that's deteriorating or crumbling. <u>Emotional</u>: You feel depressed and overwhelmed by conditions that seem to be going against you. You're paralyzed by the fear of poverty. You're feeling helpless or victimized by greedy people who take advantage of you and give nothing back. <u>Mental-Spiritual</u>: You're caught in negative think-ing, or your worldview and belief systems are falling apart, mak-ing way for something new to be built. You're "slumming it," visiting a way of thinking that's below your normal level, so you can develop greater compassion for those less fortunate than you.

smartphone: (*see telephone*)

smoke: <u>Physical</u>: You're focusing on covering up something with a smokescreen or trying to clear smoke so you can see hidden deception and truth. If you're using smoke from sage, pinon, or other natural substances in a ceremonial way, you're working to cleanse yourself, a group, or your environment. Thick smoke without fire can mean a warning, frustration, or lies. <u>Emotional</u>: Smoke with fire can indicate you're working to release intense emotion or purify something. <u>Mental-Spiritual</u>: Smoke from incense in a quiet setting means you're focusing on ancient wis-dom, inner harmony, purification/clearing negativity, respectful-ness, gratitude, inner peace, and transformation. Smoke can carry blessings and prayers to spiritual beings and people in need.

snake: <u>Physical</u>: You're focusing on life force energy (kundalini) and sexuality, instinctive drives, feminine energy and power, healing, and regeneration. You're entering a time of change and renewal. You need to have a healthy mistrust for someone.

Emotional: If you personally fear snakes, the symbol serves as a warning of potential danger concerning something in your life. You feel tempted by someone who may be sly, as "a snake in the grass." Mental-Spiritual: You're focusing on connecting with the underworld, the subconscious, goddess power, psychic energy, or the ancient wisdom of the earth. Certain snakes, like cobras, symbolize shrewdness and unwavering truth. Serpents awaken unconscious urges and increase your knowledge.

snow: Physical: You're focusing on qualities like stillness, purity, innocence, peace, and tranquility. You're making a clean start with a fresh perspective. Emotional: You feel indifferent, isolated, shocked, restricted, or neglected. Snow and sleet mean frozen or unexpressed emotions, while hail relates to feeling battered. Being snowed in means you must deal with a backlog of suppressed emotion before you can reengage with the world. Melting snow means you're facing, understanding, and releasing frozen emotions and inhibitions. Mental-Spiritual: Newly fallen snow means you're seeing the world with fresh eyes and a sense of wonder. A snowflake represents your soul's unique expression, complexity, and beauty. Your thoughts come from a quiet, neutral place.

soap: Physical: You're focusing on the need to clean and freshen your environment. You want to be free of negativity, toxins, and impurities or to wash off the residue of dealing with a draining or belittling person. You want to clean up incomplete experiences with others or make amends for an act you regret. Emotional: You want to resolve a confusing, hurtful experience that has left contracted, cloudy feelings. A bar of unopened soap means you're looking at issues that need to be cleared. Using liquid soap also means emotional cleansing but perhaps with an additional element of speed involved. The scent of soap adds an extra layer of meaning — for example, lemon, renewed energy and clarity; rose, love and spiritual blessings; sandalwood, inner peace and purification; pine, wisdom and longevity. Mental-Spiritual: Washing your hands with white soap and clear water indicates you're purifying yourself for sacred acts or healing. You want to be clear of fear and blockages so your soul and divine energy can flow through you unimpeded.

south: Physical: You need to be more physical, passionate, fiery, and sensual. You need movement and dancing. You can endure difficulties without complaint and bring projects to culmination. Emotional: You're opening your heart and warm feelings, healing emotional wounds through joy, generosity, and humor. Mental-Spiritual: You're focusing on the spirit of the earth and the power of the sun's life-giving rays. You can receive revelations and understand that what seemed secret is actually obvious through open-mindedness.

spaceship: *(see UFO)*

sphere: Physical: You're noticing your "sphere of influence" and your current reality. You're seeking to expand your business, self-expression, and "scope." You need adventure, foreign cultures, and travel. Or you need to shrink your scope to pay attention to detail. Emotional: Being at the center of a sphere means you feel grounded, safe, and inclusive. A spherical shape represents the whole world or the well-rounded self. You're focusing on being in touch with personal feelings and how others feel. You're sensitive to humanitarian concerns and feel overwhelmed that you alone can't do enough to help. You need to stimulate yourself to take chances and move beyond your comfort zone. Mental-Spiritual: You're looking for the whole story, wanting to understand all the pertinent variables in a situation, or you want holistic, complete solutions. You're zooming out to see the higher view and wider perspective on your life. You have eclectic, diverse interests. You're aware of the soul, your destiny, or what exists in the present moment.

spider: Physical: You're caught in an entanglement by someone who's trying to trap you. You need to stay away from an alluring situation. You're focusing on feminine power, the calculating nature of some women, a devouring mother, or female seductions. You're entering a highly creative, productive phase where you'll be rewarded for your hard work. You need to pay attention to your "web," the internet, your network of contacts, or your family connections. You know how to attract the resources you need. Emotional: You feel someone is sucking the life out of you. You feel trapped in a sticky or clingy relationship. A painful spider bite means you're externalizing a subliminal emotional wound. Mental-Spiritual: You're attuning to high levels of knowledge, mathematics, the neural net, and world energy grid. You're focusing on how you're creating your destiny. Spiders are considered power animal totems, spiritual guides, and protectors.

square: Physical: You need more stability in life. You're focusing on the strength, endurance, and sturdiness of your body.

You're preparing to create something physical that needs to be constructed in steps, carefully, in time and space. You're looking at qualities of solidity, focus, and tangible accomplishment. Emotional: You feel insecure and want someone or something to rely on. You're too flighty or drowning in your emotions; you need to be more practical and down to earth. Mental-Spiritual: You're defining things too much or focusing on tradition and familiar systems of thought. You need to be more imaginative and think out of the box. You want to deepen your thoughts and emotions into more universal states of awareness. You're focusing on the formal, mathematical, scientific order of the cosmos.

squirrel: Physical: You need to reserve supplies for a future time or are retaining too much and need to let go. You need to store your energy for times of need. You're entering a planning and gathering phase. You need to clear away clutter. You're overactive and need to calm down. Emotional: You're afraid of not having enough or expect the worst, or you're feeling hypernervous about danger. Your behavior is erratic, or you're dodging traps. You need to let go of the superficial things that won't sustain you over time. Mental-Spiritual: You're clever and adaptable, and you can access anything you need. You understand safety and safe places. You take no more than you need. You need to discard outmoded thought patterns, worries, and stress.

stage/theater: Physical: You're looking at your life and how you live it. Performing on stage shows roles you're playing, your current behavior, how you present yourself to the world, and how you interact with society. Being in the wings means you're observant and preparing to take action. You're learning to work with a team. Emotional: You want to be the center of attention or receive recognition. Forgetting your lines indicates you feel unprepared or inadequate where you must perform to attain success. You're putting on a false act and need to be honest. Mental-Spiritual: You're focusing on how extensive you want your reality to be; "All the world is a stage." You're practicing how to let your self-expression be inspired. *(see acting)*

stairs: Physical: You're planning the steps you need to take to accomplish a goal. Walking upstairs means material and insights are surfacing and coming to you. Walking downstairs means you're accessing deeper reserves inside yourself, you're about to experience some setbacks, or you're rejoining the world after a hiatus. Emotional: Going downstairs means there's something from your past you need to acknowledge, you're dipping into your subconscious to access repressed fears, or you're retrieving useful lessons. Mental-Spiritual: You're moving between levels of yourself or contemplating a process of either focusing, descending, or expanding — ascending your awareness and understanding. You are in a process of change and transformation. Each step is a lesson on your path. Spiral stairs signify growth or rebirth.

star/shooting star: Physical: You desire self-fulfillment, fame, and fortune. You're about to experience a new birth or changes in your life. You're entering a lucky phase. Your hopes, dreams, and wishes can come true. An opportunity is being pointed out to you; pay attention. Emotional: You need recognition and greater self-esteem. Being "star-crossed" means frustration because your desires don't line up with your destiny. Mental-Spiritual: You're focusing on high ideals, spirit, and your destiny. "It's in the stars" or "My stars" means your life is guided by higher forces; stars represent high states of consciousness and were considered by the ancients to be gods and goddesses who died and now guide us.

stargate/portal: Physical: You're wondering about having adventures in other dimensions or traveling through space to the "outer limits." This can be beyond physical reality or to find a connection to your past lives and deeper self. Emotional: You want a stimulating, surprising journey that takes you beyond what's normal. You want the thrill of discovery. Mental-Spiritual: You're expanding energetically to be able to move through a mystical gateway to discover or remember nonphysical spiritual worlds. You're looking for your home in the universe, your "people," and where you originally came from. You're seeking connecting with higher beings and new consciousness and energetic abilities.

steal: (see thief, criminal, cheat)

stomach: Physical: You need to pay attention to what you eat, and how you assimilate your food. Similarly, you need to be careful about the people you bring close to you and the kind of support you give yourself. Emotional: You're receiving emotional, instinctual information. A knot in the stomach means you sense something is wrong or false about a situation. Not being able to "stomach something" means you're disgusted, afraid, or threatened to the point of physical nausea and vomiting. Mental-Spiritual: You're digesting new ideas, attitudes, and nourishing resource materials.

storm: (*see hurricane*)

stranger: <u>Physical</u>: A new part of yourself is emerging, and you need to get to know it to see what it has to offer. You will receive news from afar. <u>Emotional</u>: Repressed, unfamiliar emotions are surfacing, and you're wary about your safety. You're focusing on a general threat or fear. Kissing a stranger means you long for a new relationship. <u>Mental-Spiritual</u>: You're experiencing a visitation from a being or spiritual guide from another realm, perhaps a deceased loved one. You're receiving guidance from a deep part of yourself.

strangle/suffocate: <u>Physical</u>: You're experiencing a situation or relationship that smothers you or doesn't give you enough space. Something or someone is holding you back. You're repressing or denying a vital aspect of your self-expression, your truth, or are hesitating to share your message. <u>Emotional</u>: Choking indicates an inability to swallow something, like a lie or an idea that's inappropriate for you. Someone is forcing you to behave in a certain way, and you feel revulsion. <u>Mental-Spiritual</u>: You need to reconnect with your inspiration, the source of life, faith, trust, and the present moment. You're focusing on expressing your true nature without restriction. (*see neck*)

subway: <u>Physical</u>: You're moving through life and reaching your goals via subliminal methods. You're exploring hidden aspects of yourself. <u>Emotional</u>: You feel claustrophobic, trapped, or lost amid a maze of confusing feelings that never seem to become conscious. <u>Mental-Spiritual</u>: You're activating your intuition and instinctual knowing, exploring the collective subconscious mind. (*see tunnel*)

sun: <u>Physical</u>: You need to be outdoors more often. You're focusing on your vitality, radiance, and what creates good health. You want strong, positive relationships where things are obvious and on the up and up. You're lucky and inclined to be productive, hardworking, and enjoy what you do. <u>Emotional</u>: You feel positive and encouraged, especially about dealing with difficulties and healing emotional wounds. You feel goodwill toward all. <u>Mental-Spiritual</u>: You're focusing on creativity, intellectual brilliance, enlightenment, and insight. Two suns in the sky mean a fortunate event on your horizon.

sunrise/sunset: Physical: Seeing a sunrise means you're focusing on new beginnings, renewal of your vitality and energy, and fulfillment of goals. You're embarking on an adventure or starting a new project. You're hopeful. Seeing a sunset means you're completing a cycle of activity and are ready to let go, relax, rejuvenate, and just *be* for a while. You feel your energy is low or that your life force is fading. Emotional: Sunrise means you feel optimistic, enthusiastic, and motivated, or you need more of these states of being. Sunset means you feel tired and need more peace, rest, and connection with your deep, inner life. It means you can let go and be satisfied with your accomplishments and progress. Mental-Spiritual: Sunrise means you're focusing on creativity, inspiration, inventiveness, and surprising ideas. Sunset means you're introspective, reviewing, evaluating, and finding higher perspective.

surgery: Physical: You're concerned about an upcoming surgery. You're removing or cutting away old issues from your life and personality. You need to eliminate something or someone from your life that isn't positive. Emotional: You're facing and healing deep emotional wounds. Mental-Spiritual: You're opening yourself up to grow in new ways. You're working at higher levels with spiritual guides to repattern your energy body, streamline your spiritual growth process, and remove karma. *(see cut, doctor)*

swamp: Physical: You're living through a period of struggle, challenges, setbacks, and slow progress. You're "swamped" with work, demands on your time, and responsibilities. You feel stuck and lack motivation but must keep on. You'll experience success through dangerous and intriguing means. Your sexuality is supercharged. Emotional: You feel anxious about mysterious dangers that can emerge suddenly and threaten your safety. You're facing unruly or depressing emotions. Mental-Spiritual: You have an abundant imagination. You're passing through a test of character on your hero's journey. *(see hero)*

swan: Physical: You're focusing on qualities like grace, beauty, elegance, dignity, fluid movement, stateliness, and balance. The swan's long phallic neck links to male sexuality. You want to be prosperous, with greater prestige and wealth. You're singing your "swan song," preparing to let go of something important, or leave a period of your life behind. Emotional: You're looking at your own inner beauty, ease of being yourself, and presence under pressure. Someone is being mean to you under the guise of beauty. Mental-Spiritual: You're focusing on intuition, transformation, ugly duckling to swan, and knowledge of the future.

swim: Physical: You want greater fluidity and less resistance in the way you move through life. Emotional: You're involved in a psychological growth process or therapy. You need emotional support. Swimming underwater easily means you're submerged in your feelings, processing deep issues you haven't been willing to face. Drowning means you feel overwhelmed by repressed emotions. Mental-Spiritual: Swimming represents movement of your awareness between realms as you explore unconscious and subconscious issues. Ecstatic feelings while swimming indicate you're flowing through higher spiritual realms. *(see pool, ocean)*

sword: *(see knife, cut)*

T

tail: Physical: You're focusing on maintaining balance, remembering something from your past, or waiting for someone or something to catch up with you. You're looking at basic vitality, male sexuality, and sexual needs. A situation is dragging out, taking too long. Emotional: A wagging tail means happiness and excitement. A curly tail means mischievous, sometimes lustful, feelings. A switching tail means you feel annoyance, irritation, or occasionally, pleasure. "Hightailing it" means you're moving rapidly, suddenly or high-spiritedly. To "turn tail" or leave with your "tail between your legs" means you're humiliated, defeated, or frightened and want to flee from difficulty. Mental-Spiritual: You're focusing on instinct and urges. Holding the tail of an animal means you're following your gut instinct. Cutting off a tail "curtails" access to the wisdom of the body and earth.

tattoo: Physical: You're focusing on your individuality and what makes you unique. You want recognition for being different from the ordinary crowd and known for certain qualities: audacious, sensitive, artistic, strong, dangerous, or spiritual, for example. You're focusing on the power of identifying with a symbol, or even a collage of images, to help you become what is symbolized. Emotional: You're gathering courage to do something you've been afraid to try. You feel vulnerable and want protection. You want others to know your story and who you are down deep. You feel isolated and want to be part of a tribal consciousness. You're acting tough and stoic as a way to convince yourself to be more authentic. Mental-Spiritual: You're going through an initiation period, getting ready to begin a new phase. You're remembering other lifetimes when you experienced belonging to a like-minded, spiritually coherent group.

taxes: Physical: You're balancing out what you give and what you receive, looking at the price you pay for your lifestyle, or acknowledging that you must pay for past actions. Emotional: You feel guilty, or you owe a debt to someone or society. You feel unfairly dominated by an all-powerful authority or have lost your self-directedness. Mental-Spiritual: Refusing to pay taxes means you're a nonconformist or rebelling against societal mores and collective beliefs. You're examining your karma.

teacher: (*see authority*)

teeth: Physical: You're grinding your teeth, or there's a potential tooth problem. You're examining the subtle balances in your body and life that maintain health. You're focusing on confidence, competence, assertiveness, aggression, and your ability to cut through or bite through tough or confusing situations. You're looking at your ability to engage and accomplish things: "I can sink my teeth into it" or "I've bitten off more than I can chew." Loose teeth or losing your teeth indicates you're losing power, courage, your grasp on a situation, or the ability to succeed. A gleaming white movie-star smile indicates you're putting on a show, or someone is too seductive. Emotional: You're self-conscious about your appearance and self-worth. Losing teeth means you fear looking foolish, being embarrassed, unattractive, getting older or impotent, or you refuse to face reality and are retreating to infancy. You've lost self-respect. Biting or being bitten means you feel angry and defensive. Mental-Spiritual: You're looking at how you articulate and express yourself. Rotten, yellow, or decaying teeth link to lies, insincerity, lack of character, and untrustworthiness. Swallowing a tooth means you may have to "eat your words."

telephone/smartphone: Physical: You're focusing on establishing and maintaining connections, having a better social life, or being popular. Emotional: You're looking at your dependence on and possible addiction to your phone. Losing your phone means you've lost touch with your true feelings or inner self and need to feel who you are without external validation and how capable you are of being alone. If the phone is ringing constantly, you need more quiet integration-meditation time. Mental-Spiritual: You're looking at the balance between extraversion and introversion in yourself. You're working with a soul group or collective consciousness. You're developing telepathy and clairaudience. You're accessing new insights and intuitions or setting up events for the near future.

telephone call/voicemail/text message/email: Physical: You're focusing on how you communicate, what you want to communicate, and difficulties communicating. Wrong numbers, disconnected calls, bad connections, lost numbers or addresses, and unanswered calls mean you're conflicted about saying or hearing something or that you have trouble making connections in life. A conversation with a specific person means you have an issue that needs to be discussed, or you need to understand that person. Emotional: Not answering a call or returning a message means you want to keep an emotional issue at a distance, you feel overwhelmed and unable to communicate, you feel unsupported, or you're involved in a relationship problem. Calling 9-1-1 means you urgently need support from yourself or others. Leaving a message means you need to be heard or need help. Mental-Spiritual: You're connecting telepathically with your higher self or others. You're receiving guidance and "getting the message." *(see cellular phone)*

telescope: Physical: You need to take a closer look at some situation or bring an aspect of your life into focus. Emotional: You feel anxious about the future and the potentially dangerous or negative outcome of a situation. Mental-Spiritual: You need to see things that are far off or understand the specifics of a coming process or event. Looking into space at stars and planets means you're developing intuition, clairvoyance, and precognitive abilities, as well as exploring higher realities. Your focus is too narrow; you're missing the big picture.

television/monitor: Physical: You're focusing on your inner process, the way your energy flows, and your self-image. Seeing yourself onscreen means you need to be more objective about yourself. Emotional: A monitor that freezes or blacks out means you need to drop into your feelings and break addictions to visual stimulation. Mental-Spiritual: You're examining your mind, thoughts, logic, and intuition and how you receive, integrate, and express your ideas. You're looking at your attention span and how distracted you are. You need to concentrate on one thing. You're receiving a message.

terrorism: Physical: You're frustrated with slow progress and acting impulsively to force movement or change. You need to develop more patience. You're disrespecting other people's individuality or experiencing this from others. You're attuning to a potential interruption or sabotage of something in your life. Emotional: You're upset and anxious from listening to the news or negative gossip. You're hurting others in thoughtless ways. You need to be more centered, grounded, and aware of your personal authority to choose how you want to feel. Mental-Spiritual: You're harboring violent, punishing thoughts or caught in too much ego or the idea that yours is the only way. You need to open your heart, broaden your mind, and cultivate tolerance and appreciation.

tests: Physical: Taking a test or exam means you're entering a new level of expertise, responsibility, and authority. You're ready for something new, to advance in your life. Emotional: You're focusing on anxiety about measuring up, meeting expectations, being worthy, dealing with the unknown, and succeeding. Mental-Spiritual: You're measuring your current level of expertise so you can plan your life. You're involved in a spiritual initiation, entering a new level of consciousness.

theater: (*see stage, acting*)

thermometer: Physical: You're looking at the level of your energy, motivation, or measuring how far along you are in a project or process. Emotional: You're measuring your level of self-worth or looking at the state of your emotions — whether you feel hot and passionate, angry and hostile, peaceful and affectionate, or frigid, frightened, and untrusting. Mental-Spiritual: You're examining your level of understanding, mental sophistication, clarity, truth, spiritual enlightenment, or love.

thief: Physical: Someone, something, or an aspect of your own mind is stealing or wasting your energy, time, or resources. Life is too demanding. Emotional: You feel vulnerable about your boundaries and need to take a stronger stand for yourself, or you're overstepping others' boundaries. You're too isolated and self-protective. You don't feel entitled to abundance. You're afraid of losing what you have. You feel limited or unworthy or that there's an unfair distribution of benefits. You feel envious of others' good fortune. You feel disrespected, manipulated, violated, invalidated, taken advantage of, and undervalued. Mental-Spiritual: An idea or issue in your subconscious is pushing into your awareness. You must re-own a part of yourself you've judged as negative. *(see cheat, criminal)*

throat: *(see neck, strangle)*

ticket: Physical: You're focusing on new goals or a new beginning or direction. Whether it's a ticket for a movie, concert, plane, train, bus, lottery, or raffle, you have permission to enter a new place or experience, travel wherever you want, see what you need to see, or win a prize. You're looking at the price you pay to get ahead and what you've earned. Emotional: A lost ticket means you feel like an outsider or that you won't be able to have or experience something you want. You feel confused or frustrated about making progress. Mental-Spiritual: You're examining your beliefs about what you deserve and are entitled to. You are about to experience a higher level of awareness. *(see keys)*

toad: Physical: You're focusing on new growth opportunities and the process of transformation — of balancing practical everyday life with mystical insights. You're trying to see the magic in changes that have happened to you. You're sensing how luck and even money are coming to you. Emotional: You may be focusing on the negative or superstitious side of this animal — that it's about ugliness, toxicity, associations with sorcery and bad luck, or evil. Mental-Spiritual: You're focusing on the power of spiritual awakening, of fertility, protection, healing, and prosperity. You're seeing the gifts in something that seems unattractive or negative.

toilet: Physical: You need to cleanse your system of toxins and take more care with your hygiene. You're losing money through inattention or carelessness, impulsive action, scams, or fraud. You're giving yourself a wake-up call concerning self-care and bad habits. A blocked toilet means you're forcing yourself to face past acts that are fear-based, unforgiven, or deeply uncomfortable. Emotional: Constipation while on a toilet represents holding back emotion and self-expression or even a tendency to control and hoard, while diarrhea connotes a lack of emotional control, a deep need to reveal feelings, release something that doesn't nurture you, or an urgency to move on with a process you're involved in. Mental-Spiritual: You need privacy and space to find peace and clarity. You're caught in overwhelm, needing to sort out what's important from what's distracting. Difficulty finding a toilet means you need an immediate shift or sense of relief for a situation you've been tolerating. You want to feel lighter, cleaner, and in balance without needing more or less.

tongue: Physical: You're hungry or sexual. You're focusing on how you communicate and use speech. You're lying, joking, criticizing, being charming, or are speaking with a "forked tongue," "tongue in cheek," or giving someone a "tongue-lashing." A wagging, loose tongue means you're gossiping, talking too much, or being talked about. Emotional: Having to bite or hold your tongue means you feel silenced, judged, and limited in your self-expression. Ripping someone's tongue out means you're extremely angry with something the person has said. Sticking your tongue out at someone means you're skeptical or taunting them. Mental-Spiritual: Having your tongue cut out indicates you need to be silent and listen, watch what thoughts you've been voicing, and find new ways to express yourself. *(see mouth)*

tornado: *(see hurricane)*

tower: Physical: You're focusing on individuality and the need to isolate yourself to discover who you are. Being in an ivory tower means you're separated or insulated from ordinary life and its problems. Coming down from a tower means you're rejoining the world and becoming accessible. You're focusing on male sexuality. Emotional: You need to be a tower of strength for someone or need unconditional support yourself. You feel you're being punished and ostracized. Mental-Spiritual: You're too aloof and cerebral and need to balance yourself with more sensitivity. You have high hopes or you feel superior to others. You need to obtain a higher worldview or broader perspective about a situation.

traffic: Physical: Traffic on streets, at airports, in hallways, or on sidewalks means you're crowded, overwhelmed, and confused and need time and space to yourself. Emotional: A traffic jam means you feel blocked and frustrated at not being able to move as fast as you want. You need to develop patience and tolerance for people's differences. You feel minimized, unimportant, and helpless. Mental-Spiritual: You're mindless and need to be more conscious. You're part of a collective consciousness going the same direction, or in many directions simultaneously. You need to be in the moment, have faith that everything is in order, and that you'll reach your destination just when you need to be there.

train: Physical: You're focusing on "staying on track" in your life. You're headed in a specific direction toward goals, social and work-related, shared with others. Missing a train means a missed opportunity. A train wreck means you're encountering an unexpected obstacle that seriously disrupts your progress and throws your life into chaos. Emotional: You feel you're conforming and not being original enough. A train going through a tunnel indicates you're experiencing a life lesson you can't avoid. A freight train means you're carrying burdens and problems. Mental-Spiritual: You need to think in an orderly, sequential way with a clear "train of thought." You're focusing on the momentum and speed of your life's evolution. A derailed train means you've gotten off track and need to realign with your life purpose.

transgender: Physical: You're looking at the experience of gender identity not conforming to societal beliefs about being exclusively male or female. You're focusing on different blends of gender identity and sexuality, from being two genders to no gender. Emotional: You're focusing on the emotional shifts, freedom, or feedback from others that atypical gender identity elicits. Mental-Spiritual: You're contemplating the sense of spiritual truth about souls not being limited to one gender or any gender. You feel "between worlds" and may act as a bridging spiritual teacher or messenger.

treadmill: Physical: You need more exercise or to improve your circulation. You're experiencing a lack of progress and you aren't going anywhere despite hard work. Something or someone is holding up a flow causing you to have to wait. You need freedom and expansion. Emotional: You're experiencing a series of relationships where the same problems repeat. You feel hopeless or depressed because you aren't making enough progress psychologically. Mental-Spiritual: You're bored and think life has become monotonous. You're caught in deeply ingrained habits or beliefs that you would like to break free from. You need a greater variety of ideas. If you're multitasking while on a treadmill, you're focusing on the need to pay attention to the moment, meditate, silence your mind, and find guidance and inspiration within.

treasure/inheritance: Physical: Finding treasure or a treasure chest means you're discovering hidden skills, talents, and opportunities or that help is coming. You're entering a period of materialistic gain and bound for success. Receiving an inheritance means you're integrating all your past talents, experiences, and luck so you feel empowered to create and do more in your life. Emotional: You need to feel more worthy and gifted. You're avoiding applying yourself and want rewards without having earned them. Losing treasure means a downturn in your luck, a loss of friends, or a period of introspection. Mental-Spiritual: An inheritance indicates you're making a leap in your spiritual growth, and you benefit from the work and experience of your family lineage. Life has more meaning and is richer.

tree: Physical: You're focusing on the power of your personal growth, individuality, and stability. A tall, healthy tree means a flourishing, vibrant life. A newly leafing or blossoming tree means your self-expression is entering a new creative phase. A thick trunk means you're strong and rugged, while a thin, narrow trunk means you're more sensitive and flexible. Climbing a tree means you're achieving your goals and reaching higher positions at work and in society. Emotional: Trees with many connecting branches mean you want to know your family lineage or have a family of your own. A withered tree means you need to activate your feelings and loosen up. A diseased tree means you're out of balance and need nurturing and healing. Cutting down a tree means you're sabotaging your own life and, in effect, killing yourself. A fallen tree means a sacrifice. Mental-Spiritual: Magnificent old grandfather and grandmother trees mean you're attuning to ancient wisdom, the divine, and the "tree of life."

trial: (*see judge*)

triangle: Physical: You're focusing on personal harmony and easy flow of self-expressive energy. You need to talk, laugh, sing, write, perform, or be more social. Emotional: You're involved in a relationship or love triangle and are dealing with emotions like jealousy, worry, rejection, excitement, overwhelm, or rejection. You're focusing on balancing and integrating your body, emotions, mind, and spirit. Mental-Spiritual: A triangle pointing up means you're aspiring to truth, spiritual knowledge, inner knowing, and evolution. A triangle pointing down means you're focusing on trusting your body, feminine awareness, the earth, and incarnation or involution.

trumpet: Physical: You're announcing your intentions: to achieve something, to be interested in something, to move forward, or to change. You're spreading the news, teaching, promoting, or you need to send your messages and creations into the world. You're preparing to lead a charge and are rallying people to your cause. Emotional: You want people to know you've arrived. You want to get attention and be recognized. Mental-Spiritual: Hearing a trumpet indicates you need to pay attention to something coming from your subconscious mind or soul, or from life.

tumor: Physical: You need to pay attention to your body's energy flow, circulation, and elimination; you may have areas that are clogged or blocked. You're focusing on a subtle buildup of energy or a bottleneck that's causing a slowdown in your progress or on a project. Emotional: You're encapsulating some repressed memories or emotions, making them more conscious so you can see and clear them. You're holding back or suppressing your feelings to the point where they dam up and cause trouble in other areas of your life. The location of the tumor gives insight to the feelings that are emerging. Mental-Spiritual: Your ideas, beliefs, and worldview are too constricted; you're due for a review of what's important *now* and a purge of those things that once were useful but are now acting as blockages.

tunnel: Physical: You're making a transition from one phase of life to another, involving a period of restriction from which you cannot escape. The period of concentration or difficulty must be lived through and learned from until you naturally come out the other side. You're focusing on female sexuality and birth. Emotional: You need security and nurturing. You feel anxiety about being in limbo, where unknown, clandestine things can happen. Exiting a tunnel means you're coming out of depression or a time of anxiety. You feel blind and punished. Mental-Spiritual: You have a limited perspective and are exploring and living out issues in your subconscious. Seeing light at the end of a tunnel means hope, and a new phase of life with new awareness is just ahead.

turkey: Physical: You're focusing on the cycle of giving and receiving, being generous, sharing yourself with others, and counting your blessings. You're looking at the ideals of family, tradition, or sacrificing your time or part of yourself for someone else. A flock of turkeys means recognition, honor, or a rise to prominence. Shooting a turkey means you're trying to acquire wealth in an underhanded way. Hearing gobbling means you're gossiping or being talked about by insincere friends. Emotional: You need to be more humble and not so prideful, or you need more self-esteem. Mental-Spiritual: You're being silly or not thinking clearly. Native Americans connect turkeys with luck, wisdom, and spiritual vision and use turkey feathers in cleansing rituals.

turtle: Physical: You have been indoors too long. You're focusing on feminine energy, the womb, fertility, conception, and pregnancy. You want good luck, good health, and longevity. You need to learn to be at home anywhere and find new opportunities wherever you are. You need to reconnect to center, be grounded, and balance the physical, emotional, and spiritual energies in yourself. You're going through a slow phase, need to slow down, or resist change just because you're bored. Emotional: You need to be patient, persistent, have good personal boundaries, respect others' boundaries, and be more self-reliant and nonviolent. You can be too sensitive, withdrawn, uncomfortable in insecure settings, or perceive danger too quickly. You need to come out of your shell, stop hiding, show your true self, and be more involved and vulnerable with others. You need to go inside yourself and honor your feelings. Mental-Spiritual: You're focusing on Mother Earth, the divine feminine and goddess energy, and ancient wisdom. You need mental and psychic protection by being centered and fully present and by focusing and meditating on what's true and real.

twins: Physical: You're focusing on accessing a hidden part of yourself that you buried or are alienated from and that contains "half" of your potential. You want a soulmate partner. Emotional: You feel split or ambivalent about an issue or are in conflict with someone who represents an unacknowledged part of yourself. Mental-Spiritual: You're balancing and integrating your yin and yang energies, your light and dark selves, or your conscious and subconscious minds. You're focusing on merging with your light body or soul. You're learning to see yourself in others.

U

UFO/spaceship: Physical: You're focusing on the sudden appearance of something or someone. You need to change direction suddenly and have no limits on what you consider possible. You're exploring a new situation that's unlike anything you've ever seen before. There are more advanced possibilities for you. Emotional: You feel alienated from others. You're too "spacey" and need to come back down to earth. You're involved in a relationship with someone you think is out of this world. You want to be whisked away from suffering or the mundane, or you want to feel special. Mental-Spiritual: You're an independent, imaginative, and creative thinker. You need a different, perhaps unusual, perspective to transcend circumstances and explore new, creative solutions. You want to connect with other worlds, find higher knowledge, and spiritual purpose. Your consciousness is moving up into the highest realms of the collective consciousness, contacting spiritual guides. *(see aliens)*

umbrella: Physical: You need to protect your finances and save for a rainy day. If you're carrying an umbrella, you're focusing on being prepared, safe, and lucky. Emotional: You're putting up a shield against worries and negative emotions or developing strategies to avoid upsets. Closing an umbrella means you're ready to face emotional issues and needs. A broken umbrella, one that won't open, or one that's turned inside out means you feel overexposed to the world and unprepared to face your problems. Inviting someone to walk under an umbrella with you means you want greater generosity, intimacy, and trust in relationships. Mental-Spiritual: There's a barrier between you and higher information. You're unifying ideas or components of yourself or your work under a common theme.

underground: Physical: You need to focus on your body's inner dynamics. You're working with your deeper senses like hearing, touch, and smell. Emotional: You're dealing with subconscious issues or painful emotions that are hidden or repressed. You want greater security, inner peace, and quiet. Mental-Spiritual: You're discovering ancient secrets and knowledge, especially pertaining to feminine energy. *(see cave, subway, tunnel)*

underwear: Physical: Something you normally keep hidden is being revealed, or layers are being peeled away concerning some person or issue so you can see what's true. You're focusing on privacy, modesty, honesty, or being exposed. You're experiencing a loss of respect or reputation. You're exploring erotic images and memories. Emotional: Being in your underwear in public indicates you feel vulnerable, embarrassed, or ashamed, or you're hesitating to reveal true feelings, attitudes, actions, or habits. You're taking an emotional risk. You're experiencing unwanted intimacy or emotional neediness. Mental-Spiritual: You're getting down to the essence of an issue, overcoming distractions and illusions.

unicorn: Physical: You want to experience more magic in life. You're focusing on the qualities of solitude, privacy, beauty, that which is unattainable, purity, healing, wisdom, and renewal. You're looking at being able to fight fiercely while also maintaining harmony and gentleness. <u>Emotional</u>: You need to let loose and welcome synchronicity and miracles. You need to focus on innocence, sweetness, and your right to freedom. <u>Mental-Spiritual</u>: You're linking the physical and spiritual realms. You have high ideals, hope, and insight into a current situation. You're opening your imagination, intuition, and clairvoyance. The horn means you're safe from all incurable diseases and poisons.

uniform: <u>Physical</u>: You're questioning your identity, the roles you play, and the specific kind of authority and power you have. You're focusing on the façade, or layer, you put between yourself and others, how you portray yourself, and how you want to feel personally. You've lost some individuality by being part of a group. <u>Emotional</u>: You feel anxious about having to conform to others' expectations to gain approval. You feel trapped by your duties to others and living in an overly regimented way. You can be deceived by appearances. You feel rebellious and antisocial, and it's getting in your way; you need to relax and join in with others for a purpose. You yearn to be part of a group that feels like family. Having a defined role allows you to relax, at least for now. <u>Mental-Spiritual</u>: You're focusing on thinking for yourself and being authentic. You need to develop greater depth of perception to see beyond surface behaviors. You're examining beliefs about how you express yourself, what you need to do to receive approval, and how vulnerable you can be.

university: <u>Physical</u>: You're focusing on what you can be and learning, especially a specific skill or body of knowledge. Now is a good time to try new things, experiment, and pay attention to new information and points of view. <u>Emotional</u>: You have performance anxiety, are afraid of failing, and are under stress to "graduate" or make the grade. Or you're excited to be on your own, experiencing independence and your own choices and motives. You're remembering your college years and how they affected your emotional makeup. <u>Mental-Spiritual</u>: You're learning about yourself and improving your life. You're going through social or cultural changes. You're examining how you learn, expanding your knowledge into more sophisticated levels. You're exploring higher realms, bringing knowledge back to your daily life from the collective consciousness. You're learning a spiritual lesson.

unravel: <u>Physical</u>: Something unraveling means you need to untangle the variables in a snagged situation, in your own way of living, or in a large mystery that has captured your attention.

You're slowly unwinding complexities. Emotional: You feel you're "coming apart at the seams," that your familiar social façade isn't working anymore, and your survival techniques are falling flat. You may feel you're a victim, that life is against you, that you've lost your self-worth, sense of purpose, and connection to love and creativity. Mental-Spiritual: You're living through a powerful time of transformation. You're on a journey to truth, a spiritual path filled with detaching, dissolving, and untwisting old concepts of life and self to experience the beauty, belonging, freedom, and power to be whatever you want — that exists, simply, everywhere and in everything.

upside down: Physical: You feel disoriented, as though you and the world occupy differing realities that are 180 degrees apart. You feel dizzy and need to find balance. You're experiencing chaos or dramatic change in your life. Emotional: You feel uncertain, directionless, even a little bit "crazy" and out of control. You feel like you don't fit in and are drawn to unconventional ways of being. Mental-Spiritual: You want to challenge conventional thinking and perception. You need to reconsider your understanding of a situation. If you see someone else upside down, look for how their perception is opposite from yours and possibly insightful. If you're floating and turning upside down, you're moving in and out of the spiritual realm. You're opening to personal transformation, finding a totally new sense of self.

urinate: Physical: You're releasing energy, toxins, and impurities. You're getting rid of an unwanted situation. You're involved in a territorial dispute or need to assert dominance. Emotional: You're afraid of an uncontrolled release of emotion that might prove embarrassing. You're angry (pissed off) or want someone to go away (piss off). Someone urinating in your space means you feel invaded, intimidated, violated, or even threatened sexually if there's exposure of the genitals. You feel put down or fouled, as though someone is "pissing on" your work or character. Mental-Spiritual: You're experiencing a release of tension and worry. Ideas that have served their purpose need to be eliminated.

urn: Physical: Urns can represent personalities, open and waiting to be filled with life experience and wisdom. You're remembering precious memories and shared experiences with loved ones. You're connecting with someone who has died. You're focusing on the feminine side of your being and on keeping things safe, cherished, and nurtured. Emotional: You're focusing on loss, especially of someone, or a loving pet, who has died. You need to pay attention to the valuable, timeless, beautiful things and experiences of your life — things you wish to endure and become permanent parts of your being. Mental-Spiritual: Ashes in an urn speak of transformation; your past has been released, and you have risen from the ashes anew, like the phoenix.

U-turn: Physical: You're breaking habits and starting a new regimen. You're altering the course of your life, changing directions, and beginning a different path. You have passed the point of no return and must continue on the path you chose. Emotional: You feel ambivalent about your life and are subject to vacillating emotions. You're afraid of missing out if you take only one direction. Mental-Spiritual: You need to refocus or change your way of thinking. You realize you forgot something or made a wrong decision and are remedying it. Seeing a "No U-turn" sign means you cannot take back what has been said or done. You're focusing on being fully present in the now.

V

vacation/resort/spa: Physical: You need a break from your daily routine to do something different and recharge yourself. You need to acknowledge the good work you've done and reward yourself. You need to lose weight, get some bodywork, and improve your diet. Emotional: You need to feel there is joy to be had in all things. You're being too dutiful or too escapist, feeling you must please others or rebelling against authority. Mental-Spiritual: You're examining how you lose energy and enthusiasm. You're focusing on how relaxing the present moment is — that resting in your true self is the best vacation of all.

vacuum: Physical: Vacuuming a room means you're cleansing your body of impurities. You're too overwhelmed and need to be empty and still, as though in a vacuum, to regather your energy. You're experiencing a void, waiting for the next phase of life to unfold. Emotional: You feel isolated, empty, depressed, or in panic. You need to clean up your act and rid yourself of negative emotions and habits. You feel sucked in by, or helpless to resist, someone's drama and neediness. Mental-Spiritual: You need to suspend your inner chatter, enter a deep meditative state, and experience what's beyond form and the mind. A higher part of you is calling you out and up to receive guidance.

valley: Physical: You've finished a cycle of creativity, and you're preparing for a new one. You're exploring the highs and lows in life. Being in a valley means you're at a low point, which can be a peaceful, restful, regenerating paradise or intimidating as you look for a pathway out. You're focusing on female sexuality. Emotional: You want to feel sheltered and protected. Entering a valley that connects to ideas of dying or an end to something, brings up anxiety and sorrow. You feel gloomy and troubled about problems, losses, setbacks, or disappointments. You feel blind. Mental-Spiritual: You're focusing on being in your lifetime, versus being in spirit, and the containment of being physical. You need to relax and allow yourself to be taken care of by higher forces.

vampire: Physical: You're drained and exhausted by events or people. Others are taking from you without giving back, or you aren't noticing what you're receiving. Someone is invading your space or trying to make you do something against your better judgment. Emotional: You're acting like a victim, giving your power away to charming seducers, or dealing with people who feel victimized or are addicts. You're obsessing about something. You greedily want someone else's energy or success. You feel anxious about being sexually pressured, losing your virginity, or making an unhealthy commitment that traps you. You're facing dark, repressed emotions and desires. Mental-Spiritual: You're looking at the contrast between being civilized and noble and being ferocious and without morals.

vehicle: Physical: You're examining how you focus yourself in, and move through, different realms of consciousness. A car, bicycle, motorcycle, or train symbolizes your physical body, personality, or life. Elevators and stairs symbolize moving between realms. Driving the vehicle means you're controlling your journey and choosing your direction. Emotional: Boats or other water vehicles symbolize how you traverse the emotional realm. Being a rider in a vehicle means you've given your power to another and are being passive. Mental-Spiritual: Airplanes, hang gliders, rockets, or UFOs symbolize how you move through the mental and spiritual realms. Cotravelers mean you're part of a group consciousness where people share a similar path and life lesson. A stolen vehicle means you've lost your connection to a particular reality or focus and need to put attention on recreating it.

veil: (*see hood*)

vein: (*see artery*)

violin: Physical: Hearing a violin means you're balancing the energy in your body, tuning up to a higher way of functioning. You're focusing on peace, beauty, and harmony. Fiddle music means you need to have more fun and move spontaneously. Emotional: Hearing a violin means you're focusing on emotions like yearning, sadness, bereavement, passion, or angst. You're accessing emotions and memories from your subconscious. You hunger for romance — to make "beautiful music with" someone. Playing a violin means you're attuning to feelings of nobility, refinement, and uplift. Mental-Spiritual: You're focusing on hopes and dreams. Hearing a violin means you're connecting to deep states of timeless love and compassion. You're moving into higher realms of devotion and inspired creativity.

visitor/visitation: Physical: To have a visitor means that news or information is coming to you. You're focusing on beginning a new relationship. You're accessing parts of yourself that haven't become normal yet. Emotional: Being a visitor means you need to feel that you're welcome and belong. You want to feel like family with others and integrate the moods and feelings of different places into your makeup. Mental-Spiritual: You're connecting with nonphysical beings, like people who have died or spiritual guides. You're receiving an important message from higher dimensions. If you know the visitor, you're focusing on integrating the quality you associate with them into yourself. *(see stranger)*

vitamins: Physical: Taking vitamins means you're attuning to your body's actual nutritional needs. You're focusing on strengthening yourself and your self-expression in an area of your life. Emotional: You feel drained emotionally and need to feel cared for, included, and that you're entitled to be happy and successful. Mental-Spiritual: You're examining your ideas about natural, preventative healing versus traditional medicine. You're focusing on the ideas and insights you need for a new phase of creativity and expanded self-expression.

voice/voices: Physical: You need to speak your truth. You're focusing on how you express yourself and what your message is. Emotional: Your subconscious is contacting you, bringing forth important feelings, or you feel fragmented, neurotic, and paranoid. You need to pay attention to inner needs. Mental-Spiritual: Hearing a literal voice speaking to you means an important message is coming from your soul or spiritual guides. You might hear a single word, a phrase, an entire message, or even detailed instructions. If the voice belongs to someone you know, you may be receiving a telepathic call for help or important information you should act on in waking life.

voice mail: (*see telephone calls*)

volcano/lava: Physical: You're focusing on tension in yourself or in a relationship that has built to the breaking point. You need to relax and let off steam. You're experiencing pressure or an unavoidable crisis or challenge. Emotional: You feel extremely frustrated or angry and need to be careful not to explode violently. You're dealing with someone who has an explosive temper. Lava means you need to express your pent-up feelings. Mental-Spiritual: Your mind is inspired and intensely creative, spewing forth ideas rapidly and in no particular order. New ideas from the depths of your soul and subconscious are surfacing.

vomit: Physical: You need to purge yourself of something that is toxic or unhealthy for you. There's a person or situation you can't stomach and that isn't nurturing. Emotional: You need to reject or discard an aspect of your life that is revolting. You refuse to accept a situation, change, or relationship. Mental-Spiritual: You recognize and reject what is untrue or doesn't align with your life purpose.

vote: Physical: You need to speak your mind, express yourself authentically, and share yourself with others. Voting for an unpopular choice where others know your position means you need to stand up to judgment. Emotional: You're too passive and apathetic. You want to belong to and contribute to the functioning of a group. You need recognition, conviction, courage, and passion. Mental-Spiritual: You're too opinionated, or you need to examine issues open-mindedly, clarify your positions, and take a stand for what you believe. You're highlighting what you want in your life.

vow: Physical: You're focusing on keeping your word and following through. You need to make a commitment. Emotional: You're afraid of letting others down or being weak and unprincipled. Mental-Spiritual: You're examining your behavior and habits and where you fall short of doing your best. You're realigning with your destiny and intending to live as your soul.

vulture: Physical: You're focusing on the approaching death of a part of your life, the need to eliminate dead or unwanted parts of your personality, or to recycle old aspects of yourself for new uses. Aggressive, opportunistic people are hanging around waiting to feed off your creations, and you must vigilantly chase them away. You need to be a hardy survivor. Emotional: You feel lonely, ugly, unloved, discriminated against, and misunderstood. You need to watch your tendency to be greedy or gluttonous. You feel you're getting the dregs and leftovers, scrounging for nourishment and recognition. You need to face something in your own underworld. Mental-Spiritual: You're disrespecting or judging others to feed your ego. You're receiving a warning about the death of someone, the failure of something, or a disaster.

W

waiter/waitress: Physical: You're focusing on catering to the demands of others. You need to notice the people who are helping and serving you. Emotional: You need to develop more gratitude, humility, patience, and tolerance. A surly, unconscious, inattentive waiter means you feel unsupported by friends or colleagues. You feel used and unappreciated. Mental-Spiritual: You need to focus on the true purpose of service, and how you receive as you give. You're overcoming your ego, practicing the Golden Rule.

wall: Physical: You're encountering obstacles, barriers, and boundaries to your progress. Jumping over or breaking down a wall means you can overcome difficulties and succeed. You need to stop, pay attention to your path, and possibly shift your direction. Emotional: Building a wall means you need more privacy and introspection, or you're protecting yourself from danger or from people you don't like. You're stubbornly refusing to move forward or express your feelings. Mental-Spiritual: A hole in a wall means you can see through a limited way of thinking, old habits, and resistance. You're becoming aware of the boundaries and transitions between possible realities. Walking through a wall means you can use your intuition, faith, and positive attitude to turn obstacles into opportunities.

wallet/purse: Physical: You're focusing on your personal identity, financial resources, and the things you consider necessary for survival in the world. Emotional: Losing a purse or wallet means you aren't paying attention to what's valuable, or you're too attached to security, definitions, and habits. <u>Mental-Spiritual</u>: Losing your wallet means you need to let go of an aspect of your identity and refocus on who you really are underneath.

war: <u>Physical</u>: You're being affected by actual current events. You're focusing on chaos, disorder, and conflict in your personal life or business. Someone has attacked you, challenged your authority, or manipulated you, or you've done this to someone. <u>Emotional</u>: You're being too assertive or not aggressive enough. You feel reactionary, rebellious, defensive, desperate, angry, self-righteous, or frightened of losing control. You feel torn between several choices. <u>Mental-Spiritual</u>: You're caught in a struggle between wants and shoulds — between the instinctive forces of your subconscious and the rules held by your conscious mind. You're trying to understand two opposing points of view or are caught in a battle of wills.

warehouse: <u>Physical</u>: You're focusing on the energy and reserves you have stored in your body. You need to either use some of what you've been holding onto or renew your supply through rest and self-care. You're looking at hidden resources or talents you didn't know you had. You're putting plans on hold, waiting for something to happen before you act. <u>Emotional</u>: You're hoarding what you consider valuable and need to focus on being generous and releasing or distributing the "goods." <u>Mental-Spiritual</u>: You're examining memories stored in your subconscious mind. You need to sort through old ideas and habits, get rid of what's outdated, and express yourself more.

wash: <u>Physical</u>: You're cleansing and purifying part of yourself. Washing your hands means you're releasing yourself from a relationship. Washing anything — a car, clothes, vegetables, or your face — means you want that thing, and what it represents, to function optimally, like new. <u>Emotional</u>: You're tending to your ordinary world with kindness and respect. Trying to get a stain out means you feel guilt or shame. <u>Mental-Spiritual</u>: Washing yourself ritually, as in a river or fountain, means you're cleansing yourself of sin, inviting forgiveness.

watch: (*see clock*)

watching: <u>Physical</u>: You need to be more mindful and alert and notice what you're noticing. Each thing you "see" has deeper meaning — a message to you from your inner self. You're trying to monitor your behavior, bad habits, self-destructive behaviors, and resolutions to stay true to your decision to improve. Emotional: If you're being watched, you're receiving the attention you need to feel better about yourself. You're looking at past shameful behavior and criticizing and judging yourself. If someone you know is watching you, you might take it as a sign to be more alert to *their* behavior. You feel slightly paranoid or self-conscious, knowing that your negative, judgmental, or envious feelings can be felt at some level by others. You fear retaliation or invasion. Mental-Spiritual: You're practicing mindfulness by observing life neutrally and merging with what you notice. You're in the protective gaze of a guide, angel, or divine being. You're never alone because you're connected by consciousness to all beings and forms of life.

water: Physical: You need to cleanse yourself. You're focusing on sexuality and letting go. "Getting your feet wet" means you're willing to try something new. Emotional: You're focusing on emotions and the subconscious mind. Cloudy, murky water means emotional confusion. Floods, tidal waves, and turbulent water mean you feel overwhelmed, threatened, and chaotic, while drought indicates being out of touch with inner juiciness and feelings. Frozen or evaporating water indicates emotional paralysis or volatility. The power to control water means you're working on controlling emotional outbursts. Mental-Spiritual: Clean water means good sense and clarity. Smoothly flowing water means contentment and peace of mind. Diving into deep water means you're exploring unknown areas of the self. Wading in shallow water indicates a cautious attitude. Breathing underwater means you're open to the collective consciousness and intuitive awareness. Walking on water means you have control over emotions and doubt through faith in yourself and the divine.

weapon: Physical: You're focusing on the need to defend yourself or an endeavor from danger. You're caught in an external or internal conflict, looking at rash ways to end it. You're looking at aggressive, dominating sexuality or behavior. Someone is threatening you. Emotional: You're facing feelings of disrespect, greed, vengeance, or hatred. Using a destructive weapon against someone or something means you have anger and resentment toward them or the part of yourself they represent. You feel powerless and insecure and want to feel important. You're taking advantage of someone or being victimized yourself. You're looking at the need to protect yourself and others. <u>Mental–Spiritual</u>: You're caught in offensive/defensive ideas and strategies to preserve your point of view. You're focused on your ego and need to shift into your heart to find a better path of action.

weasel: <u>Physical</u>: You're focusing on physical fluidity, agility, adaptability, playfulness, and maneuverability. You're examining the dynamics of someone who is clever, sly, stealthy, and sneaky and who is bringing chaos and confusion into your life. You're dealing with hyperactivity and being too keyed up. You need to stay calm. You're caught in intrigue or the use of covert tactics. <u>Emotional</u>: Your emotions are changing rapidly, often without consideration for your impact on others. You've been tricking yourself or lying to others. <u>Mental–Spiritual</u>: Your thoughts and point of view are waffling among a variety of positions. You're realizing how resourceful you are and how well you overcome challenges to succeed. You're focusing on waking up fully and activating deep powers of observation and ingenuity.

weave: <u>Physical</u>: You're making something out of nothing. You're integrating diverse elements to produce beautiful and useful results. You're creating greater strength from the marrying of weaker elements. <u>Emotional</u>: You feel you're coming apart or unraveling. You need to be patient throughout a growth process or transition. You're becoming comfortable with diverse aspects of yourself. <u>Mental–Spiritual</u>: You're exploring ideas like the whole is greater than the sum of its parts, it's important to see the big picture, and complexity contains components that work together in harmony. You're piecing together information or an explanation.

website: <u>Physical</u>: You're focusing on who you are and what you truly want to do. You're looking at who someone else is and if they're talented and trustworthy and fit well with your needs. <u>Emotional</u>: You're allowing yourself to be seen by strangers. You're being careful about how you portray yourself to others because you want to be liked. You're looking at how you judge yourself and others and how you have been judged. <u>Mental–Spiritual</u>: You're determining how vulnerable to be, how much to reveal about yourself, and how others might respond. You're focusing on the logical, left-brain view of yourself with an eye toward financial and career success. You're looking at becoming more of your true self with the help of others.

wedding: Physical: You're thinking about marriage or divorce. You're at a new beginning or transition. You're unifying or balancing two parts of yourself, like the anima and animus, the physical and spiritual, or the internal and external. Emotional: You're examining your anxiety about commitment and independence, loneliness and loss of self-expression. Being at a friend's wedding means you feel left out, left behind, or need to commit to something in your own life. Mental-Spiritual: You're giving yourself important data about how you connect with people and examining the meaning of ceremony. You're opening and expanding your heart. *(see marriage)*

weeds: Physical: You're crowded with clutter and distracted by activities that aren't on purpose. You're hardy and can flourish anywhere. Emotional: You feel underappreciated, straggly, disordered, and ugly. You're neglecting part of yourself. Pulling weeds means you need to rid yourself of negativity, grudges, and relationships that have gone awry so you have space to grow. Mental-Spiritual: You're rooting out and clearing old ideas and negative thoughts from your mind. There are attitudes and beliefs that are interfering with your personal growth. You're finding beauty in the mundane.

well: Physical: You're digging down, seeking a source of energy and motivation deep within. Emotional: You're dealing with your deepest emotional patterns and source of love. The well that never runs dry indicates your inner wealth is inexhaustible. A dry well means you feel exhausted. You need to offer nurturing to others and let people gather around you and see you as a blessing. Mental-Spiritual: You're accessing the deepest recesses of the collective consciousness, from which you're drawing up knowledge, wisdom, your divine nature, and unlimited resourcefulness.

west: Physical: You're focusing on the end of a cycle or phase, on the positive side of surrender, rest, silence, darkness, and death. It's time to stop, let go, pause a moment, or complete a project you've been involved with too long. You're concerned with finality. If something "goes west," it's destroyed or lost. Emotional: You're anxious about growing old, facing things you consider evil or bad, entering the unknown, or changing. You need to be fluid, adaptable, and able to "shape-shift" easily. Mental-Spiritual: You seek self-understanding through introversion, dreams, intuition, faith, and trust. You're focusing on reaching into other dimensions and contacting nonphysical beings and spirits of the dead. You're concerned with healing the earth. You point out truths by doing things in a contrary, humorous manner.

whale: (*see dolphin*)

wheel: Physical: You're looking at cycles of growth, the "wheel of life," or the completion of a phase or a project. Your daily routine is too repetitious; you need variety and spontaneity. A turning wheel means you're progressing steadily, or you're looking at the ups and downs of life. Emotional: You feel frustrated and anxious because you're caught in a repetitive cycle going nowhere. You need to be less serious and more "freewheeling." Mental-Spiritual: You're looking at karma, reincarnation, the wheel of rebirth, and the long-term evolution of the soul. Seeing "wheels within wheels" means you're contemplating something that cannot be understood superficially. You're focusing on parallels through the microcosm and macrocosm.

wheelchair: Physical: Even if you're actually using a wheelchair, the symbol may indicate you're exhausted and need a break. You feel you need help to move forward in life right now. You need be more independent, to stand up for yourself, and stop depending on others, or you need to stop letting others push you around. Emotional: You need to come out of your shell and offer assistance to others. You're facing feelings of dependency and fear of involvement in the world. You're frustrated because you feel trapped and immobilized by a situation. Mental-Spiritual: You need to examine your beliefs about helplessness, industriousness, what you deserve, and how much you're willing to serve. You're in a process of shifting from debilitating egocentricity to moving forward under the soul's guidance.

whip: Physical: You're contemplating being controlled or controlling something through threats, domination, or punishment. You need discipline and control in your life. You need to "crack the whip," "whip up some enthusiasm," and be more motivated to produce results. You are "whipped," or exhausted. Emotional: You're lashing out at others with hurtful remarks and accusations. You feel punished or attacked. You're dealing with issues of physical, sexual, or emotional abuse. You're focusing on issues of sexual submission and having to be obedient to others. Mental-Spiritual: You're making a point, critiquing something, or developing mental prowess; you're being "smart as a whip."

whisper: Physical: You're focusing on gossip, either toward you from others or from you about others. You're allowing yourself to participate in something partially, without full understanding. Emotional: You're focusing on feelings of insecurity. You need to *want* to know what's trying to be communicated to you. If you're whispering in the dream, you want to keep something secret. Mental-Spiritual: You're hearing your inner voice — your intuition — guiding you, giving you a message or warning. You're receiving guidance from a higher spiritual source but need to pay closer attention to hear accurately.

white: Physical: You're focusing on purity, perfection, goodness, innocence, simplicity, virginity, sterility, and cleanliness. You're beginning something. You feel complete and whole. You're stuck with something that cost a lot but has no useful purpose, like a white elephant. Emotional: Being "white as a sheet" means you feel frightened or are ill. You're protecting yourself by "telling a white lie" so you don't upset someone. Mental-Spiritual: You're attuning to spiritual light, the sacred, joy, transcendence, radiance, spiritual birth, enlightenment, ecstasy, faith, and the yang side of the divine.

wig: Physical: You want to cover up the effects of an illness. You're focusing on making a good impression on others or representing yourself deceptively as someone you are not. You're activating the quality in your personality that you're role-playing with the wig. Emotional: You feel ashamed of an aspect of yourself. You're hiding feelings of inadequacy and fear of being unattractive or not powerful enough. Mental-Spiritual: You're not being true to your own beliefs. You need to start thinking for yourself. You're playing and experimenting with ideas about your identity, stretching into new possibilities. Losing a wig means you are losing your composure or "wigging out."

wind: Physical: You're focusing on your basic life force, energy, motivation, and the dynamics of how things move in your life. You're considering upcoming changes or being buffeted by troublesome change, especially if the winds are strong or stormy. Emotional: You're feeling stirred up and pushed to confront repressed, unsettling emotions. You're tired from resisting an overpowering force or from being victimized. You need to trust the "winds" to take you to the perfect next experience. Mental-Spiritual: You're being renewed. You're becoming conscious of invigorating, influential ideas or a cultural or global movement where people share an ideology. Gale force winds mean your mental structures and worldview are breaking down — that it's time to let go.

window: Physical: You're focusing on your worldview, your outlook on life, looking outside to external things, or inside to your inner self. You're looking at how much of the outer world you let in. The type of scene you see gives an indication of what's coming in your life, or what you expect. Emotional: Being outside looking in can mean you feel excluded from belonging, or you're in an introverted period. Curtains that are drawn indicate a refusal to see clearly because you're withdrawing. A broken window means greater vulnerability and contact with the world. Mental-Spiritual: Washing windows means you're clearing your perception and intuition. You need to pay attention to the moment and "a window of opportunity."

wings: Physical: You're focusing on the tension level in your shoulders and arms. You want to escape the heaviness, drudgery, and problems of daily life. You want increased freedom. Emotional: You're focusing on activating feelings of sweetness, kindness, and lightness. Mental-Spiritual: You're being visited by nonphysical relatives, spiritual guides, or angels. You need a clear, higher perspective on a situation, one that includes spiritual purposefulness. White wings mean you're focusing on the ultimate truth.

winter: Physical: You need to hibernate, be more introverted, and take some time to rest and recuperate. You're focusing on a health problem, the aging process, or other challenges that seem difficult. Emotional: You feel anxious about possible misfortune or are caught in depression, hopelessness, emotional coldness, isolation, or paralysis. You feel unloved or that you don't belong in an emotionally warm group. Mental-Spiritual: You're focusing on the need for celebration, playfulness, and having quality time with loved ones — on opening your heart, your experience of generosity, gratitude, and peace. You're reconnecting with your spiritual path.

witch: Physical: You're focusing on something that might be an ill omen or superstition. You're looking at negative ideas about women. Emotional: You're dealing with a suppressed aspect of your feminine energy that you've judged negatively and that needs to be understood. You want more magic and ease. Mental-Spiritual: You're focusing on the destructive aspect of the subconscious. You're aware of "the witching hour" when the mundane shifts to the magical reality when witches are most active or babies are most fussy. Since witches' original roles were as priestesses and representatives of inner wisdom, you're focusing on intuition and healing and connecting to a deep understanding of the universal laws.

wizard: Physical: You're focusing on attaining power and having your life move more easily and quickly through exertion of clever, tricky, secretive means. You want to be able to control a situation or are feeling controlled by others in ways that are hard to recognize. Emotional: You feel helpless, weak, or paralyzed. You want to avoid reality by experiencing more magic. Mental-Spiritual: You're looking at arrogance, too much dependence on personal willpower, and cleverness. You're addicted to fantasy. You're looking for advanced knowledge about secret things.

wolf: Physical: You're focusing on healthy family values and loyalty. A ravenous part of yourself or a life situation is devouring your energy or creativity. Something threatening is at the door. You're being too much of a "lone wolf" and need more nurturing social activity. Emotional: An innocent part of you has been seduced. You're afraid of aggressive, lustful, male sexual energy. You're afraid of your own tendencies toward self-destruction, aggression, rage, or uncontrolled sexual desire. You've been "crying wolf," and no one will help you. Mental-Spiritual: You're learning about your instinctual wildness, intuition, the seasons of life and death, and the deep wisdom of group relations. You're connecting with a spiritual guide and protective companion on your life journey.

women: Physical: Any female figure represents your anima or the way you use and understand feminine energy. You need to express more, or less, receptivity, unconditional love, appreciation, and presence. Emotional: You're facing unresolved issues with your mother or female relatives. Mental-Spiritual: How the women are dressed provides a clue about the area of your life that needs more yin energy. You're focusing on intuition, empathy, faith, and inspiration.

woodpecker: Physical: You need to be industrious and dedicated to results. You're activating qualities of dedication, diligence, consistency, and precision in your personality. Emotional: You feel attacked or pounded on by others' critical remarks or belligerent ways, or you're being this way. <u>Mental-Spiritual</u>: You're examining stubbornness, pushiness, and unrelenting attitudes. Instead of being sharp and critical, you're looking at opening your heart and speaking from your soul. The pileated or ivory-billed woodpecker means you're being open to divine inspiration and work and remaining open and loyal to the sacred.

worm: <u>Physical</u>: You're focusing on sneakiness, or something entering your life by covert, even cowardly, means. You need to be practical, down to earth, and humble. Something is decaying and on its way out of your life. You're focusing on male sexuality. <u>Emotional</u>: You feel low-down, dirty, and disgusting or downtrodden and oppressed. You've felt weak and passive but sense that it's time for "the worm to turn" — for you to take control of your life. <u>Mental-Spiritual</u>: If you have a "worm's eye view," you know or understand a small, often lowly, part of a situation. You're creating pathways through fixed beliefs systems and a dense worldview.

write: <u>Physical</u>: You're communicating to yourself about a situation in waking life. You're out of touch with a loved one and need to make contact. If "the writing is on the wall," it's evident that something is not going to succeed. <u>Emotional</u>: You're expressing or clarifying and defining your feelings and creativity. <u>Mental-Spiritual</u>: A deep part of you is sending you important guidance about life direction and personal growth. If someone else is writing, this shows an aspect of you that is seeking to express itself. *(see letter)*

X

X: <u>Physical</u>: An *x* by itself can mean you're focusing on canceling a project or event, an agreement with someone, or a mistake that needs to be made conscious and corrected. You may want to edit or "cross out" something you've written or said. As a symbol, *x* can represent a missing or mysterious element, as in "Project X", or it can serve as a signature for an illiterate person. You may be focusing on relationships and connections — for example, an "ex" partner. An *x* might mean you're focusing on a crossroads, a meeting point, or the endpoint of a treasure map (achieving a goal). <u>Emotional</u>: You're focusing on multiplying the emotional effects of something or giving an issue too much attention. You're focusing on affection (x being a placeholder for kisses). <u>Mental/Spiritual:</u> You're focusing on the unknown — to experience it or to find insight. You're focusing on the meeting and integration of heaven and earth, the spiritual and mundane. You're focusing on sacred geometry or personal transformation. In its Greek meaning as *chi*, it can indicate you're tuning in to Christ consciousness. Today, *x* is often used to show that two entities are cooperatively connecting, collaborating, and exchanging knowledge and energy, creating a synthesis experience without losing individual identity.

X-rays/X-ray vision: <u>Physical:</u> You're focusing on the inner workings of your body, scanning for things that might be out of harmony. You're penetrating into the hidden problems in your current life situations. <u>Emotional:</u> You need to look more deeply at the cause of emotional upsets. If you're being X-rayed or viewed by someone with X-ray vision, you feel vulnerable and exposed, as though your secrets are being revealed to the public. You're worried that a deception will be discovered. It's advisable to stop defending yourself. <u>Mental-Spiritual:</u> You desire greater inner knowledge, to see past surface appearances to the true nature of things. You have penetrating insight into relationships, problem-solving, and diagnosis.

Y

yardstick: <u>Physical:</u> You are focusing on how well you're performing, comparing yourself against your own or other people's standards. <u>Emotional:</u> You feel anxiety about measuring up or being exactly right. <u>Mental-Spiritual:</u> You need to soften any rigidity or unyielding qualities in yourself. You're looking for a new way to understand yourself, wanting to dissolve the usual constraints society imposes.

yarn: <u>Physical:</u> You're focusing on a problem having many strands of causality — factors that weave together into a complex situation. You're following a thread from a current situation to related situations in the past and future. You're weaving a large pattern, creating your life work, from the streaming flow of your talent. <u>Emotional:</u> A ball of yarn coming unwound means you feel you're falling apart, losing your center, or following leads to the very core of a matter or emotional issue. Tangled yarn means your emotions are confused and knotted. <u>Mental-Spiritual:</u> Winding yarn into a skein or ball means you're putting your thoughts in order, organizing your goals and choices, and getting ready to create something. You're "spinning a yarn" — making up a tall tale or a complicated series of lies. You're exploring the idea that everything in life is interwoven.

yellow: Physical: You need energy, especially the vigor of muscle energy. You want to attract attention or promote yourself. Emotional: You need to cheer yourself up and develop warmer feelings toward yourself and others. Yellow promotes happiness, spontaneity, humor, naturalness, and enthusiasm. You need to develop greater courage and decisiveness. Mental-Spiritual: You're actively and open-mindedly working with your intellect, creativity, imagination, memory, and communication.

yin/yang sign: Physical: Seeing a yin-yang symbol means you're focusing on balancing yourself between various pairs of opposing character traits to experience unity. You're learning to flow harmoniously and integrate your male and female energies. Emotional: You feel either too receptive or too aggressive and need to use both aspects of yourself. Mental-Spiritual: You're focusing on the two universal, primal opposing but complementary principles or cosmic forces found in all objects and processes. You're experiencing how the feminine or yin is dark, downward-seeking, passive, receptive, and moist, while the masculine or yang is light, upward-seeking, active, expressive, and dry. You're realizing you move through these cycles throughout your life.

yodel: Physical: You want to make your voice heard by many people across distances. You want to experience the power of intense sound vibrating through your body. You're alerting yourself about change or letting others know of an accomplishment. You're learning about sound healing. Emotional: You need to express strong emotions, especially the pure joy of your true self. You want to discover your deep gifts and habitual limiting patterns by dislodging them from your subconscious with vibration. Mental-Spiritual: You're communicating across dimensions, modulating your frequency to create an uplifting musical effect instead of a linear verbal one. You're attuning to a major shift in your life and reality, helping it materialize through sacred sound.

yoga: Physical: You're focusing on developing self-discipline and physical precision in your performance, either in a physical practice, like athletics, or in your work. A particularly convoluted or difficult posture means you feel you must play an unnatural and uncomfortable role in waking life. Emotional: You're focusing on calmness and being centered. You need to feel the subtleties of your own emotions and how they affect your body. Mental-Spiritual: You're learning to control your mind and body, finding the balance and integration of the parts of yourself and, thus, harmony with the universe.

yo-yo: Physical: You're being pulled or pushed in two directions, or you're focusing on how what you put into the world comes back to you. You want to play and feel more carefree. You're learning how to keep your cycle of creating and materializing results in motion without it slowing down and stopping. Emotional: You're frustrated or overwhelmed because life seems to change direction too rapidly, and you're not able to finish things. Someone is playing with you, manipulating your feelings. You're confused because someone seems one way and then the opposite. Mental-Spiritual: You change your mind too often; you need to stick with one direction for a while longer until the flow naturally turns into the next direction and idea. You're focusing on how life flows toward results and then back to new inspiration in repeating cycles with no real gaps.

Z

zebra: Physical: You're focusing on how to camouflage yourself in an environment where you stand out too much because of polarized beliefs or actions. Emotional: You feel too exposed when out in the open. You feel too caught in conflict or struggle. A zebra, or any black-and-white animal, symbolizes the need for integration of the dark and light, good and evil. Mental-Spiritual: You're focusing on ideas of right and wrong, the attraction of opposites, or two distinctly different roles in yourself. You're seeking balance, unity, and harmony.

zero: Physical: You're focusing on loss and emptiness, on what you don't have, or what you're not. You've wasted your energy. You need silence and space or have too much silence and space. Anything is possible and you have absolute freedom. You can create or dissolve what's been created. Emotional: You feel alone or unimportant. Someone is cold toward you, or you to them. You're seeking relief from too much pressure. Mental-Spiritual: You're focusing on what you don't know or on the unknown or collective unconscious. You're looking at the concepts of completeness and the void, where there is no beginning and no end. The circle of zero links to infinity, eternity, wholeness, the soul, unlimited potential, timelessness, and perfection. You're looking at the irony of this world of form being, in the end, meaningless and dissolving back into the all that is.

zigzag: Physical: You're taking a back-and-forth route to your goals, possibly for evasive purposes. You see you're drawn toward something and change direction when you become bored. Emotional: You feel defensive and wary about being dominated or trapped. You're confused and focusing on your erratic avoidance behaviors. Mental-Spiritual: You're focusing on being indecisive or decisive. You're showing yourself that the best path to a goal is not always a straight line. The zigzag represents the lightning bolt, so it can mean you are receiving inspiration or insight from higher dimensions.

zipper: Physical: You're focusing on quick action, closure to a situation, or the need to be quiet ("zip your lip"). A stuck zipper indicates a frustrating situation that must be untangled. Emotional: If clothes are unzipped, you're experiencing a loss of control or feeling of exposure in your life. Mental-Spiritual: You are focusing on ideas that are sexually exciting or that connect two separate realms of thought. You are in a process of deconstructing ideas or creating new understanding.

zodiac: Physical: You're focusing on flying through space, exploring the energies of stars, planets, constellations, and galaxies and how you respond to them energetically. You're becoming more deeply in tune with your own cycles and the timing of major events. Emotional: You're accessing insights about yourself and timing, as well as deep-seated desires, motivations, and fears. You're allowing yourself to receive guidance directly from the consciousness of celestial bodies. Mental-Spiritual: You're looking at the stars and constellations, interested in experiencing the entire circular path of the zodiac and understanding its ancient history, both astronomically and astrologically. You're focusing on your own astrological signs and chart, looking at abilities and possible mistakes of expression. You see the interweaving of the heavenly/nonphysical realms with the physical flow of evolution for humanity and the earth itself.

zombie: <u>Physical</u>: You feel exhausted and dull or are struggling to keep up with others or societal changes. You want to avoid responsibility or tasks that seem difficult. You act like an automaton and don't engage fully, or others who are like this irritate you and interfere with progress. You aren't moving on. <u>Emotional</u>: You're becoming aware of feelings of anxiety, overwhelm, stress, and numbness. You're struggling to eliminate bad habits, negative reactions to people and events, and unhealthy attachments that keep you upset. You avoid life with apathy, unconsciousness, unresponsiveness, and lack of sympathy and empathy. You feel disconnected from loved ones and life. <u>Mental-Spiritual</u>: You need to be more curious and focus on what's interesting. You need clear mental boundaries and a sense of your own vitality and authentic energy. You're resistant to change and letting go. You need to reconnect with your deeper life purpose. It's okay to totally let go and experience pure being, without body, mind, and emotion.

zoo: <u>Physical</u>: You're involved in a situation that's chaotic and wild. You need to create more order and neatness in your life. <u>Emotional</u>: You feel a loss of freedom, that your talents are unnoticed, or that you're on display or being caged in an artificially tame world. <u>Mental-Spiritual</u>: You're looking at ways to find harmony among diverse people or are integrating unusual ideas.

3

The Part of Tens

Discover ten useful techniques for exploring dream messages.

Explore the meanings of ten of the most common dreams.

IN THIS CHAPTER

» Expanding the detail and scope
of a dream

» Adding extra characters to the dream

» Writing or making art to discover
extra meaning

Chapter **7**

Ten Techniques for Exploring Dream Messages

Dreams are little realities that are entirely fluid, intuitive, and responsive to a change of thought or intent. This means you can play with their form to discover insights without feeling as locked in or helpless as you might in everyday life. You can expand the scope of a dream, change the action, bring in imaginary helpers, talk to an imaginary dream expert, or use a creative process to find hidden connections between symbols. In this chapter, you can explore ten helpful methods for finding the messages in your dreams.

Back Up and Extend a Dream

If you don't remember a whole dream sequence, you can imagine it as a filmstrip and rewind it; then extend it further and see what's there.

1. Pick a dream with clear images, where you remember the beginning, middle, and end.

In your imagination, run through the dream. Familiarize yourself with the symbols, feelings, actions, and characters.

2. **Return to the beginning and instead of running it as is a second time, imagine you're backing it up so you can see what happened just before the dream began.**

   Make a note of the predream activity. Replay it from the new starting point to where it stopped before.

3. **Keep playing the dream past its normal endpoint.**

   See what happens next. Use the new insights about causes and outcomes to help you find the deeper messages in your dream.

Add an Extra Character

If you get stuck in a dream scene, you can imagine a new character in the dream to give you advice or shift the flow.

1. **Pick any dream, but a frustrating or frightening one works especially well.**

   Review the beginning, middle, and end, remembering the feelings, symbols, and actions.

2. **Just at the point where you get frustrated or terrified, introduce a new character into the dream.**

   Let your imagination invent someone and continue the dream with the intervention and help of the new person, entity, or animal. What happens next? How does the dream resolve?

3. **How does the new character represent a new part of you that might want to be activated?**

   What is the lesson your soul is trying to teach you?

Expand the Scope of the Dream Environment

To attain more perspective and information, you can adjust your zoom lens, seeing what's farther away or close-up.

1. **Enter your dream and review it from beginning to end, go back to any point where you're centered in a location — inside or outside — and slow the speed way down or freeze-frame the action.**

   Look around. What direction are you facing: east, south, west, or north? What's to the left, right, and behind you? Where's the light coming from? Are there other people nearby you didn't notice before? If you're inside, go outside. If you're outside and there's a house or vehicle, go in. Try zooming up in the air and see the lay of the land. What's just beyond the horizon?

2. **Notice what extra information you receive.**

   How does that data help you understand the dream process and message? You can repeat the process with other dream locations within the same dream and see how the expanded knowledge helps the pieces fit together.

Dialogue with Symbols or Dream Characters

In your imagination, create a conversation with a character or symbol. See what's revealed.

1. **Create an imaginary dialogue with a dream character.**

   The conversation can be between you and the character or between two characters. Have the characters ask each other questions. Why are you here? What's your complaint or biggest problem? What are you good at doing? How are you supposed to help me? How can I help you? What do you want to do next?

2. **Create an imaginary dialogue with a dream symbol.**

   Focus attention on a symbol, give your energy to it, and let it give its energy to you. Enter and merge with the symbol, become it, then speak directly in first person about what you represent, what your expertise is, and why you appeared at this time. Describe how you feel and why. What do you need help with? What is your message?

Face Your Monsters and Take Your Power Back

If you're being chased or threatened by a dream monster, wild animal, serial killer, science fiction character, or violent family member or ex-spouse, you can turn things around quickly.

1. **Review the dream later in a meditation, moving to the point where the anxiety reaches its crescendo, when you feel the most helpless and panic-stricken.**

   In the meditation, stop running or acting like a victim. Turn and face your pursuer. Pull out an imaginary weapon that is more powerful than your opponent. Ask your pursuer some questions: Why are you chasing me? What do you want from me? What do you need to tell me?

   See what the character says. If the scene wants to progress into a dialogue, let it. You might demand of it: Give me a present!

2. **Once the tension resolves and you find understanding, let the image of the "opponent" melt and dissolve.**

   As it does, the energy that was in it flows back into you and you become stronger, more confident, and full of yourself.

Make Quick Associations

Without thinking too much, you can find connected meanings with word and phrase lists that pop to mind.

1. **For each symbol, write a string of associated words, as fast as you can, without reading back over the list.**

   For instance, if the symbol were camera, you might write things like lens, shutter, film, eye, click, blink, view, zoom, look, pictures, color, format.

2. **Write a series of words or phrases that convey emotions or a feeling-state you associate with that symbol, such as, private view, enjoy, preserving a moment, being close to people and landscapes, magical images, loving details, perfect framing.**

3. From the new associations and meanings, see what insights are freed from your subconscious and what feels real and useful when connected to a process in your waking life.

Redream and Change Your Dream's Outcome

If you have a troubling dream (someone steals your car, you plant a garden and it dies, you flub a speech in front of a thousand people), you can go back later in a meditation and re-dream it.

1. **Sit quietly and bring the dream to mind, review it, and reenter it.**

   At the point where things start to go awry, shift the plot. The thief is about to hotwire your car and a loud squealing alarm goes off, attracting the attention of neighbors or passersby, scaring the thief away. Your garden is planted, and just as it begins to wilt, you spray magic fairy dust over the whole thing, and it starts to glow with extra light. You're struggling with your speech, and you see the Dalai Lama sitting in the front row, smiling and nodding encouragement, and you immediately relax and become eloquent and funny.

2. **After changing your dream so it flows to a new conclusion, which may surprise you, notice what you've been trying to show yourself about a real issue in your life and what you're capable of doing.**

Invite a Hero or Expert to Give You Insights

Imagine yourself sitting casually at a sidewalk cafe with the feeling that you'd really like to talk to an "expert" about what your dream means when someone suddenly slips from the crowd and sits down at your table. The person says, "I'm sorry I'm late for our appointment. I got word you wanted to talk to me. I'm _____. How can I help you?"

1. **Notice the person's face, eyes, clothes, the energy of their body, the feel of their maturity, the light coming from them.**

2. **Explain your dream and let them tell you what the parts of the dream mean, what's going on inside you, and what you need to do next.**

   Allow the experience to unfold spontaneously. When it's finished, thank the person, come back, and record what happened.

3. **Ask yourself questions about the experience.**

   Why did that particular person appear to you? Is there a symbolic meaning? Do they have a quality you want to activate in yourself?

Write a Story, Fable, or Poem from a Dream

Turning your dream into a story or poem, or writing more of it in a stream-of-consciousness way, can bring new feelings and insights to assist interpretation.

1. **Write a children's story or fable based on your dream.**
   This is especially fun to do with a child or a friend. Or role-play your own inner five-year-old, or 100-year-old self, and alternate between yourself and your role. First tell your dream or a single dream scene. Then let the other person or your pretend self add a made-up scene. Then you add more. Keep going this way until it comes to a natural end. If you get stuck, ask yourself, *What else could have happened at this point?* The next day, you might take the dream you had that night, add it to the end of the storyline, and continue the process. You might actually make a blank book by folding sheets of paper and stapling them together. Then write and illustrate the dream story, and finally, create a title for it.

2. Every dream can be written as a poem; try it!

You can excerpt powerful pieces of the dream and turn them into three-line haikus. Write a poem around a list of words from your dream or draw a picture of your dream. Then make lists of word pairs from the dream (red mountain, spiral cloud, rushing mud) and write a poem using those phrases tied together in a meaningful way. Your intuitive poetic voice often interprets the symbols naturally as you write. You might try writing your dreams in both narrative form and poetic form side by side in your dream diary.

Make a Dream Collage

Moving into a more sensory mode and using your dream to create artwork can bring a deeper "felt sense" of the meaning.

1. Cut up old magazines and save pictures of wild animals, cars, airplanes, monsters, flowers, trees, toys, dolls, dogs, cats, birds, fish, foods, kids doing different things, old people, adults in sunglasses, mountains, lakes, backyards, bedrooms, shoes, and sky.

2. Paste images that connect to your dream on a big sheet of paper, overlapping them or making connections between images, perhaps doing some pencil drawings of the dream alongside.

You'll find the dream expands as you add related images and meanings. As the dream collage grows in complexity, tell yourself the new story that's taking shape.

3. When you're finished, write the complete story from beginning to end on the back of the collage or in your dream diary.

What is the hidden message? What guidance do you receive from your inner voice?

TECHNICAL STUFF

There are 700 references to dreams in the Bible. The longest recorded dream is three hours and eight minutes. People forget 95-99 percent of their dreams. Only about 12 percent of people dream in black and white. And you can't read in dreams because that part of the brain isn't being used.

Chapter **8**

Ten Common Dreams and Their Meanings

You've probably experienced one of these ten common types of dreams in your life; they focus on themes universal to most people. Under these dreams are emotions everyone shares and is preoccupied with but that no one especially likes to deal with consciously. By working with the inner messages in common dreams, you can maximize your confidence, creativity, and effectiveness in waking life.

My Teeth Are Falling Out!

It's especially popular now to have gleaming white, movie-star teeth, so if your teeth are dirty, diseased, disintegrating, or falling out in your dreams, you're probably worrying about how pleasing and attractive you are to others and to sexual and romantic partners. You may be afraid of getting old. Teeth also relate to self-expression and effective communication, so losing teeth can mean you're embarrassed about something you've said, or you're having trouble saying what you really mean. The real essence of teeth is their ability to bite through, to cut, tear, and grind. As human animals, you retain a vestige of snarling — showing teeth as a "stay back" warning — in our disarming smile. If your teeth fall out, you lose personal power and your ability to be assertive, decisive, and self-protective.

You might ask yourself these questions:

>> Where do I lack confidence or feel powerless?

>> With whom do I feel self-conscious or insecure?

>> How am I angry or frustrated?

>> Where should I act to "bite through" something or chew something thoroughly so I understand it?

I'm Naked in Public!

You're going about your business and suddenly realize you're naked or in your underwear at work or at the grocery store. Exposure dreams bring to light the things you don't want others to know about you and places where you feel vulnerable. Suddenly everyone sees through you. Being naked in front of others also implies being caught off guard or being unprepared, uninformed, uneducated, or unpracticed.

Try asking yourself:

>> What have I been hiding?

>> Where do I feel like a phony?

>> What's wrong with being seen for whom I *really* am?

>> Where do I feel invisible?

>> Can I tolerate, or even love, my imperfections?

>> Who am I really, down under all the coverings?

>> What am I telling myself I need to be prepared for — for my *own* sake?

A Monster Is Chasing Me!

You're running, trying to outpace or outwit your pursuer, and that monster is gaining on you! Suddenly your legs are paralyzed! Chase dreams often represent fears of facing up to something you've judged negatively, like your own rage, shame, or irresponsibility, for example. Or you may feel threatened by someone or by a possible failure. If you become paralyzed, you probably need to stand still and meet your pursuer to receive an important message. You also may be experiencing the normal "paralysis" that occurs in the REM (rapid eye movement) sleep state.

Consider these questions:

>> What do I feel threatened by?

>> What am I avoiding?

>> Who have I given my power to?

>> Where have I surrendered my right to "take up space"?

>> Where do I feel helpless or unsupported?

>> How do I deal with conflict?

I'm in My Childhood Home; It Has New Rooms!

Houses are symbols of the self, so returning to an old house means you're looking back at an old way of being, past habits, identities you've held, and outdated concepts you've been operating from. Perhaps you need to bring repressed memories to the surface to be healed. Trying to live in an old house that might be too small for you now or seeing things that need repair means you're becoming conscious of how much you've grown and what you're renovating in yourself. When your old house has new rooms, you've added new talents, experiences, people, and components to your life.

You might ask yourself these things:

>> What parts of my house need refurbishing?

>> Am I comfortable in this space?

>> Which room is my favorite?

>> What do the new rooms symbolize?

I'm Making Love with a Movie Star!

Sex dreams are often about merging several aspects of yourself together or loving a part of yourself you've judged or rejected. Sex with a celebrity can mean you want more visibility, self-worth, and recognition, or you're activating qualities in yourself represented by the famous person. Sex with an authority figure like a professor, doctor, or boss can show how it feels to have greater power and knowledge so you can be more effective in the world. Sex with a foreigner or someone of another race might mean you are integrating the character traits of that culture or racial consciousness into your personality. Sex with someone of your own gender may simply show you how to better accept and love yourself.

Try asking these questions:

>> What quality or experience am I activating in myself?

>> What do I admire about this lover that is a key to a new ability of mine?

I Lost My Wallet and Keys!

Dreams of loss point to areas where you are too attached to something; you're telling yourself, "Let go and see what comes next when you don't have it all locked down." Losing your wallet can indicate it's time to reexamine your identity. Losing your car may mean you need to look at your need for movement, freedom, and independence as you've defined it. Losing keys points to a fear of losing authority or access to an opportunity. Losing money can mean you're letting go of what's been valuable to you so you can revalue your core self.

Consider these questions:

>> How have I outgrown ideas of who I am?

>> Where do I need to let go and trust the unknown part of myself to provide for me?

>> Where do I need to experience space and emptiness instead of clutter?

I'm Taking a Test and Didn't Study!

You have an exam and can't find the room, you're late, or you haven't studied. You're in a play and forgot your lines. Performance anxiety dreams point to areas in your life where you feel judged by others or unprepared for a challenge. There is pressure to be successful and move ahead in life. You fear if you don't do well, you'll be rejected and ridiculed. If the setting is academic, you probably need to pay attention to new knowledge or to a lesson that's part of your personal growth process. If it's a play or a keynote lecture, you may be ready to express yourself more fully — to be more articulate and confident in the world.

You may ask yourself:

>> What new opportunity do I want but don't feel ready for?

>> How could I feel adequately prepared?

>> How do I feel I might let others down?

>> What do I love to do that I'm always ready for, and how can I transfer that feeling to other things?

I Found Money or Jewels!

Dreams about finding valuables are often about a new positive phase of your self-expression: You're gaining in emotional well-being, confidence, and power. You may be preparing to increase your creativity and abundance level and to feel that having more is normal. They may be showing you something about your beliefs concerning your comfort level. You may be awash in debt, fear that you'll never have enough, or that you'll lose what you have. You want to feel lucky, influential, and rich, so you try it out in your dreams. Under these worries often lurks a deeper fear — that you don't deserve to be loved, supported, or cared for. Your deep self is showing you what it feels like to be blessed.

Try asking yourself:

>> Who gave me the money or valuables?

>> What or who does this person represent to me?

>> Where did I find the valuables and what do the place and kind of item represent to me?

>> What's my attitude as I receive: greedy, worried, egocentric?

>> How do I act after I've received: powerful, generous, relaxed?

I'm Having Surgery on My Eyes, Brain, Heart, or . . . !

Hospital and surgery dreams are often symbolic of a fundamental change you're making in the way you live, the way you work with energy and run your body, and how you constrict or allow your authentic self-expression. On rare occasions, they're warnings about actual health problems, or they indicate you're exhausted and need to rest and be cared for so you can shift to a new phase of self-expression. You may need to get something out of your system, change your habits, move to a new location, or release a person from your life. You may need to open yourself to emotional healing and new experiences. If you experience anesthesia in the dream, you're probably avoiding your feelings, worries, or responsibilities. If you're bleeding profusely in the dream or feel pain, you're telling your conscious mind that part of you feels out of control, severely drained, and wounded by trauma or cruelty.

Ask yourself these questions:

>> What or who has caused me to feel so wounded and helpless?

>> Why am I focusing on this particular area of my body?

>> What are the surgeons doing to help me?

>> Is there a change occurring in my subtle energy body? After I heal, what will I be capable of doing?

>> How is the pattern of my awareness changing?

My Car Won't Stop or Go!

"Difficulty with your vehicle" dreams usually arise when events in your waking life seem out of control, you feel powerless over something, or you're afraid you're about to fail or "crash." Your car is rolling backward, the brakes won't work, you're trying to steer from the back seat, the tires are flat, the ignition doesn't catch. Vehicles are symbols for the way you move through experiences in your life. Cars, motorcycles, bicycles, buses, or trains represent physical experience and your body; boats signify emotional experience; planes connect you to mental experience; and rockets and UFOs represent spiritual levels.

Once you see what level of yourself you're focusing on, determine whether you're the driver or passenger. This shows how you feel about being able to direct your life. Driving from the back seat means you need to step up and be more responsible. Someone else driving means you've given your authority away. Next, look at how the vehicle is functioning. Problems indicate problems you may have in real life. The steering or brakes don't work: You're going too fast and about to make a big mistake. The tires on the right side are flat: You're afraid to move forward and take new actions. The starter won't work: You need to renew your motivation and passion.

Try asking yourself:

>> In what area do I feel disabled or powerless?

>> Who did I give power to?

>> How am I out of control?

>> What in my life needs to work properly?

>> What can I do to move freely?

Appendix
Dalaam Diary
Writing Prompts

As an extension of your dream diary practice, I want to give you some additional writing ideas to prompt informative, insightful responses from your deeper self. Asking the right questions can be very powerful, especially if you remain neutral and receptive and allow your intuitive voice to answer spontaneously. The responses you receive can open and refine your dreamwork process and intuition.

Motivating Yourself

If you've become distracted from your dream diary practice, these suggestions can reboot your interest, momentum, and interpretation success.

1. **Start with the following phrases and write several paragraphs on each until you feel finished.**

    You might want to repeat the phrase several times as you write to maintain a fresh connection with your source.

    - If I could remember what I do in my dreams, I'd . . .

    - If I knew my dream activities were real, it would change my experience of myself because . . .

- If I knew I could try anything in my dreams and not get hurt, it would encourage me to . . .

2. **Write from your body's point of view, in first person (starting with "I"), about why you're not remembering your dreams as well as you might.**

When you finish that part, write about your body's recommendations for increasing your dream life.

3. **Answer the following statements, repeating each one ten times, allowing yourself to get a variety of responses:**

- If I could know anything in my dreams, I'd like to know . . .
- If I could go anywhere in my dreams, I'd like to visit . . .
- If I could meet anyone in my dreams, I'd like to get to know . . .
- If I could create or invent anything in my dreams I'd like to create . . .
- If I could avoid dreaming about a particular subject, it would be . . .

4. **On a scale from 1 to 10, with 10 being the highest or best, rate the following abilities and write about the reasons for the scores:**

- Your ability to be consistently enthusiastic
- Your ability to be calm and centered
- Your stress and anxiety level
- Your level of depression or apathy
- Your energy level in the early morning, the late morning, the early afternoon, the late afternoon, the early evening, the late evening

Afterward, write about how these factors affect your attitude about dreams and your ability to dream.

5. **Write about your specific dream goals for the week.**

As you write, notice which one or two appeal to you the most. Write about why.

6. **Write about your "innocent expectations" in life.**

- What do you assume will come to you effortlessly?
- What do you expect you will never attain?

- What do you expect to be difficult?
- How might these expectations affect your dream life?

7. **Describe your ideal bedroom in detail. What colors, style, furniture, lighting, windows, or decor would it have?**
   - What would you do in your ideal bedroom?
   - How would it feel to dream there?

Remembering Your Dreams

You can use these prompts to jump–start your imagination, which is so important for recalling dream details.

1. **Write about the animals you consider to be your allies, especially those you could imagine helping you remember your dreams.**
   - What is each animal's specialty, and how would each animal guide you?
   - What message might each animal give you now?

2. **Describe in detail a dream recall ritual that comes to you from your inner self — one that will work specifically for you; meditate for ten minutes and write about the process you experience.**
   - How did it feel to your body?
   - What happened to your emotions?
   - What images did you notice?
   - How long could you maintain it?
   - How did you feel afterward?
   - Did you recall any fleeting dream images?

   The process can be anything and different each time you do it.

3. **Pick three well-known people or characters from books, from any time in history, who you think could help you with your dreams.**

   Write about what each person would do for you and how they'd do it.

Energizing Your Dream Diary

The following prompts give you ways to focus on your sensory imagination, which motivates your body and emotions to recall more detail.

1. **Describe a collage of images you might assemble to decorate the cover of your dream diary.**

    What goes next to what?

2. **List ten reasons why you can't possibly do a daily writing practice — then list ten ways you could.**

3. **Write a paragraph completing each of the following prompts:**

    - If I were Picasso, my dream journal would be filled with dreams about and would look like . . .

    - If I were Mother Teresa, my dream journal would be filled with dreams about and would look like . . .

    - If I were Robert Redford, my dream journal would be filled with dreams about and would look like . . .

    - If I were Taylor Swift, my dream journal would be filled with dreams about and would look like . . .

Enhancing Your 24-hour Awareness

The following prompts help you enhance your attention to both your dream time and your waking time.

1. **Write about your sleep process.**

    - Describe your process of falling asleep and the bodily sensations you experience.

    - Do you have sleep disturbances during the night? What happens to your body then?

    - Describe your experience of waking up and how you could refine the process.

2. **Write a presleep prayer asking for help remembering and recording your dreams and aligning with your own higher dimensions, your soul, and the divine.**

3. Write a blessing to say after your prayer, one that addresses your desire to help those you love, or people who are in need in the world.

4. Repeat the following ten times: If I were fully conscious 24 hours a day, I'd feel capable of . . .

5. Write an imaginary account of your journey into dreamland.

Pretend you can remember every detail of what you're doing from the moment you close your eyes until you open them again. Don't allow any blank spots.

6. Write about how some of the themes from your daily life may have carried over into your dreams.

Look for parallel themes, repeating symbols.

7. Write about how some of the themes from your dreams may have carried over and affected what you subsequently did in your daily life.

8. Write about what you observed by being mindful of a mundane task.

9. Write about why you forgot to pay attention to something.

What are your justifications? What do you lose by skimming across the surface?

10. Write about a time when activity in another dimension (such as, someone's death) interrupted your ability to concentrate while you were awake.

11. Notice the times today or recently that you "left your body" and blanked out.

Write about what triggered you to leave.

Sorting through Love and Fear

These prompts can help you discern the expansion feeling associated with love and the contraction feeling that occurs with fear.

1. Make notes next to all the dreams you've remembered this week.

How many are primarily love-based? How many primarily fear-based?

2. **Using stream of consciousness — writing whatever comes into your mind — make up three love-based dreams, writing nonstop without rereading.**

   Take five minutes to do each.

3. **Using stream of consciousness, make up three fear-based dreams, writing nonstop without rereading.**

   Take five minutes to do each.

4. **Make a list of the subconscious and superconscious symbols and actions in your dreams from the past week.**

   What might each signify? Write about how each might relate to your daily life.

5. **Write about what you label as good, desirable, or pleasing; then write about what you label as bad, undesirable, or upsetting.**

   Why do you hold these judgments?

6. **Pick a "bad" dream, think back through your life to earlier similar episodes, and write about as many as you can; then pick a "good" dream, think back through your life to earlier similar episodes, and write about as many as you can. What old beliefs do you notice?**

7. **Transform a nightmare into a useful dream and write about what you needed to do to shift the outcome and the insights that came as a result.**

8. **Looking back at your dreams and waking experiences for the past few weeks, write about what your soul is trying to do to help you.**

9. **List five "shoulds" that affect the way you act with other people, how you progress in life and attain success, and how you view yourself.**

10. **Write about the negative consequences that your subconscious thinks underlie each of your "shoulds."**

    For example: *I should be quiet. If I'm too loud, people will think I'm selfish and reject me.*

Programming Your Dreams

The following prompts can help you maintain better focus and concentration about creating what you want.

1. **Make a list of five problems you'd like to solve, or questions you'd like insight about.**

   Pick the most important one and program a dream to help you with it. Write about the response you get. If you don't receive a dream, make one up with stream-of-consciousness writing. And try the real experiment again!

2. **Loosen your "question-answer" imagination by pretending to be your body giving you advice.**

   Write spontaneously about the following:

   - If I were my body, giving me a dream about how to heal my (backache, carpal tunnel syndrome, insomnia, and so on), I'd project the following images . . .

   - If I were my body, giving me a dream about what I want to eat and don't want to eat, I'd project the following images . . .

   - If I were my body, giving me a dream about how to improve my energy level and regulate the flow of my energy, I'd project the following scenarios . . .

3. **Write a detailed description of how you see yourself optimally expressing a new skill and program a dream to practice the skill.**

4. **Imagine you're a famous (painter, sculptor, dancer, architect, musician) with no creative blocks and write a stream-of-consciousness dream sequence involving your creative genius as if you are that person.**

   What did you learn about the creative process and yourself?

Interpreting Waking Dreams

The following prompts are meant to help you sharpen your perception and expand what you notice during the day. Many ordinary experiences can be interpreted as dreams.

1. **Make a list of ten images from daily life that stand out to you.**

   What might each of them mean if they occurred in a dream?

2. **Make a list of the signs or waking dreams you notice for one week and write about the underlying themes and the connecting threads; also relate those themes to the**

themes you notice in your sleep dreams for the same period of time.

3. Make a list of the subtle signs or signals you notice in one day and write about the underlying messages.

4. Write several paragraphs describing a time your body acted directly from instinct and led you to discover something interesting.

5. Write several paragraphs about a time a sign or waking dream connected meaningfully to your future.

6. Write about how you are either ahead of yourself (in the future) or running behind (in the past).

   What influences you to go forward or backward in time? Write about what you might be avoiding, the seeming benefits of being elsewhere, and what happens when you bring your entire awareness into the present moment.

7. Write several paragraphs about your recent experiences of synchronicity.

   What were you bringing to your attention?

8. Try to catch as many of your daydreams, fantasies, preoccupations, and flashes of insight today as possible, and record them in your diary, writing about what conversation is going on inside yourself under the surface.

Interpreting Sleep Dreams

The following prompts are meant to help you sharpen your perception and expand what you notice about your sleep dreams.

1. Scan through your dreams and make a list of scenes where you experienced fear, worry, or anxiety, then list scenes where you felt uplifted, excited, or inspired.

   Write in first person as your soul about each scene, such as, "I caused myself to experience this so that . . ."

2. Pick a dream, center yourself, and ask your body to write what it knows about the core purpose of the dream.

   Let yourself write in a stream of consciousness, without editing or rereading. Begin by writing: The core purpose of this dream is to show myself ____. I chose the symbol of the <blank> because to me it represents <blank>. Let yourself write, word by word, until you feel complete.

3. **Examine your recent dreams and notice their structure.**

Have you dreamed in fragments? What does one powerful fragment give you that a longer dream might not? Or have you dreamed in epic movies? Were they composed of two, three, or four scenes? Write about why you like the style of your dreams. Why might your subconscious like to have a beginning, middle, and end?

4. **Write about what one of your dreams means, as though you are (Sigmund Freud, Carl Jung, Buddha, Jesus, your grandmother, your inner five-year-old).**

5. **Pick a dream, go back through it in your imagination and while you're in it, look to the left, to the right, and behind you, then write about what you see.**

6. **Pick a dream where you woke before the action was complete, or where an action taken by a character was ineffectual. Write about why your subconscious caused the flow to be interrupted.**

7. **Review your dreams and make a list of all the statements, directives, specific questions, or words or phrases you saw or heard in the dreams.**

As you see them now, grouped together, out of context, write about the impressions you have about what you're really telling yourself.

8. **Examine your recent dreams for puns, exaggerations, and opposite meanings then write about the hidden meanings you find.**

9. **Go through your dream diary, pick three dreams then write your opinions and judgments about what occurs in each.**

See how those statements show you about your deeper self.

Working with Symbols

The prompts in this section can guide you to first relate with a symbol, then enter it and become one with it to find deeper meaning.

1. **Make a list of the symbols in your dreams from the past week and write about how each might relate to your physical and emotional life right now.**

2. **List five symbols from your dreams this week.**

Write about the vertical path of their essential meaning, then the horizontal path of their associative meanings.

3. **Pick five colors, other than the seven standard rainbow colors (pick, for example, turquoise, chartreuse, olive green) and merge with the experience that each one represents.**

Write about your body's primal responses. What emotions do you feel? What impressions do you receive? What happens to your mental clarity with each? What does each color "know about"?

4. **If the numbers of your home address appeared on a house in your dream, what would they mean?**

Write about the qualities your home is activating in you based on the archetypal meanings of the numerals.

5. **List the people in your nuclear family, including grandparents, aunts and uncles, and cousins.**

For each one, decide what color would symbolize them. What kind of food would symbolize them? What other odd symbol pops to mind for each?

6. **Draw a symbol that represents**

- The essence of your creativity
- Your future success
- Your personal truth
- Your current health
- Something from your shadow self

7. **Write a paragraph about what your full name means.**

What characteristics, sensations, and emotions does it elicit? What impressions might it give others?

8. **Pick three to five symbols from one dream and write directly as each one, then write directly about their interrelationships with each other.**

9. **Pick three dream fragments and write a short interview with your dream self about each one.**

10. **Pay attention to the clichés and puns you hear this week, even in your own mind, and write them in your diary, exploring the underlying meaning of each.**

Empowering Your "Life Dream"

The prompts in this section are designed to guide you toward deeper understanding of your own life pattern.

1. **Pick three dreams from your diary and write about what has happened to you since you dreamed each one, placing special emphasis on insights, ideas, experiences, and even other dreams that tie in thematically.**

   How has your understanding of the dream meaning deepened over time?

2. **Pick three dreams and determine the message; then decide what actions you are going to take to integrate the dream's advice — and act! Write about what happens.**

3. **Go through your dream diary with an eye to finding the life lessons peppered through your recent dreams; list the themes and specific issues you're working on.**

4. **Examine your dreams for the personality traits of the various dream characters.**

   If each trait is something you might want to activate or balance within yourself, how would doing this help you learn a life lesson?

5. **Make up a life/work vision for yourself that has the elements of a mission or a calling.**

   Totally blue-sky it and don't listen to your inner skeptic. How much do you think you're capable of doing?

6. **Examine your dreams to see what they're telling you about your life dream.**

   Have they been indicating a new direction, new goals, or old ways of being you want to change?

7. **Scan through your diary and write about the types of decision-making dreams you've had.**

   How have they given you direction, and about what issues?

8. **Write about your life dream as extensively as you can; then write about your desires and things you want to do after you've felt the reality of your life dream and list the actions you could take to bring that reality closer to you physically.**

9. **Look through your dream diary and make a list of ten dream characters you had relationships with.**

   For each, write about what your dream self was showing you concerning how to relate more successfully.

10. **List ten people or animals you have relationships within your daily life; then write about what character traits each represents and why it's important to you to develop or fully understand these traits.**

Improving Relationships

You can become more conscious of your relationship dynamics by working with the following prompts.

1. **Think of one of your friends who seems to be troubled or in need of help.**

   Ask for a dream to shed light on their problem, and to show how you might counsel them. Incubate a dream and when you receive one that seems like the answer to your request, call your friend and tell them about it. See if together, the two of you can interpret it.

2. **Finish the following sentences with as many answers as you can:**

   - If I could know anything about my relationship with *<blank>*, I'd like to understand . . .

   - If I could help *<blank>*, the most appropriate thing to do or say would be . . .

   - If I could find true forgiveness for *<blank>*, I'd need to let go of/understand . . .

   - If I could begin a new relationship with someone, I'd like them to have these qualities . . .

3. **Go through your dream diary and list the romance or sex dreams you've had.**

   What, besides wishful thinking, might have been the purpose of these dreams?

4. **Write several paragraphs about the taboos you've broken in your dreams.**

How did it feel? What did you learn? Why did your dream self want to experience that particular area? Did you feel increased or decreased energy as a result?

5. **Write about the times you've experienced telepathy, in ordinary reality and in dreams, with someone else.** How did it feel? How did the communication occur? Was it in a visitation from someone far away, or in the spiritual realm?

Enhancing Healing

You can use the writing prompts in this section to tune in to what affects health negatively or positively, and how healing occurs.

1. **Scan through your dream diary, noting any dreams that might be about your health or body and write about each.**

   - If this were a forecasting dream, what would your dream self be trying to tell you?

   - If this were a therapeutic or healing dream, what would your dream self be trying to tell you?

2. **Write about three possible scenarios that would put you in a state of deep peacefulness; include the sensory detail, how your body responds to being there, how you feel when your mind is quiet, and how you would use each setting for maximum benefit.**

3. **Make up three dream scenarios where you're healed of some problem you currently have — mental, emotional, energetic, or physical.**

How does it happen? Who helps you? Where are you when it happens? What advice do your helpers have for you? Are you really healing yourself?

4. **Write out three dream scenarios depicting yourself in optimum health.**

How do you look? What are you doing? How are you interacting with others? How do you remain healthy?

5. **Let yourself fantasize and write about how you would help heal a friend, relative, or even a public figure who suffers from an injury or illness.**

Imagine that anything is possible, and you can use any technique that comes to mind.

6. **Examine your dreams and write about symbols and imagery pertaining to possible imbalances in your system, illnesses, accidents, parts of the body, or even problems other people might be having.**

Are you dreaming about your own health, the health of another, or both simultaneously? Is it literal or symbolic?

Index

binoculars, 99

birds, 99. *See also specific birds*

birth, 99

birthday, 99

bisexuality, 99

black (color), 100

black hole, 100

Blake, William (poet), 16

blanket, 100

blind, 100

blindfold, 100

blockage, subconscious, 20–21, 30, 34, 52

blood, 100

blue (color), 100–101

boat, 101

body. *See also specific body parts*

    messages from, dream diary, 60

    physical zone/symbols, 33

bomb, 132. *See also* explosion

bones, 101. *See also* skeleton; spine

book, 101

boss (authority), 93. *See also specific authority figures*

bouquet, 101–102

bowl, 96

box, 102

brain, 102

brainwaves, 15

brakes, 102

bread, 102

break, 102

breast, 103

bridge, 103

brown (color), 103

bubble, 103

buffalo, 103–104

buildings (architecture), 91. *See also specific buildings and features*

bull's-eye (arrow), 91

burning, 104

bus, 104

butterfly, 104. *See also* caterpillar

buy, 104. *See also* bargain

C

cactus, 105

cage, 105

calendar, 105. *See also* datebook

Calvin, Melvin (chemist), 16

camel, 105

camera, 106

cancer, 106

candle, 106

captivity, 106

car, 106–107

cards, playing, 107

castle, 107

cat, 107

cataclysm, 107–108

catastrophe, 107–108

caterpillar (butterfly), 104

cattle, 108

cave, 108

ceiling, 108

celebrity, 134, 282. *See also* fame; famous people

cellular phone, 108–109. *See also* telephone

cemetery, 109

change points, as interpretation start, 54–55

characters, dream, 28, 56, 272

chase, 109

cheat, 109–110. *See also* steal

chess, 110

chest, 153. *See also* heart

chicken, 110

child(ren), 110

    dreams and nightmares of, 14

    sleep amount needed, 36

    sleep pattern, 15

chin, 110

church, 111

circle, 111

city, 111

cliff, 111

climb, 32, 111

clock, 112. *See also* watch

clothes, 112, 280. *See also specific clothing items*

clutter, 112

cobwebs, 112

coffee, 112–113

collage, creating, 277

cologne, 204. *See also* perfume

colors, 113. *See also specific colors*

column, 205–206. *See also* pillar

companionship, 140

competition, 113

complete the day, sleep preparation, 23

computer, 26–27, 113–114. *See also* laptop

horizontal awareness,
45–47

horns, 90

horse, 156

hospital, 156, 284–285

hotel, 156–157

house, 157, 281–282.
*See also specific parts
of house*

Howe, Elias (inventor), 16

hummingbirds, 77, 157

hunger, 158

hurricane, 158

hypnagogic/
hypnopompic, 31

hypnosis, 158

hypnotize, 158

I

ice, 159

iceberg, 159

icicles, 159

ID card, 159

igloo, 159

images, as interpretation
start, 56

imagination, growth of, 11

immigrant, 159–160

impression dreams, 51

incomplete dreams, 52,
275

infestation, 160

infinity sign, 160

inheritance, 243–244,
283–284. *See also*
treasure

inhibitors of dreaming, 17

ink, 160–161

innovation development,
11–12

insects, 160. *See also
specific insects*

instruments, surgical,
284–285

interdimensional
communication, 37

internet, 161

*The Interpretation of
Dreams* (Freud), 48

interpreting dreams, 14.
See also dream diary;
symbols

archetypal meanings,
42–45

common dreams,
279–285

daydreams, 31

exercises, 60–63

finding meaning, 51–63

horizontal awareness,
45–47

past dream dictionaries,
48

personal meaning,
43–47

sample dreams, 66–72

sample interpretation,
58–60

sleep dreams, 294–295

starting to interpret,
52–55

types of meanings,
42–47

vertical awareness,
44–45

waking dreams, 293–294

intruder, 161

intuition, 19–20

development, 11–12

invention, 161

investments, 162

invisibility, 162

iron, 162

ironing, 162

island, 163

itch/itching, 163

ivy, 163

J

jaguar, 163–164

janitor, 164

jaw, 164

jewelry, 164, 283–284

jewels, 164, 283–284

jigsaw puzzle, 165

job, 165. *See also* dream
diary; symbols

joints, 165

journey, 165

judge, 166

juggler, 166

jump, 166

Jung, Carl (analyst), 63

jungle, 166–167

junk, 167

junkyard, 167

Jupiter, 207

jury, 166

K

kaleidoscope, 167

kangaroo, 167–168

keyboard, 168

keys, 168, 282–283

kick, 169

kidnap, 169

kill, 169

killer, 169–170

kiss, 170

kitchen, 170

kite, 170

knee, 170

kneel, 170

knife, 171. *See also* sword

About the Author

Penney Peirce is an internationally respected clairvoyant-empath, visionary, and pioneer in transformation dynamics, intuition development, expanded perception, and dreamwork. Penney has worked throughout the United States, Japan, South America, South Africa, and Europe, training and advising coaches, business and government leaders, psychologists, scientists, celebrities, and seekers of all types. She is known for her commonsense approach to spirituality and the development of expanded human capacities. She is the author of 11 books, including the first edition of *Dream Dictionary For Dummies* and her Transformation series (Atria Way): *The Intuitive Way, Frequency, Leap of Perception,* and *Transparency.*

Penney is known for sophisticated, useful, intriguing insights into the hidden dynamics of well-rounded success. She weaves together teachings in psychology, philosophy, personality typing, and metaphysics with her experience in writing, advertising, design, and corporate art direction. She lives in Florida. You can find her online at www.penneypeirce.com and https://penneypeirce.substack.com/.

Author's Acknowledgment

I've been blessed with family, friends, and clients who are good at both giving and receiving. It's so empowering to have stimulating conversation and honest feedback and to be able to explore dreams and imagination with them. I've been tremendously entertained and educated by the dreams these people have shared with me over the years. Plus, working and just talking with them has taught me a huge amount about perception itself.

I've enjoyed working with Alicia Sparrow and Charlotte Kughen at Wiley; their enthusiasm and cooperative attitude made the production process clear and fluid. I'm especially grateful for their interest in expanding the original *Dream Dictionary For Dummies* to its present, much more complete edition. I want to thank Cassie Hessler-Smith, a dream-savvy psychotherapist and friend, for her professional review of the manuscript. And finally, great gratitude goes to my friends and clients who contributed dreams to be interpreted for Chapter 6; I love your rich imagination and hope I provided a few fun insights!

Dedication

To my sister, Paula, who has been my friend and sounding board all my life. Though she doesn't remember her dreams as much as I do, she generously makes time to listen to me rattle on about mine.

Publisher's Acknowledgments

Acquisitions Editor: Alicia Sparrow

Project Editor: Charlotte Kughen

Peer Reviewer: Cassie Hessler-Smith

Managing Editor: Sofia Malik

Production Editor: Umeshkumar Rajasekhar

Cover Image: © gremlin/ Getty Images

Printed and bound by CPI Group (UK) Ltd, Croydon, CR0 4YY

19/03/2026